ONLY THE RIVERS ARE PEACEFUL

ONLY THE RIVERS ARE PEACEFUL

THOMAS HART BENTON'S MISSOURI MURAL

By Bob Priddy

For the Smiths,

with best wishes

Bob Priddy

5/6/04

Independence Press/ Herald Publishing House
Independence, Missouri

ONLY THE RIVERS ARE PEACEFUL
Thomas Hart Benton's Missouri Mural
by Bob Priddy

Copyright 1989
Independence Press/ Herald Publishing House
Independence, Missouri

Library of Congress Cataloging-in-Publication Data

Priddy, Bob.
   Only the rivers are peaceful: Thomas Hart Benton's
Missouri mural / Bob Priddy.
      p.   cm.
   ISBN 0-8309-0534-0 : $20.00
   1. Benton, Thomas Hart, 1889-1975. Missouri
mural. 2. Benton, Thomas Hart, 1889-1975—Criticism
and interpretation.   3. Missouri in art. I. Title.
ND237.B47A73   1989
759.13—dc19   89-30682
                                                      CIP

Printed in the United States of America

5 4 3 2 1   93 92 91 90 89

This book is for the thousands who have walked into that room and asked, "What does all of this mean?"

Thomas Hart Benton, about the time he painted the Missouri mural   (courtesy of *Kansas City Star/Times*).

CONTENTS

FOREWORD

This book is about Thomas Hart Benton and a mural he painted in Jefferson City, Missouri, where I live and work.

Here are some things it is not:

It is not my analysis of Benton's technique or my considered evaluation of his social and political motivations. I have never taken an art course in college, so I am not acquainted with high-sounding technical words that render me enough of an expert to pass judgment on Benton's value as an artist or for me to step into his mind and interpret either his motivations or his symbolism.

I rather resent those who claim though their obviously superior taste that Benton is not a major artist or even a good one but is a person who wandered from a more worthwhile career as an abstractionist and settled into an inferior role as a regionalist.

Benton's paintings are alive and exciting. They strike a chord within me. I do not need those who think culture is contained on the Atlantic side of the Alleghenies telling me that Benton should be beneath my appreciation.

I like Thomas Hart Benton. The more I researched this book, the more I liked his intellect, his frankness, and his disdain for (often) self-induced pomposity. And the more I read his writings and heard recordings of his voice, the more I realized he's right about art.

I like him and what he did. And that's enough.

This is the story of an artist and one of his works. It might be seen as a defense of Benton. If it is, that's fine.

A lot of people have helped me reach this point. Many of their names are scattered throughout this book. They are people who have shared their experiences and advice in this project for the last four years. In addition to them, some specific people deserve thanks.

The Missouri Committee for the Humanities and Professor Jim Bogan at the University of Missouri-Rolla began this project. Jim called and asked if I would like to be part of a lecture series about Thomas Hart Benton. All I had was a recorded interview I had done with John G. Christy the day Benton died. All of this began with that. There were two seasons of lectures in which I was joined by Professor Doug Wixson, also at UMR, and folk singer Bob Dyer, at Kemper Military Academy in Boonville. I appreciate the opportunity given me by the committee and by Jim.

The trustees of the Benton Testamentary Trust, most particularly Lyman Field, who was Mr. Benton's attorney, and Steve Campbell, who assisted me at United Missouri Bank in Kansas City, provided me with copies of sketches and notebook pages that were important in discovering the story. Henry Adams at the Nelson-Atkins Gallery in Kansas City shared some of his research and insights. The State Historical Society of Missouri in Columbia was extremely helpful with its clipping files and microfilmed newspapers. The librarian at the *Kansas City Star* and *Times* let me prowl through the newspapers' clipping and photo files. I appreciate *The Star's* permission to use some of those photographs in this book. Sid Larson gave me some important insights into the character of Mr. Benton and the care of the mural in the half-century since its completion. The State Museum at the Capitol provided the color photographs used.

My family, of course, deserves thanks and sympathy. They tolerated my spending hours in the basement den. "Is that Benton again?" they would ask. I would nod as I watched new letters appear on the screen, and they would quietly leave.

Most of all, I thank Tom Benton for being Tom Benton.

Bob Priddy
Jefferson City, Missouri
March 1989

10

To go into painting in all of its aspects and with all your heart is to live really a life. You're always in a battle royal. You work away full of steam and genius and all of a sudden something pops up in your picture you never figured on and you stand back, full of Freud, Jung, Holt Hart, and you say to that something, "You son-of-a-bitch where did you come from? Get out of my way" And you sail in to put that something out of the works and when you do get rid of it, it turns out to be just what you needed and you have to set to and coax it back again. And believe me, that coaxing exercises your ingenuity and enlarges your acquaintance of many, many things that you'll never read about and that you can't write about. It's one "desperate situation" after another, but by God, let me live desperately. I'll let the literary gigolos do the "thinking" if I can keep tangled up in situations.

Thomas Hart Benton
letter to Alfred Stiegletz
January 1, 1935

Chapter 1

The Beginnings

To *St. Louis Star-Times* reporter Paz vanMatre, the diminutive artist working high on his scaffold in the cavernous room reminded him of "a fly on a window pane—industriously moving toward some great unfathomable, mysterious future, oblivious to time and speed."

But Thomas Hart Benton knew precisely where he was going with his art and with this painting in particular. When vanMatre wrote his article, Tom Benton knew the stories he wanted to tell and the design he would use to tell it. Sketches covered the walls of the room. They had been months in preparation and would be months more in the painting. When he was done, Benton would have finished a milestone work in his own life and would have triggered the most vituperative controversy in his artistic career.

The idea began to form in the minds of others in 1934. One of the nation's leading artists, a son of Missouri, should be hired to paint a great mural for his home state.

Tom Benton, native of Neosho, son of a congressman and grand-nephew of Missouri's second United States senator, was in New York, becoming famous for his historical murals. He had shaken off his early training in abstract art, was growing tired of a New York sapped of its energy by the Depression, and was growing out of the pretensions of a modern art movement that fed upon itself.

He felt himself being drawn back to the Middle West. His mural of the social history of Indiana for the Chicago World's Fair of 1933 strengthened his move closer to his roots.

The route Thomas Hart Benton took back to Missouri's capitol was a long one personally, philosophically, and artistically. He would later say in his first autobiography, *An*

American in Art, the Missouri mural "completed the last phase of my development as an artist. While various modifications of my pictorial style were made later...all the basic structural procedures I would ever use had been arrived at."

He often said that what he put on the approximately 2,000 square feet of walls in the lounge of the Missouri Legislative Assembly represented things he had experienced from life. Indeed, it might be said that the first forty-five years of the life of Thomas Hart Benton were spent growing toward this mural.

It began with his own heritage.

I was raised in an atmosphere of violent political opinions, exploded when the Democrats of the East and West were at odds over President Cleveland's policies. I was in the habit of hearing these opinions bolstered by views of historical fact. This was always going on at the dinner table, where there was always company; and though it didn't have meaning for me in a political sense, it did have significance of an emotional sort.[1]

Benton came from a historical family. His father was a federal attorney who dealt with outlaws for the Western District of Missouri under President Cleveland, then a congressman. His great uncle was a senator from Missouri. He was raised in a southwest Missouri town "when the section reverberated with the great Oklahoma rushes." Benton recalled going hunting in what was then the Indian Territory and attending "innumerable old settlers' and old soldiers' reunions."

I heard a lot of hot stuff which the old boys thought I didn't understand...I know what camp meetings are, and the political rallies of the backwoods, barbecues, schoolhouse dances (with a jug in the bush), and I know—as well as I know the skyscrapers of New York, or better—what men look like who break new land.

Benton's contacts with the past were carried through his family line. "What happened in Oklahoma in my lifetime happened in Missouri in my father's and in Kentucky and Tennessee in my grandfather's,'' he wrote.

...and living words from people, not books, have linked them up in feeling and established their essential sameness. What constitutes the real break in this historical progression is the machine, and I can almost fill that gap in direct experience, for I have ridden on, and well remember, the wood-burning locomotive that used to thump over the old split-log railway in southwest Missouri.[2]

Mural painting came to Benton when he was six or seven years old, and he used charcoal to draw on the cream-colored wallpaper of his home a train chugging up a stairway. "It began with the caboose at the front of the steps and ended at the top with the engine puffing long strings of black smoke—because of the heavy grade,'' he recalled.

The kind of appreciation accorded this early effort was the first intimation I received of the divergency of view on the subject of mural decoration. The question of appropriateness, which later and on other occasions I was to hear a lot about, was then brought up for the first time. Decision in this case was against me and, after a good lecture, my labors were obliterated with bread crumbs.[3]

He recounts in his two autobiographies his first formal instruction in art came at the Corcoran Gallery in Washington, D.C., where he took special classes on Saturday mornings while his father was in Congress. He was not inspired by drawing from wooden geometric figures "the very appearance of which was forbidding.'' Benton preferred to copy engravings found in his father's history books. He also was especially taken by the famous "Custer's Last Stand'' painting that hung in many taverns, as well as an engraving of the destruction of the Battleship *Maine*.

It was, in fact, a barroom picture that pushed Tom Benton into the world of commercial art. He was fifteen, self-proclaimed tough, working in the mines near Joplin. One

Saturday night when he was in the "House of Lords," a prominent saloon in the town, he became fascinated by a painting that was famous in the community. It showed a masked, naked woman who had been stabbed by her brother, standing in the background. He was about to dispatch himself the same way. When some older fellows began to poke fun at young Tom he told them he "wasn't particularly interested in the naked girl, but I was studying the picture because I was an artist and wanted to see how it was done." An artist? "Yes, by God! And I'm a good one!"

"By a little quirk of fate, they made a professional artist out of me in a short half-hour," Benton later recalled. The group at the bar led him to the new newspaper in town, the *Joplin American*. Benton went in, asked if they needed an artist, and was told to sketch a man at a drugstore counter across the street if he wanted a job. It was the first drawing he ever made from a live model, but it brought him a job at $14 a week.[4]

His first real insights into the structure of art came when he went to the Chicago Art Institute. There he "acquired some knowledge of the human figure." From Japanese prints that were popular at the time he learned to "arrange...pictures in definite patterns and acquired a taste...for flowing lines which lasted all my life." It was while he was in Chicago that he began to paint with oils.

From the moment I first stuck my brush in a fat gob of color, I gave up the idea of newspaper cartooning. I made up my mind that I was going to be a painter. The rich, sensual joy of smearing streaks of color, of seeing them come out in all sorts of unpremeditated ways, was too much for me and I abandoned my prospective fortunes in the big-time newspaper business without a qualm.[5]

In 1908, Benton was in Paris to study at the Academy Julian. But he found most of the teaching would not lead to any kind of art he wanted to create. For the next dozen years in Paris and later in New York, Benton sought his kind of art.

About the only things that permanently impressed me were the weekly lectures on anatomy, which were graphically conducted with a living and usually muscular model on hand for comparison with the diagrammatic expositions of the anatomist. These lectures, unlike the visualistic copying of the regular drawing classes, provided a real body of knowledge—something which stuck in the mind.[6]

However, by 1911 he found "the art of Paris appeared to be feeding wholly on itself, paintings were growing out of paintings rather than out of any discernible cultural situations."

Weighing my situation, it seemed to me that I must make a choice. Either I would paint in the realistic traditions of Western art with some kind of identification with the natural world, and thus risk being "unprogressive," or I would follow the new movements toward an unknown goal, a goal which a number of farsighted critics were already saying might turn out to be an empty square of paint.[7]

In 1912, Benton returned to New York, after "a few depressed months at home in Missouri" and three weeks of no success in Kansas City. While in Kansas City he learned the Art Institute was looking for someone who had just returned from Paris—"only it turned out that they were all homosexuals in the place, and I didn't get along," Benton recalled for Robert Gallagher in *American Heritage* magazine many years later. In the article published in June 1973, Benton said Kansas City in those days was a "vaudeville and carnival exchange center...a place where the chorus boys would be stranded for weeks at a time."

And somehow or other, Kansas City had become a quite developed homosexual center...and it had reached into the art institute. Now listen, I'd been through Paris, and I'd never seen anything like that. It shocked the hell out of me. They had a party for me, and they all came in women's underwear and all that stuff. That was something I was absolutely innocent about, and I couldn't stay there.

One of his first allies when he returned to New York was "a poet at the beginning of his writing career," Thomas Craven. When Craven was not elsewhere teaching the classics in small colleges, he and Benton roomed together.[8] In later years, Craven would be one of Benton's greatest boosters and stoutest defenders. He remembered Benton as twenty-three, looking old and sad, his face lined and deeply drawn. He called Benton "a sight, with his tight French clothes, his flat French hat, and his Balzac stick—the antithesis of everything American."

He talked of abstract beauty and the subtleties of Gallic philosophy; of Platonic visions of art, and French poetry, an interest which, in light of my own aspirations, was most impressive. The nostalgia of Verlaine, the perverse sadness of Baudelaire, the attenuated dreams of the symbolists— those neurasthenic imaginings of the French genius of the period which today no one would associate with Benton's life and thought, seemed to compose the fabric of his being.[9]

Craven wondered if Benton might have been "the victim of some strange irregularity of development."

Benton's paintings of flowers based on illustrations in seed catalogues brought him his first significant commission—five large floral panels for a dance pavilion on Coney Island. He was paid $35 each.

The next year he got a job researching and drawing elevations for movie backgrounds. While watching the scenery painters he became interested in "distemper," or glue painting, which in turn led to experiments that ultimately took him to egg-tempera techniques used extensively on works in the 1930s, including the Missouri mural.

His style fluctuated in the years after 1908. "I was by turn visual realist, Impressionist, Neo-Impressionist, Cezannist,

Synchromist, Constructivist, or I zigzagged between these,"
he wrote. His search for a technique outweighed the content
of his canvases in those years.

Another turning point came in the summer of 1918 when
Benton got into the Navy through some political string-
pulling that overcame an earlier rejection because he wasn't
tall enough. While he was stationed at the Norfolk Navy
Yard, he found the four-volume history of the United States
by J.A. Spencer and was attracted to its illustrations.

I began to ask myself questions. Why could not such subject pictures
dealing with the meanings of American history possess aesthetically
interesting properties, deliverable along with their meanings? History
painting, religious or secular, had occupied a large place in the annals of
art. Why not look into it again, I asked, and try to fill the contextual void
of my own painting, give it some kind of meaning?

He wasn't aware of it then, but Tom Benton was
changing. The experience would eventually separate him
from his Parisian background and "give a new and, this
time, permanent direction to my painting."

Back in New York, he became dissatisfied painting still
lifes and landscapes. He sought a more solid compositional
structure for his works and found it in his studies of
sixteenth-century artists, most specifically in the description
of the way Tintoretto created his famous version of "The
Last Supper" in the Venetian Church of Saint Giorgio
Maggiore. Tintoretto had made small, sculptured figures
which he used to work out positions in various shadings of
light. Benton decided to try that in the historical paintings he
wanted to do. In 1919 and 1920 he perfected his version of
that technique.

In a short while a veritable chasm came to exist between what I had done
previous to the winter of 1919-20 and what I did afterward...I would come
to draw people and landscapes, even fruits and flowers, much like
sculptural carvings.

This change further separated Benton from many of those with whom he had associated in New York and Paris. He wrote, "Because of that and of the early use of the method to represent a nationalistic subject matter, it would arouse sharp animosities among artists and critics and catapault me into twenty-five years of controversy."[10]

Benton decided after the war that he would not return to European patterns of thought but would instead search for American meanings in art. It was not an arbitrary decision but one he felt was a product of his raising and ancestry. "When it reveals life, art becomes a form of history—and of the most vivid kind," he wrote in *An American in Art*.

We revive and can relive the past through the reflections provided by its art. We know the actual life of mid-nineteenth century France better by the pictures the painters and novelists made of it than by all other records. So art is not only art but a regenerative force and because of that, permanently valuable to men. Forgotten meanings may come again to life, and the dead artists who represent them live again.

It didn't take long for his new style to attract attention. An exhibition at the Architectural League in New York drew some attention and identified Benton as a possible muralist.

Benton rediscovered his roots in 1924 when he returned to southwest Missouri for his father's last days. He watched as his father's longtime friends came to say good-bye and to reminisce.

I got a renewed sense of the variety and picturesqueness of his life and of the life of the people of my home country which the infatuated artistic vanities of the city had brought me to regard as stale and stuffy. I discovered that underneath the dry practicalities of his friends...there was a deep run of common human sentiment which I shared....I liked the people who came to my father's bedside.

He reflected on the Missouri of which he had lost track in his career in Chicago, Paris, and New York, noting that the state was "rural-minded," an area where the "flavor of premachine-age past'' remained in the speech of a people who are not known to "rush wildly to decisions."

Outsiders may laugh at its skeptical slowness, or the radical-minded fume because their significance is not recognized, but there are no gag laws on the Missouri statutes and its people as a whole are pretty genuinely democratic....Its rural conservatism has preserved, in prejudices and action, a large residue of that old-time American individualistic psychology with which we are going to need a large measure of acquaintance if we are to avert disaster in our further social travels.

Something began for Tom Benton on this trip that shaped his artistic philosophy and led to the kind of muralist he became. Even he did not understand what came over him as he watched his father die and saw and heard the old man's friends who came to share the last hours.

I know that when, after his death, I went back East I was moved by a great desire to know more of the America which I had glimpsed in the suggestive words of his old cronies...I was moved by a desire to pick up again the threads of my childhood. To my itch for going places there was injected a thread of purpose which...was to make the next ten years of my life a rich texture of varied experiences.[11]

Something else happened to Benton on that trip, a circumstance he didn't think about until many years later. Benton's father had been a frequent visitor to Kansas City, sometimes falling victim to pickpockets. Although the visits preceded the rise of the Pendergast factions which controlled city—and later, state—politics for years, the Pendergasts must have grown to appreciate him anyway because Kansas City Democrats helped make the elder Benton the president of the state constitutional convention of 1922.

In 1924 Tom Pendergast led a group of Kansas City politicians to the hospital to visit the artist's father. The group silently filed in to M. E. Benton's room to shake the old man's hand, Pendergast going in last. When Pendergast came back, he reached out a half-closed fist to the old man's son. When Benton grasped Pendergast's hand, he felt a hard object left in his palm. Pendergast said it was "from his friends for any little things he might need." Pendergast walked out. Benton looked down in his hand and found a roll of money—$800!

I was dumbfounded and much disconcerted. I dared not tell my father about it. Long out of practice or political perquisites he was at the end of his financial rope. I was broke and my brother, as a cub attorney, was earning little...."Well," my brother said, "we can damn well use the money but for Christ's sake don't ever say a word about it to anybody."[12]

Benton would ponder this incident years after the capitol mural was finished, wondering if it wasn't part of the mural itself. But the significance other than that of the moment escaped him in 1924.

The next ten years would become a decade of travel, observing, and sketching.

These were the days when there was a great questioning of the American system through the 20s up to the Great Depression and part of my view, my nationalistic views, were regarded by radical groups as being chauvinistic, non-humanitarian and so forth, you know, that I didn't fit within the patterns of radical thought because during the 20s everybody thought this American system was not only on trial but about to go down.[13]

His travels convinced him otherwise. Ten years after his father's death, the time was ripe for Tom Benton to return to Missouri.

His paintings at the New School for Social Research, the Whitney Museum of American Art, and, in 1933, the Indiana exhibit at the Chicago World's Fair, increased his reputation and reestablished his ties with the Middle West. By the mid 1930s, Benton, John Steuart Curry, and Grant Wood were the premier painters in America. Benton said their style of painting coupled with interest in the works of American history by Charles Beard and James Truslow

Adams moved them to the top of their field in American art, despite criticisms that they were reactionary, chauvinistic, and provincial. "However, the public temper of the thirties was with us and nullified the fulminations of our critics. We were successful," Benton recalled.[14]

But his friend and defender, Thomas Craven, wrote in 1934 that Benton's style—"restless counterplay," he called it—captured the realities of American life with its "tumultuous forces...its manifold dissonances, and its social anarchy." Craven claimed those who said Benton's work lacked poise or serenity were unwittingly affirming "its truth, its connections with its time and place."

While art, historically, has been the servant of various idealisms, it has drawn its vitality, not from the ideal, but from the exploration of the ways and habits of people...Today, as in the past, it is the artist's business to see the world clearly, and to allow no convention of ideology or technique to obscure his vision or stand in the way of representational truth.

Craven felt Benton's best works were ahead and that Benton was still searching for "more intense relief, deeper space, unprecedented contrasts of form and subject." Craven admitted he found something he wished Benton had done differently in almost every painting. He called them "mawkish clashes and unrealized intentions."

Given the co-operation of the architects—for he is essentially a mural designer—he should become the most influential of American painters.[15]

In 1934, Benton was given the first job in the Treasury Department's projects under the Roosevelt Administration. But he struggled with plans for a mural in the new post office in Washington, D.C. He disagreed with the department's committee, "the aesthetic temper of which was less than sympathetic to my way of doing things."

When word came that the legislature in Missouri had voted to hire him to paint a mural for his home state, Benton immediately stopped his work in Washington. He figured "it would be easier to deal with the state legislature than with a bunch of art experts."[16] He told the *New York Sun* in an interview published April 12, 1935, the dominant forces in New York art—the National Academy, which he said represented officialdom, and the Communist groups which represented the propogandist view of art—were so locked in conventional beliefs about art that "they are unable to turn out anything but dead conventions."

The Middle West has no inhibiting cultural patterns wrapped up in a lot of verbal logic, or tied to practicing habits that stop action.

I'm leaving New York to see what can be done for art in a fairly clean field less ridden with verbal stupidities.... Do I think I'm going to escape stupidity in the Middle West? Of course not. Wherever people talk, idiocy thrives.

He was embarking on the most important step of his life so far. Tom Benton

—who had drawn murals since he was six or seven;

—who liked to draw trains;

—who had been attracted to action pictures such as the famous "Battle of the Little Big Horn" painting that hung in many taverns;

—who learned the flowing lines that typify his paintings by studying Japanese art;

—who abandoned career plans to be a newspaper cartoonist the first time he dipped a brush into a gob of paint

—who learned to mix egg-tempera paint through his experience painting movie backgrounds;

—who, by studying etchings in history books, became convinced historical painting would be his life;

—and who discovered his own heart in the days he watched his father die and in the decade of exploration that followed—was going home to create what one art expert has called "Missouri's most famous painting,"[17] a mural

Benton himself termed "the most controversial one I'd done."[18]

Notes

1. Thomas Hart Benton, "My American Epic in Paint," *Creative Arts* magazine (December 1928). Reprinted in *A Thomas Hart Benton Miscellany*, edited by Matthew Baigell (Lawrence, Kansas: The University Press of Kansas, 1971), 19.

2. Baigell, "My American Epic in Paint," 19-21.

3. Thomas Hart Benton, *An Artist in America*, Fourth Revised Edition (Columbia, Missouri: University of Missouri Press, 1983), 13.

4. Ibid., 18-21.

5. Ibid., 31.

6. Thomas Hart Benton, *An American in Art* (Lawrence,Kansas: The University Press of Kansas,1969),15

7. Ibid., 26.

8. *An Artist in America*, 39-40.

9. Thomas Craven, *Modern Art: The Men, the Movements, The Meaning* (New York: Simon and Schuster, 1940), 340.

10. *An American in Art*, 43-49.

11. *An Artist in America*, 75-77.

12. "The Thirties," unpublished manuscript by Benton in the files of the Benton Trust, Kansas City, Missouri.

13. Interview with Bob and Betty Lewis on October 12, 1962, in Tucson, Arizona, on file in the Rogers and Hammerstein Archives, New York Public Library.

14. *An American in Art*, 70.

15. Craven, *Modern Art,* 353. The comment was made at the end of Craven's article about Benton in the 1934 edition of the book.

16. Lewis interview.

17. Interview by author with Sid Larson of Columbia Missouri (December 18, 1983). Larson, professor of art at Columbia College, was an associate of Benton for twenty-five years, helped restore the capitol mural four times, helped Benton on the Truman Library mural, and is curator of art for the State Historical Society of Missouri.

18. Jefferson City *Missouri Times* (January 10, 1983).

Chapter 2
The Mural

Since discovering his niche as a historical muralist more than a decade earlier, Thomas Hart Benton had painted a series of controversial works that everybody but the public seemed to attack. First was the mural in a classroom at the New School for Social Research in New York, for which he was paid nothing but from which he drew enormous amounts of public attention that later paid off. Art historian Thomas Craven recalled in a *Scribner's* magazine article in October 1937, the publicity Benton received was "fabulous and invaluable."

If he was not famous according to the whims of the anemic intellectuals, he was the most notorious of living painters. The critics condemned him for his "tabloid art," his "cheap nationalism," and his "modernist effrontery"; the conservatives cried out that he had degraded America; the purists attacked his vulgar subject matter, and the radicals said that he had no real political conscience—but the public was delighted.

Four decades after the New School mural was done, Benton told an interviewer,

The controversy from the political point of view was that it didn't carry what the left wing wanted, a message against the capitalist system and that made it politically undesirable for the intellectual groups in New York and for the aesthetic people, the emphasis on subject matter was considered nonessential, so I was considered reactionary on both sides of the fence, the political and the aesthetic.[1]

It was the kind of criticism Thomas Hart Benton grew accustomed to and, ultimately, enjoyed. In fact, his zest for jousting with his critics grew in coming decades.

His first major midwestern mural, for Indiana's exhibit at the 1933 Chicago World's Fair, attracted critics who objected not only to his style but the content of his

27

work—largely because Benton had included the Ku Klux Klan in his portrayal of the history of Indiana. That became something of a political skirmish which Benton shrewdly blunted by calling in his biggest critic along with some state senators during his "children's hour," during which everybody became fairly crocked on illegal Brown County, Indiana, whiskey (Prohibition had not yet been lifted) and the critic left, winking at Benton and saying, "You win."[2]

Back in New York, Benton's feud with those he sometimes called "ass-thetes" and with the left-wingers was becoming so long-winded and strident that the *New York Times* noted, "...this art debate will probably continue until the reading public is too sick of the whole mess to read another line...."

Craven added his voice, noting that the strongest criticism of Benton's works came from "the cliques in New York—the indoor esthetes and neuralgic professors to whom art is an excuse for verbal exercise, the display of dead learning...."

Benton's America is not their world; their America is the sidewalks of New York, the gallery, and the high tea. They will never know anything about America, for they are incapable of entering into any form of American life outside their own little circles. Benton, at home anywhere, goes happily about his business, adding to his fund of knowledge and painting America as he understands and enjoys it. He has not slandered our country, but by the volume, truth, and power of his art, he has done more than his share to discredit the East Side-Harvard school of esthetics.

Craven also said Benton's "first-rate mind" coupled with his bold style baffled his critics. "A painter with the ability to think is something criticism has not had to reckon with for many a day," he wrote.

He is, like Dreiser in the novel and O'Neill in the theatre, a pioneering force in American art. He has battled with academic stupidity for twenty years, and his murals announce the doom of the pseudo-classical

28

antiquities disfiguring the walls of our state houses and municipal buildings....[3]

In October Benton was invited to a dinner in New York given in honor of another midwestern artist, Grant Wood of Iowa, soon to be referred to by *Time* magazine as "the chief philosopher and greatest teacher of representational U.S. art."[4] Wood was already promoting the Midwest as an unspoiled region in which artists could discover the genuine soul of America and, thus, an American art. The friendship begun at that dinner lasted for the rest of Wood's life.

Benton's work was gaining such prominence despite the carping from critics that when *Time* printed its first full-color cover on December 24, 1934, it was a self-portrait of Thomas Hart Benton. Inside, the magazine devoted four pages to the blossoming of the United States' opposition to the pre-war French art which the magazine characterized as "arbitrary distortions and screaming colors."

U.S. painters...cheerfully joined the crazy parade of Cubism, Futurism, Dadaism, Surrealism. Painting became so deliberately unintelligible that it was no longer news when a picture was hung upside down.

In the U.S. opposition to such outlandish art first took root in the Midwest. A small group of native painters began to offer direct representation in place of introspective abstractions. To them what could be seen in their own land—streets, fields, shipyards, factories and those who people such places—became more important than what could be felt about far off places...Of these earthy Midwesterners none represents the objectivity and purpose of their school more than Missouri's Thomas Hart Benton.

The magazine referred to Benton as "the most virile of U.S. painters of the U.S. scene," and said his paintings "have a nervous electric quality which is peculiarly Benton's and which his pupils often try but fail to imitate." The article said Benton, in all his works, "almost ferociously strives to record a contemporary history of the United States."

To critics who have complained that his murals were loud and disturbing, artist Benton answers, "They represent the U.S. which is also loud and not in good taste." "I have found," he explains, "the U.S. a standardized mortuary and consequently have no sympathy with that school of detractors whose experience has been limited to first class hotels and the paved highways.

"At the same time I am no sentimentalist," he told *Time*. "I know an ass and the dust of his kicking when I come across it. But I have come across enough of it to be able to discover interesting qualities therein."[5]

Benton was growing dissatisfied with New York, its values and pretended values. During the winter of 1934-35 he went on a nationwide lecture tour. When he spoke in Des Moines on January 20, 1935, Wood introduced him. Three days later Benton was in Iowa City, where Wood was on the faculty at the University of Iowa. Wood entertained him in the quarters of the Society for the Prevention of Cruelty to Speakers, an informal two-room clubhouse garishly decorated in—as Wood put it—"the worst style of the late Victorian period." (Wood knew first hand about the decoration. He was in charge of it for the club.) It was a popular place where guest lecturers could unwind, have some refreshments, and sometimes pose in various costumes for portraits. The first guest to enjoy its hospitality was Benton. Benton and Wood, dolled up with fake moustaches and beards, struck a formal pose beneath a "Home Sweet Home" sign for the first official photograph of the club's guests. Benton then entertained club members with a harmonica performance.[6]

It was during this visit that Wood asked, "Why don't you come out here and live where you belong?" At the time, Benton couldn't see how he could afford to do it, but the comment stayed with him.[7]

Benton lectured January 28, 1935, at the Kansas City Art Institute. The *Kansas City Star* told its readers on January

12, "Rossiter Howard, director of the Institute, says he has it from Grant Wood...that Benton is a brilliant speaker, able to project his ideas with words as vigorous as his brush strokes in the scenes from American life he has painted for some of the more permanent walls, including the Indiana Statehouse." Benton met his brother Nat, then the prosecuting attorney in Greene County, Missouri, while he was there. Nat Benton convinced Tom to go to Jefferson City to meet some of the "Democratic boys."[8] Forty years later, the man who was Speaker of the House in 1935, John G. Christy, recalled some of the participants at the gathering decided it would be a good idea to have Benton do a painting for his home state.

Guy B. Park was governor and they called him sometime early in the morning with the suggestion and I think the figure, if I recall correctly, that they talked about was $50,000....The Governor was something like President Truman. He was rather pithy in his statements and with a few oaths he said, "Don't you know there's a depression goin' on? Can't you do it for less than that?" And Thomas Hart Benton said, "Yes, I could do it for nothing."[9]

But he wasn't about to do it that way.

The meeting at a Jefferson City hotel was "one of those regular hotel room parties where you pour liquids down you and stories out of you until the world begins to spin," Benton recalled. He was feeling no pain when Senator Ed Barbour of Springfield suggested to him that he ought to do a mural for his home state. Benton said he was willing but gave the matter no more thought.

Now the world was spinning for me and I took Ed's proposition just to be a part of the spinning and forgot about it. I went back to New York and fell into a lot of worldly controversies again. But it seems that Ed and my brother Nat had talked over the business of a Missouri mural before the hotel party, that they had made rather extensive plans which I knew nothing about, and that Ed's question to me was no mere party question but one that had substance to back it.[10]

Another version of the story says Benton was noticed to be sketching by Senator Barbour, who was amused to see a drawing of himself chatting with a lobbyist. Benton told him he intended to make a painting of it entitled "A Western Senator and a Lobbyist." Although the sketch wasn't too flattering, Barbour was flattered that he would be the topic of a painting. The *St. Louis Post-Dispatch* said on August 9, 1936, Barbour began to tell his friends in the Senate, "Benton knows real Missourians. He's an honest-to-God Missourian himself. He's honest. Why he'd rather sit in a store window and talk houn' dog stories and drink whiskey than do anything else."

Legislative journals show Barbour introduced Senate Concurrent Resolution 6 shortly afterward. It was passed on March 5. Later that same day, on a motion by Representative Roy Hamlin of Hannibal, the House concurred.

The resolution noted that Benton had become recognized "as one of the greatest living painters; is accredited as the leading exponent of a style and content of paintings distinctly representative of the characteristics of American life; and has gained special eminence as a painter of mural decorations depicting the scene and activities of American life"; and that his works had been permanently installed in various museums, galleries, and public buildings. But, the resolution said, no public building in Missouri had a Benton painting in it. At the same time, the capitol had not yet had "adequate and appropriate mural decorations." The resolution said it was time to honor Benton by having him do a mural for the capitol. Three senators and three representatives were to consult with the Board of the Permanent Seat of Government to find an appropriate subject and place for the mural. John Christy recalled that the original thought was to put it in the Senate Lounge. But the Lounge was already decorated with Lorenz Kleiser's tapestries. The only place in the building large enough would have to be the House Lounge.[11]

The Lounge was one of the few places that had not been decorated by a special commission appointed to place murals and sculpture in, on, and around the building depicting Missouri's history and greatness. The architect for the capitol, Egerton Swartwout, had told the Capitol Decoration Commission in a letter dated September 22, 1921, the Lounge was 'bald and forbidding.' He thought the only thing to do with the room was to place oak paneling on the walls from the top of the wainscot to the cornice. Perhaps portraits of governors could be displayed there, he suggested. He advised against any kind of mural paintings in the room: "It should be remembered this room is not a monumental room, but is a Lounging Room or large waiting room for the members and it should be warm and attractive in appearance which never could be obtained by the stone and mural treatment."

The money for Benton was in the thirty-first amendment offered to a House-passed appropriation bill in the Senate. Senator James Rollins' amendment provided Benton's $16,000 salary was to include all expenses of the work. Two days later the bill went to a conference committee. On May 27 that committee recommended Amendment 31, among others, be accepted. It took another trip through that conference committee, though, before another snag could be worked out. Later that day the House approved the bill containing the money for Benton's mural, 92-12. The Senate approved it the next day. The job was to be done by January 1937.

Tom Benton now had a reason to get out of New York.

On the same day he received word that he had been commissioned to do the mural, Benton received a letter from Ross Howard, the director of the Kansas City Art Institute. Benton had visited with Howard in late March about joining the teaching staff at the Institute. The letter from Howard said that Benton had a job there if he wanted it. "I made up my mind suddenly to leave New York and go home to Missouri for good," Benton later wrote.[12]

The agreement with the Institute was finalized in early April. Benton was to head the department of painting and drawing. Institute president W. Rickert Fillmore said,

The Midwest has been calling the strongest men in the art field, one after another, and I am satisfied that the influence of Thomas Craven, noted critic and author, has been brought to bear upon his favorite painters, among them Benton and Curry, with the idea of inducing them to join Grant Wood in the Middle West. With Benton at Kansas City, Curry at Manhattan, Kans., and Grant Wood already painting in Iowa, the strategic points are well covered. We should be able to make a strong stand.[13]

Others knew the kind of artist the Midwest was getting, even if Missourians who would later strongly oppose Benton's mural did not. His later opponents apparently had not read reviews such as the one by Ruth Pickering who said Benton "refuses to paint subjects that are merely sweet and friendly and calm."

He never paints the pleasant or the pretty. For all his volatility there is seldom joy. This is love and sorrow, pity, and wit but no playfulness. He is harassed by what he sees in American life. This is why his canvasses are restless.

She found something disturbing in his "strident, clear colored paintings and murals....His paintings are full of energy, never quite peaceful, a kind of crying in the wilderness against something."

To the critics who complain that Mr. Benton's work is "not in good taste," he announces that the life he paints is not in good taste, either. To those who condemn his pictures because "they won't be flat on the wall," he says they are realistic representations and that he has not found life flat.[14]

About the same time, the *New York World-Telegram* said on April 13 that Benton "brazenly glorifies life in the raw, unpretty life that is splendid because it is true."

He catches America as America is, the shoddy and the singing, the rugged and the pitiful. And in himself and the powerful beauty of his loud and uncouth art he shows the power that is in all this nation, if it follows truly the maxim, "To thine own self be true."

Benton was glad to be going back to the Middle West, he told *Art Front* magazine in its April issue, because it was the least provincial area in America, lacking stereotypes such as those in the East. Benton admitted the heritage of the Midwest was dotted with "crudities and brutalities." But he argued they are inseparable from a frontier opportunism that "has provided the substance for every democratic drive in our history."

Because, unlike the East, as a whole, it has never had a colonial psychology, that dependent attitude of mind which acts as a check on cultural experiments motivated in the environment.

...The Middle West is going to dominate the social changes due in this country and will thereby determine the nature of the phenomena to which the artist *must* react if he is to make forms which are not imitations of other forms.

He also felt the young artists in the middle part of the country were less affected by "that dependent, cowardly and servile spirit" he found among his artist associates in the East.

Benton also felt the big eastern cities were outworn. "Humane living is no longer possible within them," he wrote as the movers were packing up his household goods. He felt New York was "highly provincial," harboring people who had become dependent upon "attenuated political, artistic, and economic ideas of Europe."[15] In later years he told interviewer Mike Wallace that cities are "coffins for living and thinking."

I just feel that life within them is simply not good enough anymore. You don't get enough out of it. The pressures are too great. The dirt's too much. The stinks are too much. And the intellectual world stinks too when it's shut in and doesn't get out into the world. I think that the intellectual world in New York is even worse than the Congress of the United States if you're dealing with ideas....It's repetitious, common, redundant, and boresome.

[Wallace:] A bunch of people who get together and...

[Benton:] ...Got to get together and mouth at each other.[16]

There might be a little more to the story than a hotel party, a resolution, and an appropriation bill, though. Polly Burroughs, in her book, *Thomas Hart Benton: A Portrait*, quotes him telling an old friend, "I paid off a politician five hundred dollars and that did it."[17] The accuracy of Burroughs' account is questioned by some members of Benton's family. His sister-in-law, Eleanor Piacenza, notes Benton has left at least two written accounts of that payment, which went to Senator Barbour. In one account, Benton speaks of it as a lawyer's fee charged for representing his interests before the legislature. In another account he says his brother Nat suggested he give $500 to Barbour for his help. Regardless, Mrs. Piacenza says it is likely the money was paid after the mural was finished or while it was being painted.[18]

Benton was "welcomed [in Kansas City] as a celebrity, half hobo and half highbrow, the scion of a distinguished family, whose life had been rich in escapades and provocative irregularities."[19] But he walked into controversy from the beginning. His $16,000 was more money than Missouri paid the governor.

All of his expenses came out of that money, though. Even Benton didn't know how much the work would cost because of "a thousand expenses that are unavoidable."

I use real people as models. When I represent a farmer I get a farmer, when I represent a night club girl I get one of them too. The farmer doesn't cost more than a ten-cent cigar generally, but the girl is likely to be more expensive. She has to find it entertaining to pose or she won't do it. Now while some of my mural expenses come pretty easy because they have other than strict working values, they are nevertheless expenses. You can't exactly charge them up against anything when you make out your income tax, but they cut down profits just as do other more generally recognized items of expense.[20]

Benton also said his material costs were high. "When I start a mural I have come to expect to be constantly shelling out money for this, that, and the other."

He estimated, however, that after taxes and all expenses, he kept about one-third of the $16,000 as his payment—a good enough amount, given the Depression era during which the mural was done.[21]

Philosophically, Benton was ready to go home. He sensed in his lecture tours a "sort of distrust with big cities, caused by the Depression, and of the values the cities represented." He saw an increased interest in culture in smaller cities. He had seen museums springing up, universities starting new art courses, and newspapers commenting about it without poking fun. "This was a revolutionary change from my boyhood days in the West when the word 'art' was mentioned only self-consciously in the obscurity of ladies' clubs, and when the few art schools that existed away from the big cities were regarded as the resorts of nuts and cranks."

I had large and friendly audiences in my western talks and while I did not lack hecklers, the majority of these seemed to be better informed and to be more sincerely interested in getting at my meanings than did those of the big cities. Everywhere I found what appeared to be a genuine interest in the expressive arts....I felt that whatever forces were at work, there was growing, particularly in the Middle West, a belief that values could exist in things beyond immediate usage and that these values should be nursed and cultivated.[22]

He arrived in Kansas City September 23, 1935, to take up

residence at 905 East 47th Street.[23] About 1,400 people turned out for a reception to honor him October 6. Some of his paintings had been put on display at the Nelson Gallery of Art and at the Institute. The one that attracted the most attention was "Preparing the Bill," the painting Benton had done featuring Senator Barbour. The *Kansas City Star* reported the next day some other paintings drew attention: "The Jealous Lover of Lone Green Valley," by Benton and Wood's "American Gothic."

A group from Haskell Institute, an Indian school in Lawrence, Kansas, performed at that tea with music, Indian dances, and stories of Indian customs. Later, when Benton was looking for an Indian for the mural, he remembered the people he met that day from Haskell.[24]

The newspapers covered Benton's announcement of plans to travel throughout Missouri four days a week to accumulate material and sketches, teaching at the Art Institute other times. The mural would be "Missouri from start to finish," he told an interviewer. He hoped to begin work by the first of March.

But in legislative halls, there were already voices of dissent. David Hess, a young representative from St. Louis, recalled years later that Senator Michael Kinney of St. Louis was "the most vigorous opponent" Benton had. "He said he was a hack....Said he was a good cartoonist and that was about all."[25]

Benton originally thought he would do a Huck Finn mural as a tribute to Mark Twain. He had written in *The Modern Monthly* in May 1934, "It takes a Mark Twain, with direct national experience and a properly attuned psychology, to write a *Huckelberry Finn* and make a work of art which is actually an expression of its locale. An imperfect work of art, but a real one." When he learned the space provided was as large as it would be, he changed his mind. "But don't worry,'' he told the *Post-Dispatch*, "Huck will be in it and so will the King and the Duke and their raft.''

He was faced with one wall fifty feet long, and two others of twenty-five feet. A fourth wall fifty feet long was broken up by windows. His panels would have to be sixteen feet high and would have to be fitted around those windows as well as three prominent doors. The joining of the walls at right angles presented the first time he had to contend with an established architectural setting while painting a mural.

Whatever I did had to be adjusted to them. It would have been simple enough to handle this situation with flat, decorative forms, but it was difficult with the illusionary, three-dimensional projections to which I was now committed.[26]

Benton made no secret that the mural would not be a hodgepodge of well-known Missourians. The *Post-Dispatch* reported, ''Benton's idea is to show the history of Missourians, and not to emphasize heroic figures or epic events.'' When the newspaper suggested his portrayal of Missouri's history might lead to the same kind of criticism he had heard in other works, Benton refused to soft-peddle his intentions. "Now get me right,'' he said, ''None of my stuff is propoganda. I'm a realist. I paint what I see. You supply the materials. I can't always be painting pictures of people going around in frock coats and carrying Bibles. They don't act that way.''

Benton worked for about two years on the mural, much of the time traveling the state and sketching people, buildings, equipment, and animals.

After I had my subject worked out, found out what I was going to do, I had to design it. I had to get all the models to take their poses for...the positions I had designed. I had to go and find people so as to individualize the characters and make 'em all look like Missourians...It took eighteen months to prepare the picture and six months to paint it.[27]

He took two months to build the biggest, most detailed plastilene model he had ever made. It was fifteen feet long, twenty inches high. He told Betty Chamberlain of *Time* magazine, in an August 1940 letter, that he intended to give the model to the state museum, "but souvenir hunters picked nearly all the figures off it while I was away."

Although some credit him with inventing the technique, it is actually quite old, dating back to the sixteenth century Italian artist, Tintoretto, or the Spanish artist, El Greco.

And you can nearly always tell these sculptural type of paintings from paintings which are just pure visual realism, looking at nature. But, to understand here, I wanted the thing to be real. But in order to make it real I had to have some sort of reality to refer to. So I made the reality out of clay.[28]

The model was on a basic plane that was tipped back at a forty-five degree angle to give Benton the perspective that viewers would have. "Had that plane been raised to a vertical position as would have been necessary for use as architectural decoration," he said, "not only would my design have been lost, but all the forward figures would have appeared to be falling off."[29]

Sid Larson says the clay models "were never intended to become bronzes. They were only there, and only to last, until he had time to do his color sketch, his value studies from them, and then he didn't care what happened to them."

He used paper clips, little straws from brooms, chunks of tobacco mixed with wax, or sometimes mixed with wax and any kind of material that might have been around the studio, pencils—anything for an armature on which he could put a glob of clay or some of these other mixtures to get a shape. Because his paint would cover all of this, it was never done with great detail.

Larson said Benton believed "the paintings could be energized if he would, in effect, defy gravity by having the figure lean out toward the observer."

To do this, he would take two flat boards and fasten them at the horizon so that the bottom one was still sloped from back to front....The sky, meeting at that point, would then not be totally vertical but would slope also, and on that sky he would often put a bas relief cloud. On the others he would put in, perpendicular to that slanting surface, these little figures. He would paint them the local color, move them around in the light from that north window of the studio, or get in the artificial light, just to see how dramatic he could make the lighting for it for his initial studies.[30]

He also had to be careful in organizing the elements and transferring them to the wall because a mural looks different to the artist working close to it than it does to a spectator on the floor below. Benton told an interviewer, "Every inch of it must be planned beforehand, its effects pre-calculated far more than those of an easel picture." He warned that a painter who changed his mind on the scaffold risked having everything go awry. "You must solve your problems before you get up there," he asserted.[31]

Larson recalled that Benton said "that when he had finished planning a painting he had really done everything except the last and almost minor consideration and that was the execution of the final product." Larson said he knows of no other artist about which that could be said to the degree Benton meant it.

Planning and preparation were incredibly extensive and thorough, and I often felt too much so. But that was his approach. And we discussed this. I said, "Gee, you don't allow any room for intuition. You don't allow any room for the painting to talk back to you." And he said, "All those things can happen in the planning."[32]

Benton insisted on total control of his creation. He refused to allow any government commission to watch over his shoulder. As the *Kansas City Times* put it on March 4, 1937, "Neither prosaic legal pronouncements nor the perhaps plebian tastes of politicians were set up to interfere with the artistic freedom of Thomas Hart Benton." He never submitted any preliminary design to the Board of the

Permanent Seat of Government. The Capitol Decoration Commission, which oversaw the earlier decorative work of the building, was not recalled.

When Benton realized that the effort to have him do a mural for his home state was serious, he contacted his brother and outlined the conditions under which he would agree. But when the contract was delivered to him, he found "a small article" that indicated he was to work with a supervising commission. He wanted no part of that. "I was pretty certain that a Missouri Art Commission would be quite as fearful of my way of seeing things as was the Treasury Dept. Committee," he wrote.[33]

Benton feared that his plan to include figures such as Jesse James and Frankie and Johnny and others would be "subjects too unconventional to submit to the timorous judgments of any official art commission." But he also feared he would jeopardize his chance to do the work, and the large fee that went with it, if he objected too strenuously to controls over it.

On the other hand, I looked on the mural itself as the greatest opportunity I had yet had to realize my artistic dreams. Unlike the Post Office mural its theme offered immensely interesting and congenial subjects, many so familiar from boyhood memories that their representation would automatically have the qualities of that specifically Missouri spirit I wanted my mural to express. I could make it almost like a painted autobiography if I had freedom to act as I saw fit. Without that freedom I could be channeled into producing a commonplace official work full of trite and mushy symbols.

Benton had to weigh "the dreadful chance of losing the sixteen thousand dollars against that of having my mural ideas emasculated," he gambled. He sent the contract back to Senator Barbour with a note saying he would not do the mural unless the supervision language was removed. A week later the contract was returned without that troublesome clause. "I was completely free," Benton wrote.[34]

The contract required only that the mural be a social history of Missouri, "to include a comprehensive presentation of the evolution of the life and customs of the people of the state." The detail and the content of the mural were left to Benton.[35]

He traveled the state, looking for "types" of Missourians.

There's a north Missouri type, a Bootheel type, an Ozark type, But there's a distinct Missouri accent. I lived in New York for 24 years and I could tell a Missourian up there any time.[36]

He found his "types" throughout Missouri and sketched them. He recalled in *An Artist in America*:

I met all kinds of people. I played the harmonica and wore a pink shirt to country dances. I went on hunting and fishing parties. I attended an uproarious three-day, old settler's drunk, in the depths of the Ozarks. I went to political barbecues and church picnics. I took in the honky-tonks of the country and the night clubs of Kansas City and St. Louis. I went to businessmen's parties and to meetings of art lovers' associations. I went down in the mines and out in the cornfields. I chased Missouri society up and down from the shacks of the Ozark hillbillies to the country club firesides of the ultimately respectable.

His notebook, which survives in the Benton Trust in Kansas City, contains his early notes, sketches, and thoughts about the segments of his mural. St. Louis is a "rough place: 'Wine, Women & Song' in the regular frontier way," he noted; trade in furs was the accepted currency there before statehood: small coins of the period were made from Mexican dollars cut into pieces or bits. At times, he referred to history books for notes about bull boats or other features of early Missouri. At the top of one page, he penciled, "Get Houck's History," referring to the landmark books by Louis Houck, a southeast Missouri historian, developer and railroad builder.

Benton wrote to himself on one page, "In depicting an early trading town, look up types of houses. Notice division of 'common' field in French towns. Depth as contrasted with width.'' A rough sketch of two houses and the narrow common fields that went with French communities was included. He was already thinking in terms of groupings.

''3rd group will have to represent the Santa Fe Trade & Oregon trail,'' he wrote. ''Outfitting western expeditions (This is a matter of national importance).'' Then later on the page he suggested keel boats be shown in the background on the Missouri River.

The fourth group, he suggested to himself, would include the ''Annual Bonnet Show at Big Shoal Church''—Liberty, Mo., 2nd Sunday in May. Spring landscape out of the door. Room of ladies in new Bonnets.''

He noted the way buildings were constructed and what businesses existed in St. Louis when Missouri became American territory, what the early industries were, and suggested the fifth group would be ''The Duel & The organization and building of churches. The circuit riding preachers. First Baptist Church at Cape Girardeau.''

The sixth group, he thought, might involve the Missouri Compromise and slavery, showing Negro groups in chains ''led by Mo. coat of arms.''

Group 7, he thought, might be ''The Land of Zion,'' and his notes included references to accounts of Missouri's Mormon War, during which Joseph Smith's followers were driven from Missouri after months of conflict and blood-spilling.

The railroad, he thought, might be part of the eighth group, along with the stands taken by his ancestor, Senator Thomas Hart Benton, for a transcontinental railroad and against the extension of slavery in the territories. Depictions of actions of desperadoes along the Missouri-Kansas border in those years were suggested in his notes.

That led to the ninth grouping—guerilla warfare and eventually the Civil War.

The tenth group might be "the question of Negro suffrage. Banditry—James and Youngers."

They were only tentative ideas although some found their way into the finished mural.

In July 1935 Benton spent several days in Springfield visiting his brother, Nat, and was amazed that courtrooms in a city that size were crowded with spectators. He decided to paint a Missouri courtroom scene. "It may be in the state capitol but I don't know," he said, "Anyway, I shall paint it somewhere, for nothing is more typical of Missouri than the average courtroom audience."[37]

That same month, Benton took his family to Colorado for a vacation. A newspaper in Estes Park reported on July 5 that it was hard to keep Benton talking about art.

There is no affectation in the man, no "I am a celebrity" complex. He seems far more enthusiastic about playing the harmonica, for instance, than over the mural...which he has been commissioned to paint this fall.

But even then, almost a year before he started putting paint on the walls in the capitol, some folks were casting a critical eye. Springfield writer May Kennedy McCord was not impressed with Benton's painting, "She'll Be Comin' Around the Mountain." "It may be art, but it certainly isn't expressive of hillbilly life," she said. She objected to one of the figures in the painting performing on an accordion, which she insisted was a nontypical instrument in the Ozarks. But Benton said he could produce several witnesses that the accordion was being played by a member of the group when he did the original sketch.[38]

He sketched body poses, not usually putting faces on them until later. Some of his sketches were only rough outlines, hastily drawn. Some were more detailed. As Benton prepared his final drawings, his attention to detail intensified. Rossiter Howard remembered Benton spending an entire afternoon studying the hand and forearm of a model.[39]

Sometimes Benton used his students at the Institute for body poses. One of them was Jack Nesbitt who, during the summer of 1936, dropped by the school even though he wasn't taking classes that semester. Benton spotted him.

"Hey, Jack, I need a model, how about you posing for me for a couple of hours."

He sketched Nesbitt in various poses and put him in the mural not once but several times. Nesbitt recalled Benton was "a whiz" at sketching. "He could make what you might term shorthand notes and then develop it later," he recalled. "It was a real good trick that he had. I'd be taking half an afternoon to make a drawing that he could make in twenty minutes." In the courtroom scene, Nesbitt is the man seated at the table in front of the judge's bench with his back to the viewer. "That's all of me," he said, "needin' a haircut and everything else." But part of Nesbitt is depicted throughout that scene.

[Nesbitt:]There's a fella just to the left of that that's looking toward the judge, down sort of in the foreground more or less, and I posed for that figure and posed for most of the jury figures. And he put portrait heads on them.

[Priddy:] So the jury is mostly you, except for the faces.

[Nesbitt:] Except for the faces which he put on people he knew or knew about.[40]

He had his sketchbook with him at all times and made thousands of drawings, starting with tree trunks, old shoes, and other things that interested him. He told Ruth Pickering in the February 1935 *Arts and Decoration* magazine that he saw something interesting "and the formal relations follow."

Only knowledge which is deeply and profoundly a part of one can be communicated through the logical conventions of a form. Such knowledge is found, not on the intellectual fringe of life, or in the illusions of cloistered sensibilities, but in life itself where the drive of people is felt and shared.

[I paint murals] because I can include more stuff in them. I'm interested in American life. I would like to enclose it all. The mural can carry more aspects within itself than any small painting. It can therefore be more expressive of society, of the panorama. Further, it reaches more people....

Benton's travels took him to Neosho in the spring of 1936, his first visit in twenty-four years to his former hometown. The *Kansas City Star* reported on June 18 a party was held for Benton during a political rally that featured his brother, Nat, as the main speaker. The brothers were honored guests at a chicken dinner at the inn at Big Spring Park, where a number of old friends exchanged memories with Tom; some had not seen him for thirty years. One recalled the artist as "the shiftiest left-end the town football team ever had," and another recalled him as "a bearcat with his fists."

The next day, Benton spent some time looking for a Neosho lawyer, Horace Roark, who had been his father's partner. Roark, however, "neglected to appear at his accustomed Saturday morning station on the square to greet the farmers arriving in the town." When Benton tracked him to his house that evening, Roark claimed he had been trout fishing, not hiding out. Roark was willing to pose. In fact, he figured he might owe it to Benton to pose.

The other day a writer for some magazine was here and asked me about your boyhood days in Neosho. "The only thing I can remember about Tom Benton," I told him, "is that he always was being brought up in court and fined $1 and costs for fist fighting." Remember the time I paid your fine so your father wouldn't find out you had been at it again?

Roark's face later showed up in the political rally scene of the capitol mural.

While waiting for Roark to arrive, Benton went to nearby Pineville to visit with Oklahoma short story writer George

47

Milburn. (Benton's father had once so successfully prose-
cuted a man in the courthouse in Pineville that he narrowly
escaped assassination by the man's outraged relatives.)

Deep America—the backwoods, small towns and river communities—
and the problems of interpreting the American scene in art and literature
were discussed....The talk was more heady than the beer that accompanied
it. The conversation might have gone on indefinitely. But Benton had to
return to Neosho to catch his model.

The day after that Benton took his pad to Rube Rose's
farm near Springfield to sketch a mule, which was posed for
him in the barnyard by Mrs. Rose and her son. On the way
back to Kansas City, Benton suddenly stopped the car. He
had seen some heifers just the age and kind he wanted. So
the portrait of Sooky the heifer went into the sketchbook
along with Roark, Rube Rose's mule, a silo, and a coal mine.

For just the right man, just the right mule and cow, Mr. Benton traveled
more than 500 miles through Southern Missouri. This summer he will
continue traveling and searching for characteristic people and scenes,
until detail drawings make the 200-odd figures in his Missouri state
capitol mural living Missourians against a real background. Nothing will
be spared to portray the history, life and legends of the state truthful₁y and
in the spirit of modern American art.

David Hess, the young representative from St. Louis,
went into the mural as a member of the jury. He recalled he
was sitting in the legislative library working on a horse
racing bill he was sponsoring when Benton came in.

He talked to me about racing. He understood racing. He understood
breeding....And while I was sitting there, I know he sketched me at the
time because he showed it to me on two or three different occasions.[41]

The office of Adjutant General Harold Brown was in the
capitol then. Brown's son, Harold, Jr., still lives in Jefferson
City. Benton and the elder Brown became acquainted in the
capitol halls, and Benton decided to include the face of the

adjutant general in the mural. They made an appointment for Benton to call at the Brown's house across from the state prison.

But this trip became a "two-fer" for Benton—two for the price of one. And it would make little Harold Brown one of the controversial parts of the mural.

I was about one years old and I was laying on a blanket and Benton did my father and he said, "I like that baby. I need to get that baby into the mural in some way." And so I was just a victim. And he used both of these sketches....The foreman of the jury is my father.[42]

There were others who wandered into the reach of Benton's sketchbook at the capitol. Mary Tunnell Wherritt was just Mary Tunnell then, working at the state highway department. She sometimes stopped by the House Lounge to watch Benton paint when she got off work.

And one afternoon he asked me if I would mind being in the mural and I said, "Oh, no, I'd be happy to be in it." And he said, "Wait 'till I tell you what I want you to—where I want you in the mural." And he explained that it was a lady diapering a baby and I said, "That's all right with me. I don't mind at all." And he did his pen—or pencil sketches.[43]

Interestingly, this woman and the child she's diapering never met one another in those days. In fact, it was not until February 1984 that each found out who the other was.

One of the others who found himself picked from the crowd was a porter at the capitol nicknamed "Popeye." Rotha Williams was on the mop crew one day in 1935. He told Paul Watkins forty years later Benton approached him one morning and asked him to pose for a figure in the mural. "But there's a catch," he told Williams. "I'm going to say something to you and you might not like it."

He said, "Let me tell you first what the character's going to be....You're going to be—wait a minute now, I'm pretty near scared to say this to you." I said, "Mr. Benton, you won't make me mad, I don't believe you will." He said, "Well, the character's going to be Nigger Jim." His face bloomed up and he looked at me funny. But I told him it would be quite an honor to have my picture on that wall.

Williams recalled that Benton "had a little piece of paper" about the size of Williams' two hands. "It seemed like he just made three or four marks and then he said, 'Come back up here in a while. I'll have your picture on the wall shortly.'"

About 2:30, some six and one-half hours later, Benton called Williams up from the janitor room. "So I went up there and there I was," Williams recalled. "Only I was holding two fish."

Williams knew immediately what some of the others might only later have realized. "It was quite an honor. Yes it was," he told Watkins.[44]

His portrayal, however, prompted a controversy which, though small compared to others, was more national in scope than others.

The episode from Mark Twain...was all the more shocking to Benton's audience because of the prominence given to Huck's companion....Missouri was not entirely ready for people's history, however, especially if the people included Negro janitors.[45]

For years, Williams remained a familiar figure in Jefferson City, working at the Fischer Drug Store on High Street a few blocks from the capitol. He died in 1983. People who never knew his name recognized him on the street as the most prominently portrayed black man in the capitol for almost a half-century, until a bust of George Washington Carver was unveiled in 1982.

Although Benton had traveled extensively looking for the "types" he wanted to include among the faces of Missourians, he found many in his own family and several in Jefferson City.

In the jury scene of which Harold Brown, Sr., is the jury

foreman and David Hess is one of the jurors, the attorney arguing the case is Nat Benton, the artist's brother who started the whole process. Among the other jurors are Robert M. Snyder, Jr., whose father started building the castle at HaHa Tonka, now a state park near Camdenton; and Frank Canada, a watchman at the capitol, dubbed the "Unofficial Greeter" for visitors. Benton probably saw Canada often. Canada met people at the main door of the building, would "make the stranger feel at home," and tell people how to find the things they wanted to see.[46]

Greene County sheriff Scott Curtis is sitting next to the spattered spittoon. The judge who appears to be dozing is Guy D. Kirby of Springfield, a crusty circuit judge who had been on the bench more than nineteen years when Benton painted him. When Allen Oliver interviewed Kirby about his presence in the mural, the *Springfield News and Leader* published a photograph with the article showing the judge dozing in his favorite chair in his office.

He lifted his chin from the folds of his shirt front, spat with typical accuracy at the spittoon, and looked out the window partly, we thought, to conceal the fact that there was a trace of a smile around the corners of his mouth and a whimsical twinkle in his eye.

"Well," he said, "Have they got Mark Twain and Senator Vest and Champ Clark and Eugene Field? I'm pretty damn particular about the company I keep."

Then he hit the spittoon again and turned and gazed for a moment out the window.

Kirby was well known for his clothing—pants with legs that "lack several inches of reaching his shoetops" because he did not like pants legs flapping around his ankles as he walked, and with waist sized far larger than necessary because he hated tight belts around his midsection. He told Oliver that Benton had asked to sketch him.

So I told him he could, and the next morning I shaved and powdered my face and put on a little toilet water and let him sketch me. But I had no idea he was going to use it in the murals.[47]

In the background is the old county courthouse in Neosho. Slightly to the left and below that scene—actually part of another scene—is Benton's son, T. P., munching on a slice of bread.[48] Nearby, the farm woman rolling dough is Mrs. Caldwell, the mother-in-law of Nat Benton.[49]

And in the scene of the political rally is Benton's father, M. E. Benton, delivering the oration. Craven, in his *Scribner's* article, recalled that the senior Benton was a "character...squat and red-bearded...known in Washington as 'the homeliest man in Congress.'"

He could outtalk, outlaugh, and outdrink any of his colleagues. Though pot-hardy and convivial, he could be stubborn and dictatorial, with now and then a lapse into a secretive melancholy not uncommon among pioneers. But he was little given to moping, had strong physical appetites and indulged them, and never passed a wakeful night until cancer choked him to death at the age of seventy-seven.

The artist was definitely the son of his father. When the artist was searching for a "type" to represent the political orator, he turned to a man who did all he could to keep the son from becoming the artist who, a decade after his father's death, enshrined the image of a now-forgotten southwest Missouri Congressman on the wall of Missouri's capitol as a symbol of the state's great political heritage.

On the platform with Benton's father is Guy Park, the governor at the time the mural was painted. He is sitting with his arms folded. The other man is Means Ray, the mayor of Jefferson City then.

The man looking askance at the two scrapping kids in the same scene is Senator Barbour. The two boys are Benton's nephews. The fat man beside the platform is Sid Hamilton, commissioner of the Permanent Seat of Government. The tall man with a cane at the rear of the crowd is

Representative W.E. Whitecotton of Monroe County. Others in the crowd are Bowling Green postmaster Carroll Wisdom (a former state senator from Pike County), Supreme Court Judge C.A. Leedy, Jr., Stephen Hunter (the head of probation and parole for the state), and Jefferson City hotel manager W.F. (Doc) Simpson. The building in the background is the old Pike County courthouse.

A childhood friend of the Bentons, identified in *Life* magazine only as Mrs. Pickens, a WPA typist, was the model for the sunbonnet girl fixing the picnic lunch. In the *Kansas City Star* she was later identified as Mrs. Joseph Lilliard.[50]

Frank Brew is Huckelberry Finn. The man loading the mule in the first panel is prison warden J.M. Sanders. The trader with the whiskey jug is Glen Rounds, a fellow Kansas City artist who showed up in another of Benton's paintings, "The Ballad of the Jealous Lover of Lone Green Valley," painted in 1934. Benton told a *Post-Dispatch* correspondent he didn't think he was getting an exact likeness while he was painting the figure, but when he was done "the trapper turned out to look more like an old reprobate than the original."[51]

Jefferson City insurance agent Charles La Pierre is the "Pathfinder" in buckskins, with the two dogs. The figure is often mistakenly described as depicting Daniel Boone. The dog? "Sid Hamilton took me right across the river from here, and I sketched him there," Benton told an audience in Jefferson City. "I know the dog," said someone in the audience. "He's worth $30."[52]

Dan James, whose father was head of a group that raised money to buy contemporary works for the Kansas City art museum, was the model for one of his ancestors, Jesse James. In 1987, James recalled in an interview for producers of a film being made for the centennial exhibition of Benton's art, "He stuck me in one of his damn baroque positions where I had to stand forever with my knees bent holding this giant Colt revolver. I thought it came out recognizably.'' James said he was ''charmed to be entombed'' in the mural. He recalled Benton also used his first wife as a model for a woman wearing ''sort of a maroon dress'' in the small panel next to the main doorway into the room.

The persons in the St. Louis segment were people who actually worked in the breweries and shoe factories there. The stenographer is a composite of several girls working at the capitol.

The men at the table in the nightclub scene in the St. Louis segment of the mural are Justus Moll, once the president of the Greene County Historical Society, and W. Douglas Meng of Lexington, a former Kansas City newspaperman who was by then the editor of the state's official manual. One of the girls dancing with another nightclub patron in that same scene is Glada Longdon, an employee of the state old-age assistance office in the capitol, who would go with her girlfriend to the Lounge during coffee breaks to watch Benton paint.

He had warned us to be quiet and we would just step inside and watch him as he was sketching the figures. One day he asked us to strike a dance pose as he wasn't sure that the dancing couples were posed just right...He just turned around and from where he was working and looked at us and said, ''Would you girls strike a dance pose for me so that I can check my figures, and see if I have them right here?''[53]

The farmer milking the cow is Austin Houston, a former state representative from north Missouri's Putnam County, who was by then the assistant commissioner of the Permanent Seat of Government. Houston's daughter, Virginia Burnett, recalled years later that the picture is appropriate. The family retained ownership of its farm near Unionville even after moving to Jefferson City. She recalled that Benton decided to put her father in the mural after meeting him in the capitol. Her father, who died in 1975, was always quietly proud of his presence in the mural. "He didn't really go around making a big issue of it," she recalled, but "whenever anybody that was family was here," he'd take that person to the capitol to see the mural.

Virginia, then in her mid-teens, would go to the capitol after school in the fall of 1936 to watch Benton paint. He would acknowledge her presence by asking how her day had been. But she always followed her father's advice: "You can go in and watch but don't bother him."

Mrs. Burnett also recalled a "red-headed gal" named Nettie Buchanan who was a secretary for the Permanent Seat of Government who also was put in the mural.[54]

The most controversial segment of the mural is the last segment Benton painted. An insurance man, R. Bryson Jones, is speaking at a civic meeting in the Kansas City segment. At the tables below are J.C. Nichols (on the left) and W.T. Kemper, two prominent Kansas City businessmen. Some thought placing those distinguished gentlemen so close to scantily clad dancing girls was disgraceful, but Benton responded in a Kansas City speech reported by the Associated Press on March 1, 1937, that he had "been to many businessmen's parties here and in St. Louis, and I want to tell you that I put considerable clothes on her."

It wasn't the proximity to the dancing girls that enraged some but the inclusion of a portrait of Tom Pendergast, the longtime boss of Kansas City and, in many ways, state politics. Inclusion of Pendergast apparently was a late thought for Benton. Seeing the results of the November elections, he concluded that Pendergast was an undeniable part of Missouri tradition.[55] So in late November or early December, he went to Pendergast's office at 1908 Main Street in Kansas City and sketched a profile outline of the boss. It wasn't easy getting him to pose. "I had to do quite a bit of wire pulling. But I guess I've got a little politics in my own blood,'' he recalled for the *St. Louis Globe-Democrat* on March 8, 1937.

Benton and his only assistant on the project had sketched the outline of the scene but at that point hadn't put any faces into it. From the start, however, it was pointed out that Pendergast's appearance on the mural was to be an abstraction, a scene unto itself apart from the dinner gathering. The *Kansas City Star* reported on December 6, 1936, "Dinner affairs and public gatherings, except national political conventions, never have been a part of Pendergast's activities." At the last minute, Benton changed the Pendergast portrait. Representative Ansel Moore wrote to *Life* magazine that he had investigated the habits of Pendergast and found that the boss didn't smoke cigars, as Benton originally intended to show. "After being advised by a member of the press of his error, he changed the said cigar into a cigarette mounted in a holder,'' wrote Moore in the April 5, 1937 edition of *Life*.

It was this accumulation of faces that prompted a reporter from the *Kansas City Journal-Post* one day to ask Benton, "Interesting faces—whom do they belong to? Thinkers, orators, actors, business men? Who owns them?' It triggered a long discourse by Benton published on November 8, 1936, in which he pointedly noted, "The average businessman has an absolutely uninteresting face...because he has dealt with abstractions for so long that he has ceased to be a realist.''

The only time when he is at all realistic is when he is flat under his car, tinkering with its parts, or when he is out on the golf course whacking a ball around. On these occasions he must face actual existence.

Benton did find rare instances of a businessman with an interesting face. "But then he is, after all, more than an abstractionist. He has been dealing with actual things, not the abstraction called money,'' he said.

For Benton, the most interesting faces did not belong to well-known persons but to the unknown people "who handle things, objects, actualities....Your garage man, your coal man, your farmer—they are men with physiognomies which attract and hold attention."

The farmer is more weather-beaten, it is true, but this does not necessarily give him a more rugged face. The main difference between the farmer and the business man is that the farmer is dealing with solid things and the other with abstractions, with money which, in the last analysis, has no actual existence. This is reflected in their faces.

Benton riffled through a portfolio of sketches of faces "of vigorous men with plows, tender faces of women with children in their arms, faces of men crushed by defeat, faces of women saddened by great loss, faces of men flaming with ambition." The more interesting faces, he said, were found in steel mills, "because the faces...are more marked than others."

They stand out, are more deeply etched than the faces of a great many other men. About the steel worker there is always a certain amount of drama—tenseness—the unexpected, you see, can always happen in his life. That is what makes him so interesting.

Faces of criminals, college girls, and salesmen held little for Benton. He complained that the criminal is so "flat-eyed" that the artist is unable to find, as he sketches, "that inner life which most of us shield and keep concealed from others....With the criminal one gets nothing whatever from his face because of that flat or opaque eye of his."

The eye is a reflector of intention but, apparently, the criminal has no depth, for his eye is not revealing. Most animals' eyes are flat, but even some animals have eyes which are not nearly as flat as the criminal eye. The cat's eye is opaque, but not as opaque as a criminal's. There is nothing behind the criminal eye, no depth, nothing but a blankness.

Although he admitted salesmen "come up against life in

many of its changing aspects," they seldom had interesting faces because their "standard talking line"—their lack of originality—prevented them from developing an interesting "index."

The college girl, or the "society girl," Benton said, "has the most vapid face of all." He felt a working girl's face was more interesting because she is "in the midst of life," although she might do nothing more exciting than answer the telephone. "You have got to get next to life and away from the cloistered existence to develop an interesting face," he said. He included wives and mothers in the category of working women with interesting faces. "A wife, a mother, a homemaker is a worker. Surely she is about as close to life as anyone can get. She creates it."

The face of the intellectual varied. "The more genuine, the more profound thinkers develop interesting faces...[but] even in the intellectual life, along with the material one, it is the fundamental life struggle of the man which makes his face interesting or the contrary. The greater ease of accomplishment there exists in a man's life the less likely is he to develop an interestingly expressive face."

Your average college professor, for example, who merely brings facts together, is not an extremely interesting person to draw.

A minister? Yes, a preacher often has an interesting face, for it reveals conflict. There is often a conflict, a bout between the man and his work and his ideals and his beliefs.

The hypocrite has a very interesting face. Here, too, is conflict, pretense, acting, hypocrisy.

...A lawyer is generally an interesting type. He dramatizes many things, deals with people, facts, actualities.

But Benton admitted, "You don't have to go through the fire to be interesting and to have an interesting face."

Children are frequently interesting. They act on their own, spontaneously, with originality. They have not yet learned everything by rote.

Sex made no difference in whether an individual's face was interesting, so long as the person had "really lived." But he found that men were better models than women. "In traveling around the country I have found it very difficult to get women to pose. A woman is self-conscious, never very sure of herself," he said.

Benton spent days, weeks, sketching not only faces and figures but bodies and the clothes people wore and the equipment the people used. He spent hours sketching grass and weeds. In fact, it was Missouri's weeds that Benton claimed were responsible for the change in himself and his work. The change would become evident in the months after the mural was finished when the attacks on Benton were sometimes as much personal as political. The *Kansas City Times* on November 15, 1939, remembered Benton as "nervous and argumentative" when he had returned to Missouri, the kind of person who would sit up until 3 or 4 a.m. arguing politics. "In New York," he told the paper, "politics is something you theorize about. In Missouri it's something you live with every day."

Benton came to Missouri with a hatred of metropolitan intellectuals and the art cultists, a hatred which often flared into a torrent of colorful abuse. Today, when there is less argument and more work, he begins yawning at 10:30 o'clock, and is in bed by 11. He is less inclined to talk all night not because he has run out of ideas but because he has work to do.

"When I was working on the Jefferson City mural I became attracted to weeds," Benton says...."They grow in such immense, fascinating varieties."

"Are weeds more interesting to you than people?"

"No, not more so, but equally interesting. Weeds and people are alike in many respects. They both grow in such unpredictable ways."

Before the first gob of paint was put on the wall, extensive preparations had to be made. He took his sketches and made the models before doing individual paintings of the different scenes. Only then, said the *Jefferson City Post-Tribune* on September 1, was he ready to prepare the walls.

Over the walls of the lounge of the House of Representatives, a secondary wall of five-ply wood was built. Then linen was applied with casein glue, covered with seven coats of white chalk mixed with glue and yolks of eggs. This medium is considered permanent and capable of preserving the colors for years.

After having a draftsman line off the wall in three-foot squares, Benton began sketching in his subjects. His models and sketches are reduced or enlarged to the desired size through photography, with the perspective in one plane to conform with the single plane of the finished painting.

Preparation of the huge canvas was an exacting job in days when artists also had to do a little cooking. Benton explained, "The mural process involves chemistry, mathematics and physics, as well as drawing and painting." Sid Larson explained the canvas was coated with a ground called gesso:

In Tom's day, the gesso had to be made by hand....It consists of gypsum and French rabbit hide glue and water cooked for a long time over a double boiler—usually overnight—very slowly, not allowing it to boil, and occasionally putting drops of sun-thickened oil in it in order to make what they call a "half-chalk ground," which is not too absorbent....If the gesso got too hot and you were not aware of this, tiny bubbles would be part of this mix...and applied to the canvas then would trap these little air spaces, or even if the paint were put on too rapidly and there was a stirring up of the material to work some bubbles in there. These bubbles break down and they pit.[56]

Benton told the reporter for the *Post-Tribune* he was keeping the mural as much a secret as he could. "I do not want busybodies fussing with my subject matter—at least until I have finished."

Benton actually started on the mural in late June or early July, working each day from about 6 a.m. to about 5 p.m., sitting on a large rolling scaffold. Townsend Godsey, a freelance photographer for the Associated Press who photographed Benton working on the mural several times, remembered Benton would "bring in, of a morning, a little sack of eggs...mix up his paint and go to work."

He was detailing the tree that was the first item painted onto the canvas when Paz vanMatre of the *St. Louis Star-Times* was reminded in his July 15th article of "a fly on a window pane" as he watched Benton work on his scaffold.

Over the stark white walls of the lounge, pencil sketches of men, women, hills and trees and great industrial machines wove a vague, irregular pattern. And the only spot of color was a dark green tree up near the ceiling, spreading its leafy branches into a pale blue sky.

I watched Mr. Benton as he added shadows to the leaves. He was frowning, moving his head from one side to another and stopping, occasionally to bite the end of an unlighted pipe. Sometimes, squinting his eyes, he would purse his lips and look thoughtfully at his work.

On the scaffold he kept about fifteen jars of hand-mixed paint, about a hundred brushes, and his pipe. "When he is working high up he has to use a diminishing glass so that he can see what the figures will look like from below," reported *Post-Dispatch* correspondent Otto Fuerbringer, who visited Benton on July 18. In the article published the next day, he said Benton had been painting for about ten days and had finished the pioneers segment featuring the wagon train and the fur trader, and had done most of the Huck Finn segment, although Fuerbringer reported he wasn't completely satisfied with the face of Huck and had dispatched a friend to find an eleven-year-old boy in Jefferson City whose face he would like. He also had several fishermen out looking for a Missouri River catfish that Jim could be holding. "But so far they haven't brought him any," reported Fuerbringer.

It was already obvious, though, what the dynamics of the mural would be. Fuerbringer said Benton used vivid earth colors for his work. "There is nothing dainty about his figures. His men are tall and gaunt, his women ample. His

61

lovers are taut with desire, his orators thunder, his judge is grizzled.''

The room will be wild and alive and the walls will shout out their story of the rich and strenuous and ordinary life. But Benton has no apologies. "It's like a symphony," he says, "You're not expected to live with a symphony. You hear it occasionally. Nobody will be with this mural all the time. But those who do see it will know they're seeing something."

Fuerbringer found it appropriate that Benton's painting of "sweat and work" would be on the lounge walls because "some of the hard and sweaty work of politics has been done in that room."

Here have been held off-the-record conversations of party leaders, here a lobbyist has met and pleaded with the stubborn representative, here the minority has always held its caucus. Here, too, young legislators have slept and dreamed their dreams of future power.

The *Kansas City Times* reported on January 12, 1937, that Benton mixed egg whites with an equal volume of water in a small cup: "He dips his brush first into the egg mixture and then into the powdered colors." He then put the mixture on his palette and worked it with his brush until he had the color he wanted.

Another of those who spent hours in the lounge watching Benton paint the mural was Forrest Scrivner, a young sign painter from Jefferson City. He recalled he would watch Benton in those times when work was slack, never saying anything to him as he worked. For some reason, Benton began to pay some attention to him. One day he asked Scrivner if he was interested in art. "I've learned to paint signs, and I do some commercial advertising on walls and billboards," Scrivner told him. Scrivner stayed behind after Benton went back up on his scaffolding.

He had a pipe and he dropped it down there and asked me to fill his pipe, which I did and I said, "This is not going to be a very professional job," and I tossed it up to him. Then he wanted some brushes, a certain size fitch brush and those people that were in there didn't know what he meant by a fitch brush of a certain size so I went over there and picked them up for him and tossed them up to him, to keep him from climbing down.[57]

Benton didn't mind sharing some of his own philosophy with the young sign painter. "I paint sometimes to get people to criticize my work," he said once to Scrivner. Another time he told him, "I'm the kind of artist who likes to eat while I'm living instead of waiting until after I've passed away and then your work sells for a high price."

Scrivner recalled Benton didn't start at one end of the room and work his way to the end: "Sometimes he would skip, and one day you would find him working in one section and the next time he would be over somewhere else."[58]

Mary Humphrey was a secretary who went to the lounge to admire Benton's work one day during the lunch hour and developed enough of a friendship with the artist that they gave each other nicknames.

She remembered that it was hot in that room, cooled by nothing more than the draft coming through the open windows.

It was awful because the paints would get all runny and sometimes he would have to work with them to cool them down. Sometimes he'd stick them in a bucket of ice water, the tubes, before he'd start bringing them out on the palette.

She recalled that some days Benton worked quickly. Other days he painted more slowly, depending "on how much he had to drink the night before." For lunch, Benton often kept painting, munching on cheese and crackers, drinking a Coke out of a bottle with a straw, or a beer. Mrs. Humphrey could understand why Benton liked alcoholic beverages. "He smelled all those oil paints all through the years and he needed something to sort of cut that for him," she reasoned.

She and Benton became close enough friends that they began to tease each other.

We even developed kind of happy names for one another. He called me "Mary dear" and I called him "Tommy dear." That sounds crazy, doesn't it? It sounds like it was beneath his dignity, doesn't it? But when you got to know him he was really a very delightful person.

...He worked on a scaffolding all the time. I used to tease him about one leg being shorter than the other, like a mountain goat. And he would laugh, bless his heart.

She knew he was going to paint a secretary into one of the panels. Benton kidded her about it.

He would worry me to death with that. He'd say, "Well, I'm gonna start on you Mary dear tomorrow," like that. And I'd say, "You better not," and I was always scared to death he would.

She is not the secretary. Mary Humphrey's hair and eyes are brown. She describes the woman Benton put on the wall as "one of the secretaries who's been out too much at night. She's emaciated looking and her cheeks are sunken in and she has stringy blonde hair and he made her cheeks too pink."

Eventually the excitement of watching Benton paint the mural diminished. She didn't go back into the Lounge so often. Fifty years later, though, many of the memories remained fresh.

He was never really attractive to me as far as looks were concerned, but he was an intelligent man and he had many many good stories to tell—funny as they could be, and they weren't always clean, I can tell you. He had a great sense of humor. I witnessed it many times.

...He was a very pleasant man. He was an intelligent man but people never gave him credit for being [intelligent]. They thought he was a nut.

She recalls those noon hours as priceless. She thought Benton was ''just another person that had some artistic talent. I did not realize that I was talking...to a man that would one day be famous. I do not know another man that was ever like him....He was different. He was different.''[59]

Benton made several changes as he transformed his sketches into the finished product on the wall—changes in perspective, hair styles, and clothes. But the biggest change he made was done on the spot, and it instantly resolved a controversy. He changed a skinny white man into a portly black man.

A sixteen-year old youth who visited the capitol daily was one of the few to know about it. W. R. Utz, who in later years became a faculty member at the University of Missouri, wrote of the day he had journeyed from his home in Boonville to watch Benton paint. He was there when a man walked into the Lounge and told Benton he was representing a group that respectfully protested the undignified way Benton had portrayed blacks on the north wall. Utz recalled the two talked about ten or fifteen minutes before the black man left.

When I returned about a week later I was astonished to discover the very same black man incorporated into the mural. I went to the tables where the master sketches were lying in disarray to see what figure Benton had intended for that position and discovered it was a white man.[60]

It's the only time Benton bowed to political pressure during the painting of the mural. Only a few people apparently knew about it. Utz knew part of the story. So did photographer Townsend Godsey. Neither recalls the other being in the room at the time but both witnessed at least part of the story. Not until the discovery of his unpublished, handwritten, Benton manuscript was the full story learned.[61] It goes back to the very origin of the mural, and—years after

65

the painting was completed—it left Benton pondering a series of circumstances he had not previously considered.*

Benton realized that if he buckled to this pressure, he'd be open to other "suggestions" and his entire concept could be ruined. He quickly decided to take another tack. Governor Park had described the man as "the most important black vote 'getouter' in the town and he knows it. Plumb full of himself."

Benton decided to appeal to the man's ego.

At the time, Benton was working on the outdoor political meeting scene, but he hadn't found an appropriate face for one of the figures. Although he'd planned for the figure leaning against the tree in the background to be a tall, thin white man, he told the St. Louis black leader, "I've been looking for the face of a prominent politician of your race for this figure. I want to show the progress of Missouri's colored people from their unhappy beginnings, shown in the lead mine scene, to their present position of political importance in the State. The lead mine scene is part of our history, I'll admit, but it's necessary to show how the colored people overcame their misfortunes and rose up to the position of power that you represent." And then he played his trump card. "How about my putting your face on that figure? You'll be up there on this State House wall as permanent record of the colored man's accomplishments in our state."

"Why, Mr. Artist," the black leader said, "I think that would be all right."

The next day, the man and his friends came in, "whispered and chuckled" about the man's image on the wall, and left. That afternoon, Governor Park called Benton into his office for a highball and told him, "They say you are an artist, Tom, but you're a better politician."

Benton didn't mind if people strolled in and watched him work, but he disliked interruptions. Once he began his work,

*The manuscript is published in the appendix.

66

his concentration was total and he was not likely to overwhelm visitors with cordiality if he was interrupted. Many stood or sat quietly and watched, perhaps listening to Benton hum. "I nearly always hum the same tune," Benton later wrote. "It's one of those hill-billy tunes called 'Prisoner for Life.'"[62]

Benton sometimes entertained himself and others, especially in the off-hours, by playing his harmonica. Townsend Godsey recalled one evening he, Benton, some newspaper correspondents and others were in the basement bar at the Madison Hotel, across the street from the Governor's Mansion, when "the boys were feeling pretty good." Somebody said, "Well, we need Tom's harmonica in here to keep us in tune." Benton sent Godsey up to his room to get a harmonica. "He told me where in the bureau drawer that I'd find his harmonica....I got up there and he had seven or eight of them in the drawer!" And you know, he did not read music? The scores that he had, they were marked "blow" or "suck" on the notes....He worked it out so that he could play the harmonica without knowing any music.

According to *Time* magazine (January 11, 1937), his guests "gaped earnestly at a small, dark, wiry man painting furiously in a faint odor of rotten eggs, while the walls slowly blossomed with mule skinners, Mormons, dancing Negroes and Mississippi boatmen."

Benton was sometimes asked to speak to civic or social groups in Jefferson City about the work he was doing. He told Paz vanMatre of the *St. Louis Star-Times* he enjoyed the company, but there were drawbacks.

I don't like women's magazine salads. I'm always being invited out for dinner and having to dab around with those things. One of my most evident Missouri qualifications is that I like meat and potatoes.

In June he had complained about people who wanted to give him advice on what was to be put in the painting. "I've been through it, and I know how it is," he told the Associated Press in June of 1936. "Publicity brings a lot of people around who have ideas how it should be done."

Anyone who has any business for miles around Jeff City will come in and make suggestions. Every farmer who thinks he has raised the biggest ear of corn will think it ought to go into the painting, and a lot of busybodies will raise objections about this thing or that.

You know, it isn't the picture that causes the stink. It's what's said about it.

In an effort to reduce the interruptions that many spectators might feel inclined to make, Benton posted a letter in the Lounge, addressing visitors as "friends." He acknowledged that his guests might have questions to ask or suggestions to make. But he said he was too busy for the former and it was too late for the latter.

The "realness" of this work depends on a lot of abstract adjustments of lines and planes and gradation of color. These adjustments cannot be disturbed without causing me a lot of work, without, in fact, making me do this thing all over.

He asked that any suggestions people had be mailed to Room 100 in the capitol.

Pat Ward, a fomer Jefferson Citian, would visit the Lounge to watch Benton paint when she and her family returned from St.Louis to visit friends. She remembered Benton was "very particular. He didn't paint fast. Very slow and deliberate." Ward, who as Pat Jones taught art for many years in the Jefferson City school system, remembered Benton talked to himself while he was painting. "If he didn't like the way it was going, he didn't talk to himself very nice sometimes," she said. "I don't remember that he sang. He kind of muttered more than he sang while he was working."

She, like many visitors, found a quiet corner from which to watch without bothering Benton. If visitors did bother the artist, Ward said, "he would sometimes kind of stare them down and they would leave. If he knew them, he would make a comment or two or they'd say something to him. But nobody stayed very long. They just dropped in and dropped out."[62]

Occasionally a visitor would bother Benton, whose silent rage went beyond "staring them down." Sam Blair, whose brother was later a governor and who, himself, became a prominent Missouri judge years later, recalled that he and another young lawyer friend visited the House Lounge one day when Benton was painting. They began to fool around with some of the paints Benton had on a table. Benton never said a word but climbed down from his scaffold, walked over to them and scribbled a note: "God damn it, Keep your f---ing hands off my stuff." He then stalked back to his scaffold and his work. The chastised young lawyers retreated.[63] Benton and Blair later became good friends.[64]

The *Kansas City Star* recalled in an article February 3, 1937, the day a woman detached herself from some friends visiting the Lounge and approached Benton, then on his scaffold, to complain about some of the figures he was painting. He paid no attention to her and ignored her questions and comments. She rejoined her party. "He doesn't understand the English language," she told her friends.

Young Roy Utz watched Benton paint for about six days during June, July, and August of 1936, the year scorching temperatures killed more than 400 people in Missouri. Utz recalled seeing trees dying along the road between Boonville and Jefferson City.[65] A Cole County extension agent reported it was the summer of the worst drought in the state's history. Mrs. Frank Kliegel, a local weather observer, reported for the *Jefferson City Post-Tribune* that every day from July 5 through 18, the temperature was 100 or more. The peak came on July 13-16, when the mercury hit 110,

112, 110, and 108. Temperatures dropped into the 90s for three days, then there was another run from July 23-28 of 100-or more degrees. The temperature moved back above 100 on August 9, and except for one day when the high was only 92, it stayed at 100 or more for much of the rest of the month. On those scorching days, the west windows and the double east doors of the room were kept open.

Sometimes a visitor to the capitol or a capitol employee would stroll in and watch for a few minutes, but, so far as I know, during this period I was the only observer who came for the day.

Through a strategy of being as quiet and inconspicuous as possible I could get very close to Benton at work and, by being careful not to handle things, could visually examine the scores of sketches on the long tables of the lounge, watch him prepare tempera, etc. Neither of us ever spoke to the other and if he noticed me at all it was certainly not to the extent that I became part of the mural.[66]

Benton rested, ate lunch and chatted with visitors during the noon hour. He recalled in his autobiography, *An Artist in America*, that he never heard a seriously intended criticism during those hours. "Everyone was friendly," he said.

Occasionally a farmer would object to some detail of farm life. When his criticism was valid, I would change the detail which offended and which might stand in the way of his appreciation of my work. I wanted plain Missouri people like the farmers to like my painting, and when my total design was not affected by their objections to some detail of fact I remedied the matter for them.

Malcolm Vaughn, writing in the spring 1938 issue of *The North American Review*, told of the day a tall, lean, elderly farmer asked, "Is that there a new fangled kind of a plow?" He was pointing to the one hitched to the mule near the main door. Benton was surprised by the question and when he asked what was wrong with it, the farmer gave a detailed answer:

O' course I don't know nothin' erbout hand paintin', but I kin tell the hind

70

part o' that plow is too short for the man you got a-usin' it. Why it ain't no more'n a child's plow. And the handles ain't got enough turn to give enybody a real grip on 'em. That big mule a-pullin' it would yank the blade right up outen the ground most every step or so.

Benton enthusiastically thanked the farmer, declared him absolutely correct, and said there were several details here and there in the mural that he intended to correct as soon as he could.

He sat back one day in July, lit his briar pipe, and told a reporter for the *Post-Tribune* he was more concerned about what the common people thought of his work than what the critics said about it. "I like people, and primarily I paint for them," he said in the article published July 29. "If they can see something in these paintings out of their own lives, I don't care what they know or think about art."

Godsey, the photographer, said when the capitol guides brought people into the room to "give their speil" about the murals, Benton would stand aside and not identify himself. "He said the reason he did it was that he learned more about his murals from what the guide said than he knew himself," Godsey recalled.

Benton wrote in his first autobiography, "I had all the evidence necessary to make me believe that my realistic conceptions of Missouri's social history and life were in line with the reputedly realistic psychology of the state's people."

One day, when Benton had stopped painting for a few moments to savor a cigarette, a man and woman came in. They looked a little embarrassed. The man told Benton he had brought his wife to the capitol to see the paintings. "That's fine." said Benton, "as long as she doesn't want to help me." The *St. Louis Post-Dispatch* reported July 19, the woman blushed and said, "Oh, no. I wouldn't be good enough for that." Benton responded, "That's fine again. They don't all feel that way."

Benton occasionally took small breaks in his schedule in the lounge. In mid-August, for example, he lectured on mural art at the Ste. Genevieve Summer School of Art in eastern Missouri. He discussed the mural and showed the students some of his techniques. The *St. Louis Star-Times* published a picture of Benton at the school August 14, 1936, and said he was "gathering ideas for murals."

In September he climbed down from his platform to tell a *Post-Tribune* reporter how a person paints a huge mural. "I know what I am painting, and I feel what I am painting," he said. "...I am an ordinary American and Missourian, painting what is before me....I am a realist and the mural will be realism. I have no time for hokus-pokus." He had hoped to finish the mural in November, but he told the interviewer in the article published September 1, he didn't know when it would be done. "A painter spends a day where he has allowed himself ten minutes in an estimate," he said.

But was all of this work? "My recreation is painting," he said. "I paint all of the time, in my head."

I have a wife and a 9-year-old boy. We paint and play and live. I like sports. I hate teas. Give me plenty of good old Bourbon whiskey with water and you can have all the tea in China. One of my most evident Missouri qualifications is that I love "meat 'n taters." I loathe fancy salads. I like people. And I'd rather play my harmonica than do almost anything. You should hear me play the harmonica.

Speaker of the House John Christy was one of those who sometimes dropped in to check on the progress. He had been designated a committee of one to see how the painting was going. But he said, "I couldn't see much. They was breakin' eggs and mixing paint in them...and I had no idea what it was going to look like."[67]

Christy would later become one of the key figures in the political controversy when the mural was completed. That controversy was far greater than any that occurred during the creation of the work. In his *Scribner's* article, Craven might have pinpointed the reason, noting people came in to watch Benton "speechless before his swift, sure strokes and his exhibitions of virtuosity—for he is quite capable of showing off in the midst of his most serious work."

But they saw only the showman strutting his facility. They were blind to the import of his demonstrations, excusably indifferent to his immense preparatory efforts—the months of quiet thinking and planning, the first-hand investigations, the sketches and clay models of his characters; in short to the significance of his originality and to his basic philosophy of mural decoration upon which his substantial reputation rests.

Sid Larson recalled that once Benton climbed the scaffolding each morning, he was all business. After hours, of course, he could let his hair down. But when he picked up his brushes, there was no frivolity.

I think there are people who would just love to gossip about Benton's drinking and his work habits. Let me tell you, Benton was not an alcoholic. Although he liked to drink, he never would drink during a working day. And he worked from first light till...sunset. And it didn't bother him to work seven days a week. He was a workaholic. His work is intelligent and rational and of such intensity that there's no way he could have been a drinker and a painter at the same time.

Benton told Larson he worked very hard in Jefferson City. "He alluded several times to the fact that he had a good time...that after a day's work he did not go home and read a book," recalled Larson, speaking with the author.

There was even some scandal associated with some of these rumors. Since they are nothing but that I'm not going into them. Now, Tom Benton was a very vital man. All of his juices flowed all the way up into his 85th year, as far as I know.[68]

Benton himself wrote in his first autobiography of the intensity he felt when he was on a wall, saying that a mural was "a kind of emotional spree" which "left me in an exalted state of mind, strings up my energies, and heightens the color of the world.''

After I have gone through with my practical preparations, which are elaborate and occupy the major part of the time spent on the job, a certain kind of thoughtless freedom comes over me. I don't give a damn about anything. Once on the wall, I paint with downright sensual pleasure. The colors I use make my mouth water. The sweep of my brushes, after I get really started, becomes precise and somehow or other beyond error. I get cocksure of mind and temperamentally youthful. I run easily into childish egomania or adolescent emotionalism. When the mural is finished I have a letdown.

The last figure he painted in the mural was Tom Pendergast.

I told him that this was to be a mural of contemporary Missouri, and what the hell, it can't be complete without you, and he agreed that that was true. So he posed for me in his Kansas City office. He wanted to be in it or he wouldn't have posed. There wasn't any trouble at all.[69]

Not then, but later.

For now, though, the choice of Pendergast as one of the mural figures was considered ''a happy one'' by the *St. Louis Post-Dispatch* on December 9, 1936: ''If not an emperor, he is fellow to an emperor. He went forth to conquer the world and has pretty well done it.''

A careerist painting a careerist, with a spiritual bond forged in the crucible of the same hills and valleys and skies, the same flowers and fruits and birds, the same identical spell of the ancient sun, the same nocturns borne on the breast of the same star-freighted prairie breeze—here are all the elements, factual and psychical, for art's monumental mood.

Some of the painting in the last segment of the mural was done by someone other than Benton. Robert Rhodes was a Jefferson City teenager who went to the Lounge after school that fall to watch Benton work. He developed a slight speaking relationship with the artist. ''One day he let me take a brush and paint in a little bit of a corner in a background," Rhodes recalled more than a half century later. Rhodes said Benton let him "smear some paint around in there." His brush strokes are part of the sky in the Kansas City segment of the mural.[70]

The Jefferson City *Daily Capital News* reported on December 19, 1936, that Benton had applied the last brush stroke. Workmen with him were to put on the preserving coat of shellac, alcohol, and clear varnish, then a coat of wax before Christmas. One of Benton's last brush strokes "corrected the lines of a stump, from which a tree had just been felled. It was not exactly true to type, the artist found after it had been criticized by farmers and woodsmen."

And so it was finished, a painting which, according to the *Kansas City Star* of December 27, showed "the social history of his native Missouri...stripped of artifice and glamour."

Some observers were already wondering if the mural would last very long. The *St. Louis Post-Dispatch* had commented on August 9, while Benton was still painting the mural, "The immortality Benton will derive from it is limited,"

for although the building houses over $1,000,000 worth of art, its basement was recently cleaned for the first time in three years and the existing murals have already been marred by "blisters, scratches, holes, cracks, match burns, chipped and peeling paint, a good many tacks, pencil marks, smudges and stains," an expert recently reported.

Matthew Baigell says it is the embodiment of Benton's belief that the Midwest would be "the likely place for the springing of an original art."

It is probably not a mere coincidence that Benton's finest mural cycle and Regionalism's most representative paintings were his panels in the State House at Jefferson City....These works, based on local lore and legend, are among his most completely realized designs and cannot be mistaken for paintings coming from any place else in the world.[71]

Visitors walking into what had been a comfortable lounging room six months earlier now found vivid figures on the walls—198 men, thirty-two women, and five children; seven cows, four oxen, five mules and four dogs, seven pigs, five chickens, two turkeys, ten horses, a turtle, and a fish; four hammers, five sandwiches, a cake, an axe, and two crosscut saws; four boats and five trains, two covered wagons, a tractor, a steam engine, a farm wagon, a buggy, a silage machine, a truck, a car, eleven guns, and five tree stumps.[72]

Among the 235 people who permanently inhabit that room, 234 are Missourians. Benton had to go to Haskell Institute in Lawrence, Kansas, to find an authentic Osage Indian.[73]

Two hundred thirty-five people in fifteen segments, flowing into a whole—"The Social History of Missouri."

Benton said in his second autobiography that he, as a native Missourian, wanted his performances "to have some public effect—to be more than mere flickers in a social vacuum." He regarded the mural as a pinnacle of his career.

Although I painted a number of murals afterwards, I believe the Missouri mural completed the last phase of my development as an artist. While various modifications of my pictorial style were made later...all the basic structural procedures I would ever use had been arrived at.

Benton had made his case. But for this mural, at least, there would be no time for an emotional letdown. The storm clouds in the political and art worlds were as ominous as the symbolic smoke on the walls of the House Lounge.

Notes

1. Interview by Mike Wallace, "60 Minutes" broadcast on CBS

(April 8, 1973). Recording on file with the Encyclopedia Americana/CBS News Audio Resources Library (January 1975), #3.

2. *An Artist in America*, 253-254.

3. Craven, *Modern Art*, 352.

4. *Time* (December 24, 1934): 25.

5. The *Time* article, on pages 24-27, also considered the works of John Steuart Curry, Charles Ephraim Burchfield, Reginald Marsh, Ivan LeLorraine Albright, Charles Sheeler, and other artists from Boston, California and Taos, New Mexico.

6. James M. Dennis, *Grant Wood, A Study in American Art and Culture* (New York: Viking Press, 1975), 242 and 244. Another account is found in Wanda M. Corn, *Grant Wood, The Regionalist Vision* (New Haven and London: Yale University Press, 1983), 43-44.

7. *An Artist in America*, 258.

8. Ibid.

9. Interview with John G. Christy by author in Jefferson City, Missouri, on January 22, 1975.

10. *An Artist in America*, 258-259.

11. Christy interview (January 22, 1975).

12. *An Artist in America*, 259.

13. *Kansas City Star* (April 3, 1935).

14. Ruth Pickering, "Thomas Hart Benton On His Way Back to Missouri," *Arts and Decoration*, vol. 42 no. 4: 15.

15. The entire essay was reprinted in *An Artist in America*, 261-269.

16. "60 Minutes" (April 8, 1973).

17. Polly Burroughs, *Thomas Hart Benton: A Portrait* (New York: Doubleday and Company, 1981), 123.

18. Letter to author from Eleanor Piacenza (April 26, 1984).

19. Craven, *Scribner's* (October 1937): 38. Burroughs wrote in her book that he "was welcomed in Kansas City as a celebrity, half hobo and half highbrow, the descendant of a distinguished family, whose life had been rich in escapades and provocative irregularities."

20. *An Artist in America*, 255.

21. Nancy Edelman, *The Thomas Hart Benton Murals in the Missouri State Capitol* (Missouri State Council on the Arts, 1975), 8.

22. *An Artist in America*, 260-61.

23. The Bentons did not move to their home at 3616 Belleview until 1939. Tom and Rita lived out their lives there, in a house that is now a state historic site.

24. *The Indian Leader*, weekly newspaper published by Haskell Institute in Lawrence, Kansas, on October 11, 1935, in "Notes of Interest" column.

25. Interview with the author (January 10, 1984).

26. *An American in Art*, 71.

27. Interview by Jim Lantz, then at KCMO radio in Kansas City, in Benton's Kansas City studio, although it sounds as though it was done in the House Lounge. Lantz, interviewed by the author on November 8, 1985, was unable to recall the date of the interview, although it is believed to have been in the 1960s. Henry C. Haskell, writing in the "Scanning the Arts Column" of the *Kansas City Star* (May 28, 1967), noted plans were being made to record Benton's description of the mural.

28. Lantz interview.

29. *An American in Art*, 72-73.

30. Interview with the author (December 8, 1983).

31. *An American in Art*, 75.

32. Interview with the author (December 8, 1983).

33. Thomas Hart Benton, "The Thirties," an unpublished manuscript in the Benton Trust, Kansas City (see appendix).

34. Ibid.

35. *Kansas City Star* (March 4, 1937).

36. Bill Nunn, "Tom Benton's honkey tonks, hillbillies and robbers," Jefferson City *Missouri Times* (January 10, 1983).

37. "Midwest Art Ranked Ahead, *Durant (Oklahoma) Democrat* (July 24, 1935). Story carried a United Press dateline from Springfield (July 11).

38. United Press story from Springfield, Missouri (July 17, 1935). The clipping from the *St. Louis Star-Times* in the Nelson-Atkins Museum in Kansas City is dated August 19.

39. "In Gallery and Studio," *Kansas City Star* (January 7, 1937).

40. Interview with the author (February 4, 1987). Nesbitt, a student at the Kansas City Art Institute during 1933-38, later returned as a

teacher of etching from 1949-52. He was living in Atlanta, Georgia, when interviewed.

41. Interview with the author (January 10, 1984).

42. Interviews with the author (December 29, 1983, and January 10, 1984.)

43. Interview with the author (February 24, 1984).

44. Paul Watkins, "Thomas Hart Benton Remembered," *Missouri Life* (March-June 1975): 57.

45. Karol Ann Marling, *Tom Benton and His Drawings* (Columbia, Missouri: University of Missouri Press, 1985), 116.

46. Associated Press story (July 12, 1937). Headlined in *Hannibal Evening Courier Post*, "Moberly Man is 'Unofficial Greeter' at State Capitol; Makes Strangers Feel at Home With His Greetings."

47. Allen Oliver, "The Man Behind the Face on the Capitol Wall," *Springfield News and Leader* (August 2, 1936). Mark Twain, of course, was the pen name of Samuel Clemens, Missouri's most famous writer. George Graham Vest was a U.S. Senator from Missouri (1879-1903) and is best known for his "Eulogy on a dog," a summation for a jury hearing a damage case in Warrensburg, Missouri, in which Vest represented the owner of a dog that had been killed by a neighbor. Champ Clark was a longtime Speaker of the U. S. House of Representatives and lost the Democratic nomination for President to Woodrow Wilson in 1912 on the forty-sixth ballot. Eugene Field was a newspaperman from St. Joseph, best known as a writer of poetry about children.

48. T. P., then about ten years old, once told his mother, who had corrected his manners, "I don't want to be a gentleman when I grow up. I want to be like my dad" (*Kansas City Star*, October 16, 1938).

49. Letter to the author from T. P. Benton (March 17, 1987).

50. April 15, 1962.

51. Otto Fuerbringer, "Living Missourians' Faces Used in State Capitol Mural by Artist Benton," *St. Louis Post-Dispatch* (July 19, 1936). Names of some of the other persons included in the mural are also in this article. Names of others are picked up from numerous sources.

52. "Answers Critics of Capitol Murals," *Kansas City Times* (April 15, 1937).

53. Interview with the author (November 9, 1984).

54. Interview with the author (May 6, 1987). Mrs. Burnett recalled she

would sometimes see Rotha Williams—Jim in the Huck Finn segment—in later years, and he would always recognize her: "Oh, Miss Virginia..." he'd say. During the visitation for her father at a Jefferson City funeral home in 1975, the funeral home owner told Mrs. Burnett someone was at the door to see her. It was Rotha Williams, asking permission to come in and pay his respects to her father.

55. Louis LaCoss, "Missouri Murals Split Home Critics," *New York Times* (January 17, 1937).

56. Burnett interview (see endnote 54).

57. Benton quit smoking his pipe in 1965. "I didn't try to give up smoking," he told Shirley Althoff in an article in the *St. Louis Globe-Democrat Sunday* magazine (January 7, 1973). "I tried to keep on. But I just couldn't. And you know what? That was the same year...that I was named 'Pipe Smoke of the Year' and had gotten a year's supply of the finest tobaccos around."

58. Interview with the author (December 8, 1986).

59. Interview with the author (February 16, 1987). Mrs. Humphrey worked for forty years for the state treasurer before retiring; she lived in Fulton when she was interviewed.

60. Utz wrote of the experience in a letter to the editor of the *Columbia Daily Tribune*, published anonymously on June 12, 1976. Utz later told the story to the author at his home in February 1984.

61. The mansuscript is in the files of the Benton Trust at United Missouri Bank, Kansas City. The incident was not entirely unknown, although the background apparently was. The *Kansas City Star* noted in a story on October 16, 1938, that a "Negro politician" from St. Louis objected to the slave-sale panel. The story said Benton got a photograph from the man and put his face in the painting. "It was an act prompted by a sort of puckish humor, rather than by vindictiveness; it was typically "Bentonesque," the paper reported.

62. Benton, from the foreword to *A Descriptive Catalogue of the Works of Thomas Hart Benton* (New York: Associated American Artists), 24.

63. Interview with the author in Jefferson City (January 11, 1984).

64. Circuit Judge Byron Kinder, a longtime friend of Blair. recalled for the author on July 29, 1986, "When the Benton murals were redone, they flew Tom Benton back here from Kansas City to take part in the ceremony. His great old friend Sam Blair flew up to Kansas City

in the governor's airplane and flew back with Benton. And the old gentlemen had had a few nips to steel themselves for the trip. We went out to the Jefferson City Country Club, and I was seated at the table with them. I was next to Tom Benton, and he and Sam were sitting there visiting and reminiscing and here were all these ladies—you know, as Sam would say, 'with three-orchid bosoms'— the DAR-type ladies, and Tom Benton said, 'Isn't medical science wonderful, Sam?' Sam said, 'Yes, it certainly is, all those transplants....' And Tom said, 'Oh God, Sam, I wish to hell they had a pecker bank.' The salad forks hit the plates immediately." It was after this luncheon that the tipsy Benton and Blair, along with other dignitaries, went to the capitol for dedication of a booklet the legislature had authorized about the capitol and the Benton mural. Although Benton was on the podium for that ceremony, he was not allowed to speak until the group had adjourned to the House Lounge to see the mural. Those events are described elsewhere in this book.

65. Interview with the author (February 1985).

66. W. R. Utz, letter to the editor, *Columbia Daily Tribune* (June 12, 1976).

67. Christy interview (January 22, 1975).

68. Interview with the author (December 8, 1983).

69. Robert S. Gallagher, "Before the Colors Fade: An Artist in America" (an interview with Thomas Hart Benton), *American Heritage* (June 1973): 87.

70. Interview with the author (January 5, 1988).

71. Baigell, *Miscellany*, 36.

72. I counted them, often, while covering boring (and some not-so-boring) legislative committee meetings in that room, in the days when committees met there.

73. Edelman, 18.

Chapter 3
The Furor

"A storm broke over me," said Benton in his first autobiography. "My illusions about a good many Missouri things were broken with it. I saw that realism was not by any means a completely shared Missouri virtue, and that the habit of calling things by their right names and representing them by their factual character was not wholly agreeable to so many people as I supposed."[1]

I awoke to the fact that many of those who came to see me accepted my attitudes simply because of the strangeness and perhaps the fascination of my unusual activities which made them restrain for the moment the actual mushiness and vulgarity of their own views. But in the end they let it out to me, and I found that a lot of the very people I supposed were favoring me and standing by my work were really miles away from it.

Benton found many who could not believe he was sincere in his actions or in his painting: "I found that my basic attitudes were entirely incomprehensible to many people and that my realism and intention to be faithful to my actual Missouri experiences were regarded somewhat as pretensions or poses."

The early reviews were good, though. The *Kansas City Star* on December 21, 1936, published a lengthy article noting that "Missouri's past—sometimes inspiring, sometimes a little ridiculous and even shady, but always intensely human—has risen to confront her law-making sons on the walls of the lounge of the house of representatives in the state capitol....It is not a picture to be seen quickly. The first impression is a burst of hot color and motion....In Benton's picture only the rivers are peaceful."

The mural is not a commentary. Benton has not set himself up as a judge of events or crises. He has been amused by the way people act, but he is tolerant and records their acts with as much frankness as if he were an unprejudiced and uncensored newspaper reporter. He is partial to incongruity.

The *Kansas City Journal-Post* on Christmas day referred to the Lounge as "the most interesting room in Missouri." But it also noted early unrest, saying critics were "jumping on the murals" and forecasting things would become hotter when the legislature returned in January "and again occupy the lounge and begin the luncheon hour singing of church hymns in the room now devoted to the picturization of some of Missouri's sins as well as virtues."

More support came from the *Star* on December 28:

If discussion is to be intelligent...and not merely an expression of enthusiasm or prejudice, certain facts must be born in mind. In the first place...this is no piece of glorified wallpaper. Mr. Benton does not hold the theory that a mural painter should seek simply to decorate a given wall space with conventionally pleasing figures and landscapes. He believes, with many of the greatest muralists of the past...that a wall painting should have something of consequence to say.

But the newspaper did say every person was free to form his own opinion.

The former executive manager of the Kansas City Chamber of Commerce had quickly formed his. Lou E. Holland felt the mural "wouldn't make good cartoons."

They do not show Missouri in a proper light. Missouri is a great state and the artist has overlooked important subjects.

Missouri is not proud of hangings and Negro honky-tonks. She is not proud of the whipping of slaves, the slave block and Jesse James holdups.

There are still many subjects in Missouri which would supply mural material without resorting to such subjects as those.

The figures, themselves, in the paintings, and the execution in general are terrible and not in taste.[2]

Benton had a ready response:

With pride but without vanity I can say that there is nothing wrong with the execution of that mural and I'll wager no competent critic will say so. I do not believe the mural will offend the great majority of Missourians and I cannot see why it should. During the six months I was painting, the room was always open and hundreds of persons looked at the painting. They liked it.

T.G. Field of Kansas City wrote a letter to the *Star* published on January 3, 1937, saying the mural "got more laughs than Popeye." Field blasted the mural as not being art.

Mr. Benton's pictures are condemned not by his labored attempts to find startling subjects, but by the crudeness of his work in depicting them. One panel looks much like another and there is a sameness about all the figures because of the formula by which it is done. The work of true artists, such as Daumier, Rembrandt and Breughel, often presents unsavory subjects but does so with beauty and fluency.

For most of 1937, Benton enjoyed the appraisals of his work from both extremes—the openness and friendliness of the *Star* as well as the strong disagreements from his critics.

About the time Field was writing his letter, the political storm was about to hit. The legislature was coming into session. It is helpful to recall that the legislature and the House Lounge were different then. John Christy recalled that House members did not have offices in those days. Their books, bills, and other materials were stacked on their desks. "If they wanted to relax they went into the lounge there and they would play cards or sit in there and rest." Christy recalled going into the Lounge before the Democrats caucused the night before the session was to begin and looking at the giant figures painted on those walls.

....And they just looked like they was jumpin' out at me and I thought of these people trying to go in there and sit down and relax and play cards and I was quite concerned about it.

Christy's concern led to an embarrassing confrontation the next morning. He was eating breakfast at the Missouri Hotel when Rep. Roy Hamlin of Hannibal, the majority floor leader, came in.

When he sat down with me I said, "Roy, have you seen those damnable things on the walls in the House Lounge?" And he started jumpin' around, "Shh, SHH!" And I—nothing was going to stop me then—and I said, "Roy, that's terrible. We can't have those. You...get a resolution prepared and introduced to have those walls redone and let's get rid of those things." Well, by that time he was literally hitting me in the face and saying, "That's Mr. Benton. That's Mr. Benton."

And sure enough, seated at the next table, unnoticed by the irate and outspoken Speaker of the House, was the creator of the" monstrosity" himself.

About that time, some gushing young lady come in and said, "Oh, Mr. Benton, I've seen your murals and how beautiful they are," and, "May I have your autograph?"

He got up. He never...looked at her. He looked at me and he said, "I have just heard some remarks from one who knows nothing about art and should he study it the remainder of his life would know less."

Benton stalked out of the restaurant.[3] The resolution was never introduced, but the subject was one of debate for years.

Representative Bill Barton of Montgomery County recalled no particularly loud outbursts on the floor of the House during that session.

Most of it was out in the halls...when the chamber wasn't in session...Most of it was little groups get together: "Oughta paint that thing over; it's too outstanding; why are they putting things like that in the Capitol?" and "We shouldn't have allowed it in the first place." But that was all in gossip and usually outside....It gave them something to talk about.[4]

Among the early visitors was Alfred Eisenstadt and three others from *Life* magazine who spent most of one night taking pictures of the murals. Afterwards, Eisenstadt went with Townsend Godsey and Hugh Stephens, the head of the Exchange National Bank in Jefferson City, on a short tour of the Ozarks to study "original Benton types."[5]

On January 7, the *Kansas City Journal-Post* published a letter from Cyrus Williams of Turney, Missouri, a man who claimed to have "been raised in a Missouri feed lot." He protested the segment showing the slaughter of "a beef." If it were true, he argued, that a picture should be true to fact and be as nearly true to life as possible, and "if the Benton murals...are a truly great work of art, as we suppose they are, we are of course all wrong in our conception of what art is."

If a Missouri cattle feeder had a tubercular-looking calf on his farm like the one pictured, he would at once take it to the woods, shoot it, and bury it to keep it from his dogs. We have never seen a calf look just like this one. Who would want a steak or a roast from the carcass in this picture?

Besides this, no man ever felled a beef animal with a sledge while standing with his feet close together and his heels in a parallel line. But perhaps the man in the picture could do it with some sleight-of-hand movement, as we notice that his hand is as long as his forearm.

Williams also said a log being cut with a cross-cut saw would never be put in the position Benton portrayed it in the mural. And the coon dogs? "Our best laugh," said Williams. "No man ever went hunting in Missouri with dogs resembling those in the mural."

Walter Herren reported in the January 8 edition of the *Journal-Post* how quickly some legislators were becoming uncomfortable in the Lounge.

Several pitch games were in progress under the watchful eye of Thomas Hart Benton's "Border Dude," who besides giving some of Missouri's aborigines a nip from his jug, looks as if he might report to the homefolks on the extra-curricular activities of House members.

Stern-visaged old Champ Clark, while he's only a picture in a picture, also looks down upon the members of the House. Back in 1887 he served as a Missouri legislator. Maybe he could give the "boys" a tip or two about political maneuvering.

He reported visitors, including some legislators, disturbed the players' concentration by going in to see the mural. "The lookers can't be still while so and so finishes up making his 3-bid and the boys get the opposite jacks mixed up once in a while," he wrote.

Herren reported no middle ground in reaction to the mural. "You either like 'em or you want the wall painted a deep black," he reported. And he said those who had introduced a resolution several years before demanding that nude water nymphs in the fountains on the north side of the capitol be clothed "at least will have something else to do now."

Democratic caucus chairman Bill Lafferty wasn't shocked by the speakeasy scene or the picture of Frankie and Johnny. He admitted to Herren he didn't know anything about art, but he liked the pictures. As for the complainers who said the mural did not represent Missouri history, Lafferty retorted, "There's nothing on these walls that didn't happen in Missouri, is there?"

Not so charitable was Speaker Pro-tem Dick Dale, who thought important historical events had been left out. And Dale, from Ray County (which was mule country in those days) complained to Herren that a man is not bigger than a mule, despite the way a farmer using a mule-driven plow was portrayed. He also complained that people's feet were too big. A recent college graduate standing nearby, remembering a story that members of a famous scholastic fraternity all had big feet, remarked, "Maybe they're Phi Beta Kappas."

The portrayal of Pendergast might have intimidated some critics. "This helps keep down some criticism," wrote Herren, 'because many of the solons believe he'd never have permitted his picture to be painted into something that wasn't just right."

Other reaction from legislators was mixed. The *Jefferson City Daily Capital News* reported on January 9 that members of the legislature seemed "perfectly willing to take...Benton's word for it that the murals on the walls of the House Lounge are art, and that characterization is not out of proportion to the actual life they are intended to portray, in spite of arguments to the contrary on the part of those who claim to be in the business."

Mainly the members declare their art education has been neglected but most of them appear to get some pleasure out of gazing upon the groupings of characters portrayed.

Country members are not in sympathy with criticism of farm animals on the murals, as most of them declare they've seen cows and sows exactly as pictured.

As to the sequence of events shown, most of them are willing to admit that it happened just about that way, and ask the question, "Why try to cover it up?"

None of this bothered Benton, who spent several hours a day in the Lounge, listening quietly while he smoked his pipe. He told Herren of the *Journal-Post*:

I'm not afraid of what anybody will say about the technical execution of the mural. Those who criticize it look only at some of the picture. Nobody has said anything against silo filling, the church baptismal scene, the courtroom scene, or the panel depicting the old time country political meeting.

On January 10, Benton mingled with about 300 people who met at the Kansas City Art Institute to see for the first time a display of the various stages of development of the mural. The *Kansas City Star* reported on the eleventh that "leading citizens were heard to remark that the Missouri pioneers in the picture did not appear to be the valiant, sturdy men who were concerned in the making of Missouri.''

They disliked to think their fathers and grandfathers looked like that. They would have liked to see more idealism in a social history of their state. Some saw only distortions and regretted that not one of the figures in the mural was "natural looking."

But others "felt a new respect for the art of a painter who took such infinite pains with his sketches, his drawings, his wax model, everything down to the set of mule's ears and the angle described by a young man's torso when he stooped to wash his hands in the family wash basin."

One woman "of mature years" was critical because Benton had not referred to religion in the mural.

Why, religion took a lot of time in the old days. There were camp meetings, protracted meetings, revivals, and there were plenty of churches. He has a church or two in the mural and I am glad of that. But I would like to see people going to church or Scripture reading, something to show there were family prayers at least.

The newspaper noted that there might not be any revivals, but "there is a happy home, with the atmosphere of doughnuts cooking, and happy homes were based upon Christian teachings." The newspaper reported that Benton had little to say.

The House Lounge was flooded on January 11 with visitors on who were in town for Governor Lloyd Stark's inauguration. So many people flocked to the Lounge that the corps of honorary colonels commissioned by Governor Stark were pressed into service to keep the crowd moving. The reaction of those visitors, reported the next day by the *Star*, was as mixed as criticism of the mural would be for some time.

Rep. J. F. Bentley of Randolph County, an ex school teacher: "Mr. Benton is teaching me to appreciate art. I'm glad, in the first place, to see

90

an artist touch on the common homely things of the state's history, as he has done. I come here every day and look at these murals. Each time I've found something new in the detail and the plan I hadn't seen before.

The wife of Representative T. J. Walker of Boone County found the murals impressive but not pretty and complained the people were "terribly gaunt." They were "awful" to Callaway County representative J.R. Baker; a "waste of money" as far as Pike County's W. B. Weakley was concerned; and "too gaudy" for Senator W.E. Freeland of Taney County.

But Representative T.A. Shockley of Pulaski County said the mural, "suits me fine"; and Senator George Rozier of Perryville found the paintings garish but liked them "a lot."

Senator Phil Donnelly, later a two-term governor of Missouri, complained Benton had "no proportion to his stuff," and Representative H.S. Rainwater of Polk County thought "The artist has played a joke on us."

On the fourteenth, the *Daily Capital News* reported the mural's vividness—and perhaps the increasing flow of visitors who wanted to see it—had driven pitch players out of the Lounge. Card games were moved to the House floor and to the table where the press sat in those days. (The press wasn't moved to the present gallery above and behind the Speaker's dais until the 1960s.) "It's just not comfortable in there," complained one representative. "How can you keep your mind on playing pitch with Jesse James jumping off the wall at you?"

To Representative Max Asotsky, a Kansas City realtor, the pictures were terrible. "They'd go swell in a lot of Kansas City barrooms," he commented to *Life* magazine in its March 1 issue. If that was intended to insult Benton, it didn't work. For it was Benton who, a few years later, said, "If it were left to me, I wouldn't have any museums. I'd have people buy the paintings and hang 'em in privies or anywhere anybody had time to look at 'em. Nobody looks at

91

'em in museums. Nobody goes to museums. I'd sell mine to saloons, bawdyhouses, Kiwanis and Rotary Clubs, and Chambers of Commerce—even women's clubs."[6]

One particularly salty appraisal that Benton always appreciated came from the state engineer, Matt Murray. Benton used to chuckle recalling the time Murray told a reporter, "I wouldn't hang a Benton on my shithouse wall."[7]

Although Benton could slough off some of the criticism against him, he was stung by the sometimes-vicious onslaught that came from his fellow Missourians. Thomas Craven wrote in *Scribner's* in October 1937 that it came from the very things in Benton's background. "Notwithstanding the originality of its general folkways, Missouri harbors a hidebound, middle-class practicality which, weighing heavily against nonconformity of thought, tends to dominate expressed opinion," he wrote. "This practicality accepts the useful and commonplace sentimentalities of life, but is intolerant of flights of the spirit."

It does not arrest entertaining spurts of personality, for Missourians, like other people, often act with total disregard of professed social attitudes; nor does it suppress the bawdiest and most ruffian behavior—but it is not good for the sensibilities or conducive to intellectual discrimination. This insistence or conformity of attitude operates most viciously against the creative spirit, against the mental elasticity so necessary to the development of original thought.

Craven wrote that the mural stood out against that "mediocrity of average mental performance." He predicted the mural might "become one of the shrines of American cultural achievement."

Almost immediately Benton began getting flack from Howard Huselton, a Kansas City real estate dealer and a trustee of the Kansas City Art Institute. In time Huselton would become the most persistent critic, a man whose disagreement with Benton the artist and later with Benton the author became a personal crusade.[8] Huselton predicted "a time will come when Missouri will find the murals so odious its executives will order they be blacked out." Nothing was right about the mural in Huselton's eyes. "I'm sorry they're in the capitol of this state. I don't think Benton did justice to Missouri. He exaggerated everything. It is not satire he painted; it is caricature."

Huselton complained that R. Bryson Jones, the man speaking to a group in the Kansas City segment, doesn't have Jones' body, a failing he found with all of Benton's figures. "He imposes bulging shoulders and recessed spinal columns on every man he paints in the murals," he complained. He called the work a "low type of painting."

But Huselton was countered by playwright D. L. James, who admired Benton's courage in showing what he saw and felt. James, whose son is in the mural, was in "thorough sympathy" with Benton.

It seems to me art is big enough and wide enough in its scope to include men such as Benton, Curry and Wood as well as the conventional men whose work follows traditional forms...The side of life Benton has painted in the murals may not be pretty, but it is true....This is a big world, and there is room for more than one facet of art....Benton is one of America's great living painters.[9]

Benton confronted his critics head-on less than two weeks later in a question-and-answer session at the Kansas City Art Institute. He preferred the Q&A format to a formal presentation when he went before groups to defend his mural. As time went by, Benton seemed to increasingly relish the experiences. The *Kansas City Star* on October 16, 1938, said Benton was

...thoroughly capable of taking care of his critics, but without acrimony or hard feelings; he carries no chip on his shoulder, but confounds his detractors by his deft turn of phrase and by a politician's method of dealing with the public he must have inherited from his office-holding father, and his great uncle, the eloquent namesake who stood on the eastern bluffs, visualized a city in which his great nephew is satisfied to live and made an assertion which assured the survival of his name in at least a boulevard....

Benton does not "bristle," though his black mustache does—it has the elegance and trimness of a well-worn shoe brush. The mustache fails, however, to lend its wearer the ferocity depicted in the self-portrait which hangs over the desk in his home. If he still thinks he looks like that, this is as good a time as any to disillusion him: He looks as if he would not mind at all being stroked.

When asked in the session at the Art Institute how he designed the mural, he said straightforwardly, "Well, I sat down and monkeyed with a pencil."

The session lasted more than an hour and a half.

Although it is a historical mural, Benton said, he had no problems using people of differing generations in conjunction with each other in the various scenes. He said the picture is meant to show "the conditions under which history is made rather than history itself."

Had I treated the theme as a succession of events I would have had to receive my impressions at second hand. I never put anybody in a picture of this kind unless I have had an opportunity to become acquainted with him or to sketch him from life.

But there is one person Benton did not sketch from life. And because of that, he told the Art Institute crowd, it's a poor representation of Missouri Congressman Champ Clark, a friend of the Benton family. Benton called the Clark poster "just an effigy of the man," serving only as background for the meeting. He said it was the only "portrait" in the mural his critics said he had not caricatured. That kind of comment puzzled Benton because, he said, the photograph from which he worked was not good and had been retouched.

Had I painted my own idea of him it would have been something quite different from the photograph, which is so obviously a pale and lifeless reproduction of a retouched likeness. I can only conclude that people have

94

gradually come to base their ideas of the appearance of political candidates and others in the public eye upon photographs rather than upon the testimony of their eyes.

One critic charged there is neither "beauty nor refinement" in the mural. "There is truth," responded Benton. "Besides, all that I have put into the picture is beautiful—to me."

The mural is accurate, he argued. It had to be. "I think it is important that details be right because if a visitor sees two young men wielding a crosscut saw in a manner that will result in the binding of the saw, he won't believe anything else is right in the picture."

What about the hands and feet of the people in the paintings. They're so large. "I like the hands of working people. They are beautiful. I like to have them large enough to be seen. The feet must correspond in size, of course. The fact is that most of the hands and feet you have seen in the pictures have been painted too small."

But isn't that cow too thin? No, said Benton. If fact, she's a nice cow and a distinct addition to the picture.[10]

Editorial writers from other parts of the country started getting into it. The *New Orleans Item-Tribune* on January 24 noted, "Missourians no longer need shout that they are right up to the times, the cultural peers of New York slickers. They have one of those mural rumpuses in Jefferson City." The newspaper referred to it as "a first-class squabble," saying Missourians might tolerate modern art but would become alarmed with "a yarn that the artist used up $2751 worth of fresh eggs."

The most casual acquaintance with the Missouri mind will explain the explosive power of that egg story. Art may be almost any darned thing, but eggs are eggs. They are a medium of exchange when all other currency has vanished. They are good in some parts for gingham and hair-ribbons, pencils and scratch-pads, spool-thread and cutplug, sugar, coffee, and harness-leather. Two thousand, seven hundred and fifty-one dollars worth of eggs!

Benton quickly corrected the criticism. "He used only about 35 dozen eggs—$10.50 worth. But there may be a legislative investigation," the newspaper reported.

The legislative investigation didn't materialize. Others, however, wanted answers to their questions—the American Legion in Kansas City, for instance. The *Star* described the breezy exchange in its January 29, 1937, issue:

Thomas Hart Benton, artist, went to a luncheon of the Heart of America post and pulled off his rubbers in the private dining room at the Hotel Phillips and hung his hat, scarf and overcoat on the floor...Mr. Benton pulled at his coat and tried to make his hair stay down instead of stick up and he looked all around and it was finally decided that it would be best for Elmer and his buddies to send over some hand grenades on art and for Tom to catch them and send them back.

There was nothing personal in including Pendergast, Kemper, and Nichols, Benton told the group. "They were just different types...the people who look at them can read into them whatever they desire. J.C. Nichols is there to stay, whether he likes it or not and he don't like it."

As for criticism that he made people "funny looking," Benton said simply, "No individual who is painted there on the murals likes it, but most of his friends do."

Some of the members complained about the lack of military history and others complained about the diaper scene.

First, there couldn't have been any military history if there weren't any babies to put diapers on. Second, if I'd had more space I would have done it—that is—put in more military history. But Missouri's military affairs were mostly skirmishes when we consider the entire budget of time.

One questioner worried if Benton would ever get any more state jobs since he had included Pendergast. "I never considered it. I don't care very much," he answered. Well, another questioner wanted to know, did you depict Pendergast as a statesman, a boss or what?" Benton, chuckling, answered, "I just put him in there."

The presence of Pendergast was a nettlesome issue to many, especially some of those in Jefferson City. Former Representative David Hess recalled:

Pendergast at the time was very well thought of. There was no indication that he and O'Malley and some of the rest of them had their hands in the till. None whatsoever. This was very much a shock to his friends.[11]

Pendergast was involved in a state insurance department scandal which broke open later. One of his supporters, department director R. Emmett O'Malley, was eventually sent to prison. Pendergast, himself, later went to prison for federal tax law violations that stemmed from that incident.

Former Representative O. K. Armstrong recalled that when he was elected to the legislature in 1932, Pendergast was "completely...in control of the legislature. And his word was pretty well law among the members."[12]

Benton's final word on Pendergast came during an interview years later in the Lounge.

This is not a memorial to Tom Pendergast. He just happened to be at the time that I was painting this mural, probably the most powerful figure in the state of Missouri and the most dominant figure in Kansas City itself. And in the interests of realism I felt that he should go in the mural and so I put him there.[13]

In 1940, Professor I.G. Morrison of Columbia delivered a long lecture on the interpretation of the mural. Benton wrote him that "it corresponds to my historical conceptions—in most cases, exactly."[14] Morrison said in his lecture in the House Lounge September 2, 1940:

If that is a portrait of Mr. Pendergast then these are not murals depicting a Social History of Missouri; they cannot be murals and portraits of individuals at the same time....

We have had a political boss or bosses in Missouri from 1821 to 1940. As far as I know, in the reading of history, we have never been without one. The first political boss we ever had was the great uncle of the man who painted these murals....

Ever since Moses descended from Mt. Sinai with his two tablets of stone, business and politics have been closely allied. There is nothing new presented to us here, but Mr. Benton again calls our attention to history as it is still being made.

All of this was lost on the *Tulsa*(Oklahoma)*Tribune*, which unleashed its editorial invective on January 27, 1937, charging Benton had''grossly libeled'' his home state. The paper called on Governor Stark to remove ''this libel upon Missouri.''

Benton by his labors repudiates all the integrities and all the decades of Missouri's fine social history.

Shame on you, Thomas Hart Benton, shame on you. You have disgraced your art as you have disgraced your state.

The newspaper charged Benton had pictured degradations of society in a state that cultivated no degrading social history. ''Benton has not pictured the social history of Missouri. He has used his brush to broadcast falsehood, to bear false witness against a glorious star upon our flag's field of blue.''

Shame on you, Thomas Hart Benton, shame on you, and shame on whoever, representing Missouri's government, paid you $16,000 to buy this picture of infamy. Shame upon the people's representatives in the capitol from Governor Stark to every member of the state's legislature who will allow such a picture to remain brazenly exhibited on Missouri's capitol wall.

...The whole nation is just beginning to realize that the forces of evil in Missouri are evidencing a boldness which the country can view with alarm. If the underworld is to decorate our capitols and set up their law-defying performances as worthy of emulation then it becomes high time for decent citizens from coast to coast to protest the Benton picture in Missouri's capitol as every decent citizen of Missouri now is doing....

Or is this Mr. Benton's and Mr. Pendergast's and Governor Stark's little idea of a practical joke on the fine people of Missouri? A tragic sense of humor, if this be it.

The newspaper accused Benton of lying about Missouri, desecrating the capitol walls, and declaring through the mural that Missouri's social history is one of "utter depravity." The *Tribune* proclaimed, "Missouri's social history is a story of growing refinement and nobility."

Benton sloughed off that attack in his first autobiography, noting "it was a Democratic administration that sponsored my job in Missouri and...the paper...was a Republican paper."

A small, neatly printed handbill was circulated throughout the capitol about this time, signed by "A Bum Art Critic." It complained that the dominant figures in the Kansas City segment were a butcher "sledging the life out of a particularly meek and innocent looking cow," a speaker whose back is highlighted—his face not shown, and a boss, "his eyes toward the east where lie Jefferson City and Washington, new worlds to conquer." The "critic" complained the entire scene depicting Kansas City exuded "an atmosphere of helpless futility." The handbill complained that there was little to reflect cultural, moral, or spiritual interest in the city. But it concluded that Benton's portrait of the city was accurate although he left out some things—"an overstuffed ballot box, a $40,000 underworld funeral, a union station massacre, a bandit golf course, and a kidnappers' retreat." But, concluded the critic, "shucks, art is art."[15]

The *Kansas City Star* noted on January 17 that the discussion of the murals was "replacing the duke of Windsor and Mrs. Simpson as the popular topic of conversation in Kansas City. Which we think is all to the good, even though the argument at times threatens to disrupt friendships and lead to mayhem.''

Whether one likes the Benton pictures or not, they have vitality. By contrast many of the other murals in the capitol look merely pretty and sentimental. In the old Whittier home at Amesbury, Mass., hangs a crayon portrait of Harriet Beecher Stowe. It represents her as a beautiful lady. Her brother, Henry Ward Beecher, visiting Whittier, stopped in front of the portrait. ''Well,'' he commented, ''that's the way Hattie ought to look.''

So many paintings are pictures of the way Hattie ought to look instead of the way Hattie really looks.

For those who found no beauty in the mural, the *Star* noted:

Certainly artists never have limited their subjects to beauty. They have painted tragic things, ugly things, humdrum things and have infused a feeling in their work that gives the people who see it a new understanding of life, a real expansion of experience. Paintings with this emotional quality may not be pretty. But if they stand the test of time they are considered beautiful.

The *Post-Dispatch* came to Benton's side on January 3, noting Benton had fulfilled the expectations of both those who felt an ''uneasiness in some hearts and something like diabolical anticipation in other impish souls.'' The paper indicated it preferred Benton's philosophy that life should be portrayed ''warts and all.''

Just what should a mural be? That popular historian of art, Thomas Craven, tells us it should be ''a sweeping social commentary,'' and he tells us that Benton, along with the two Mexicans, Orozco and Rivera, has rediscovered the art of wall painting on the grand scale which has been lost since the early Italians.

Is there tragic integrity, is there symbolic sequence in Benton's journey down Missouri folkways?

The *Jefferson City Daily Capital News* added its voice on February 2. Although it thought the Tulsa *Tribune* went overboard, the Jefferson City paper admitted, ''We do not admire the mural in the House lounge...because it does not, in our judgement, fairly represent the social life of Missouri.''

We do not know why the artist chose to paint Missouri's social history at its worst—a mural that satirizes rather than characterizes....We respectfully submit that the editor of the *Tulsa Tribune* is as far afield from the facts as he claims the mural to be. Neither the representatives nor Governor Stark are responsible for the kind of a mural Mr. Benton painted, and no ''shame'' whatever attaches to them.

The newspaper felt Missourians were generally tolerant ''and are disposed to let the test of time judge the merit of the mural. We do not all see alike and what to us is a folderol with a bad taste to it, to many others perhaps more capable of judging than we are, it is a meritorious work of art, worthy of the place it occupies.''

Stronger support came from Sir Charles Higham, a celebrated art critic from London, who visited the capitol. He told the *Daily Capital News* for its February 3 edition, ''Benton's work is about 20 years ahead of modern conception. Twenty years from now this work will be more fully appreciated. Benton is an artist....One does not look at paintings like these with a fleeting eye. He studies them and envies the artist who painted them.''

One of the more celebrated confrontations took place on February 3. The *Kansas City Star* reported that day Benton had lunch with 250 members of the Kansas City Chamber of Commerce. The most vocal critic was Thomas Dods, the president of a cleaning and dying works, who complained, ''If Illinois had a mural painted on the walls of the capitol, that state wouldn't show Al Capone. The inclusion of Jesse James in the Missouri mural is a disgrace to the state.''

Benton's response: ''If Illinois had any regard for the truth, it would have to include Al Capone in the mural.''

Well, what about the slaughterhouse scene? One member

said he had lived in Kansas City for forty years and had never seen a cow like that before. "That's because you never saw a cow with my eyes," answered Benton. "Everyone sees things differently. Naturally, I am forced to paint things as I see them, and I believe my work has sharpened my eyes considerably."

Dods wouldn't be quiet. "I would suggest that Mr. Kemper and these other gentlemen who have been portrayed should make up a fund and buy enough whitewash to wash over and cover up those murals and furthermore, enough whitewash should be obtained to wash out the men who had the nerve to authorize such a painting on the walls of our capitol."

Benton explained that the mural should be regarded as a person regards a tree or a house—as a reflection of the mind.

"I think they picture the mind of the man who put them there," Dods retorted.

"That's right, they do," Benton snapped. And he blew a cloud of tobacco smoke.

Couldn't something more beautiful, in keeping with the architecture of the capitol, have been chosen? "It's axiomatic that you can't build beauty out of beauty," Benton replied. "It must be from the original. Most all of our trouble comes from idealism, too. It isn't important to me what people think. It's what they have done or what they are doing."

Benton won over most of the people there that day, especially when one member asked him if the social life shown in the mural is the only social life that could be included. "Well, not all, maybe," said Benton. Then slowly, almost slyly, he said, "But I've got *this* scene in there,"—indicating the luncheon club he was speaking to—"and you wouldn't say that social scene was wrong, would you?"

The *Independence Examiner* found little merit in the

painting.

...the whole thing is sordid and rather disgusting and it's more like a cartoon which picks out and emphasizes the weaknesses and extravagance of early Missouri life and leaves out the mighty purposes, the strong characters, the ideals of men and women who built Missouri...Missouri is not a houn' dog state.[16]

Support for Benton came from Chicago, however. Edwin C. Hill, writing in his "Human Side of the News" column on February 5, said the criticism was nothing new. Artists had been criticized for centuries, especially when they put living people into their paintings. "Mr. Benton's choice of bleak, forbidding subjects, his contorted figures, his occasional savage satire of some brutal or banal aspect of our national life have brought the charge that though his paintings may be clinical documents, they are not art," he noted.

One reason why art is long is that it is forever a wide open subject. One man's art is another man's bunk.

I believe the expression "Independent as a hog on ice" derives from Missouri. Mr. Benton, reared in Missouri, a grandson of rip-snorting old Congressman Benton, who rode hell-for-leather through several sessions of congressional flummery, is exactly that.[17]

The *Chicago Tribune* also defended Benton's decision not to paint "the Pilgrims landing at Plymouth Rock, Ceres binding the wheat, the animals entering the ark, science seizing the lightning, or Newton hit by the apple."

The artist of the murals refuses to be a society portrait painter. He will not take out the wrinkles, the double chin, or the pouches under the eye. His story of Eden is Eve being bitten by the apple. He is a commentator and interpreter of events, a pictorial newspaper, or historian. In his view of mores, instincts and usages Frankie and Johnnie are the true Romeo and Juliet, like it or not.[18]

On February 17, the *Columbia Missourian* had an

editorial headlined, "Does the Truth Hurt?" It noted those who favored removing the mural or hanging tapestry to hide it. "They are the type who prefer to forget there is 'another side of the tracks,' or a 'clay hills' section in the state."

Whatever else may be said of the murals, one conclusion can quickly be drawn: they at least have substance, otherwise there could be no significant controversy.

...Benton attempts to draw no conclusion, derive no moral. He simply gives you the picture as he sees it; what you make of it depends on your own interpretation.

The *St. Louis Globe-Democrat*, the next day, also defended Benton. "From the 'houn' dog' to the Nelson Art Gallery the panorama of Missouri life is vividly portrayed." But what the newspaper found most important was "the real characterization Benton stamped upon the faces of real Missouri people."

The face from the soil, creased, reddened, burdened with petty duties. The face from the kitchen, submissive, domesticated, toiling with menial tasks. The face of the factory worker, or the business executive. These faces one meets in the elevator, on the sidewalk, in the corner grocery store.

The newspaper answered those who complained Benton had omitted "the cornerstone characters, the high ideals of the state's great men." The newspaper accused those who said, "Missouri is not a houn' dog state," of avoiding "the fundamental essence of Missouri life. The farmers, the political meetings, the hound dogs, the industrialists—these are a living part of the color-scheme of the Missouri of today."

Ed Watson, the long-time editor of the *Columbia Daily Tribune*, noted that Benton's critics—no matter how vicious their attacks—could not match the cruelty Benton had shown his home state with his mural. "It is generally agreed that the applause would be general and deafening should

Gov. Stark order this whole 'realistic' mess obliterated,''
Watson wrote. ''It is neither truth nor art.''

The trouble may be that Artist Benton's castigators entirely fail to grasp
what an artist of the realistic school really feels, and what is required of
one who attaches himself to what they must deem a rather messy ilk of
color daubers, even though the drawing answers all requirements of art in
its nakedness. Besides the technical requirements of the school may be
three strokes up of the brush, then two down, then four across, all done
with an abandon designed to create soul, atmosphere and what have you.
It may be that Artist Benton's critics cannot reach the heights attained by
this realistic scion of Missouri who sees the past social history of his
native state through lenses of a nature that perforce produce that rough
stuff he's slung on the walls of the lounge in the Hall of the House of
Representatives, and called it art.

If that was Benton's view of the social life of Missouri,
Watson remarked, ''it seems undeniable that Mr. Benton
must have been keeping mighty bad company here of
late.''[19]

Another protest came from Robert Jones of Seattle,
Washington, whose letter was published by the *Tribune* on
March 1, ''The money would be better spent on plain wall
paper, in my opinion....Don't let those cartoons remain.
They insult the state.''

I am tired of proletarian pictures, novels, essays and speeches. Let's have
something inspiring and fine, something beautiful and impressive to
represent Missouri, because that kind of subject matter is rude to the spirit
of the state and her people.

Benton confronted his critics again on February 28 at the
Community Church in Kansas City. His critics, Huselton
and Dods, were there, too.

Huselton started it off: ''I was born in Missouri and you
were too. Are you proud of your native state?''

''I don't know,'' said Benton. ''I only know I'm
interested in it.''

Benton wrote in his first autobiography his answer forced Huselton to discard many of his questions. He said Huselton lost a chance to trap him. Benton felt Huselton was sincere but was "without the slightest understanding of the sort of thing I stood for."

He could not see or believe that I really meant what I said when I told him that I judged the world and the people in it by what they did rather than by what they said. He could not understand any more than could my Communist friends of New York that I did not believe in patterns of words and that such a pattern as "Are you proud of Missouri?" was utterly without meaning for me. Like the New York radicals, he saw my kind of realism as cynicism, as something beyond even a touch of nobility or beauty. Time and time again as I talked about my mural people would rise with questions or statements that indicated plainly that they could not get the connection between beauty, sincerity, or honesty of purpose and the ordinary straight recognition of things *as they were and are* that is behind my work.

Why, asked Huselton, was Jesse James included? Because James was a Missouri institution, venerated by early settlers, said Benton.

Why Frankie and Johnny? "They are a legend, just as Huck Finn and the James boys have become a legend. And after all I have to have my people doing something. I can't have them just sitting around long tables reading the latest news about the Constitution."

"Why are your cows so scrawny?"

"It's generally known that milk cows don't get fat. I've never found a dirt farmer yet who criticized my cows. The people who have complained are those who never milked a cow and have seen only the ones that are brought to the shows. They're good for nothing but to look at."

When Huselton asked, "Why did you make Missourians all of the hick type?" Benton responded, "You suggest there is something wrong with the hick. I found him more interesting and more intelligent."

Benton said he would make no changes or substitutions in

the mural. When Huselton asked why he left out so many of "the finest people" in Missouri history—like his ancestor, Senator Benton, and General Pershing, Benton was characteristically frank: "In the development of Missouri, General Pershing was not as important as an ordinary old bucksaw and my grand uncle, Senator Benton, was of far less importance than a common Missouri mule."

Dods, by now, had had enough. He shouted, "Not only would I whitewash the murals, but I would whitewash the heads of the men responsible for them."

'I alone am responsible for them," Benton said quietly.

'No wonder then," Dods exploded.

Leave it to a schoolteacher to put things in proper perspective. Miss Ruth Mary Weeks, an English instructor at Paseo High School, had reproduced the murals by mounting small reproductions of them on pasteboard walls. She thought Benton had taken the epic view: "We are most of us too near our past to look at it in an impersonal way as Mr. Benton has done. It is like the fable of the tadpole and the frog. The frog told the tadpole he never had had a tail like that, and the tadpole replied that the frog, then, never had been a tadpole."[20]

The *Kansas City Journal-Post* commented on March 3 that Benton was proving to be 'as skillful in debate as he is with his brush. He has definitely come out on top in his argument with the buttercup school of art criticism."

The partisan alignment in the mural controversy is an old one. On one side are those who believe that not only life but history as well is just a bowl of cherries, and they like them painted large and ripe. On the other are those who are awed by the sweeping drama of human affairs; who believe that no artistic or literary treatment of them can be taken seriously if it sees only pink sunsets and pious motives.

The same argument was heard in the cases of Sinclair Lewis and Eugene O'Neil. It ran: Of course that's true, but there is enough ugliness in the world. Why write about it?

O'Neil and Lewis are the only two American writers who have

displayed sufficient vitality to win the Nobel prize for literature. Or should it have been awarded to Harold Bell Wright?[21]

The popularity of the mural in the Lounge focused attention on the capitol generally, not all of it good. The *Kansas City Star's* bureau reported on March 4 that visitors to the legislature and the crowds wanting to see the mural were openly critical of the upkeep of the capitol. The reporter noted the capitol "is rapidly gaining the reputation of being one of the dirtiest and abused" in the country. The reporter said the condition detracted from the works of art and other features of the building.

Adding to the situation is the fact that the bars have been let clear down on the uses to which the capitol was intended. On numerous occasions, particularly in recent months, it has been turned into a playground and almost a night club. A young Democratic organization has held two or three rallies in the House Lounge under the...murals. The rugs were rolled back and an orchestra played into the late hours. Frequently it has become a task for janitors to clean up the debris and empty bottles after some of the soirees.[22]

Hugh Sandidge suggested in a letter the *Kansas City Journal-Post* published on March 5 that "Benton painted with his tongue in his cheek, knowing in advance that there would be a lot of criticism and having the answers ready when it came."

After viewing the murals I use language of the street and say that I wouldn't like them if they were *good*, but I admire Mr. Benton in standing up for his beliefs, and believe that he is enjoying himself in the stand that he takes.

...Like all pioneers, Mr. Benton will make mistakes, but I firmly believe that he is opening the way for the average person to get a better understanding of art. The painter and musician have played to a select few too long and the quicker they come down off their high horse and bring their art to a common understanding, the better off they will be.

Sandidge concluded, "At least he has given us something

108

to discuss at the luncheon clubs besides the supreme court and as to whether we will have group singing or not.''

His reference to ''group singing'' went back to Benton's Chamber of Commerce appearance. Group singing was dispensed with that day.

Benton moved on to St. Louis a few days later to defend his works before the Junior League. The day before that meeting, he met with reporters at the Forest Park Hotel. One with the *Globe-Democrat* wrote on March 8 ''there is little in Benton, the artist, to suggest the scion of politicians and statesmen.''

He likes Bourbon whiskey, and has a man-of-the-people preference for meat and potatoes instead of *pate de fois gras*, but there the resemblance ends. He is too short in stature for the pontifical pose of statesmanship, and his speech is crisp rather than oracular. He has a short black mustache, sharp features and dark hair that lies back in a rough pompadour.

He explained the difference between ''mere history and social history.''

Many famous characters are not of sufficient social importance to find a place in social history. For social history is concentrated on the general behavior of the whole people. Famous people to be effective in social history must effect the behavior patterns. On that score, General Pershing is not as important as a buck saw. He commanded an army but he did not change the social habits of his people.

He also defended the lack of so-called ''nice people.'' By that, the reporter meant ''the gentry in silk hats and evening clothes.'' They were there, Benton said, but ''without their scissorbill coats and soup and fish manners.'' They're doing things in the mural they often did ''when not on parade,'' Benton said.

Benton took time to explain the distinctive American art he and others were trying to develop--art stemming from the American environment. This was described in the *St. Louis Globe-Democrat*:

For the saints and madonnas of renaissance art they substitute steel mills and cotton pickers, huskies, political spellbinders, etc., because these figures have the same indigenous vitality in the modern American scene that monks and madonnas had in the medieval.

And Benton noted his unpopularity with a large number of people and groups: "I've been called many things by many people. Good Communists say I'm a Fascist and conservatives say I'm a 'damn Red.' But I'm trying to make an objective picture of American society. I know, of course, I bring an attitude to my work. But I am not using my stuff as propoganda for a predetermined conception of what society ought to be."

At the Junior League the next day, the *Post-Dispatch* reported, "the swart little painter's dark eyes twinkled" as he fielded the usual questions. Why Frankie and Johnny? Because they are St. Louis' most famous characters.

The space could have been filled with portraits of governors, but more people throughout the nation have heard of Frankie and Johnnie than of any of Missouri's governors....Frankie and Johnnie are a rough symbol, but a good one, of what is happening all the time in a certain stratum of our society.

Benton noted that some who think the mural is a sordid portrayal overlook some obvious limitations of space and content. All kinds of people had to be shown, and those people—he said—didn't feel sordid. He went on to say that artists throughout history have been under pressure to "pretty up their work to conform to an ideal rather than a reality, or simplicity." And he recalled that Michelangelo was told by the pope that his paintings on the Sistine Chapel ceiling didn't have enough gold in them.

On March 10, Representative T. E. Roberts of Benton's home county of Newton introduced a resolution in the House noting, "there is a great danger of [the] murals becoming marred, marked, scratched, touched, soiled and

110

defaced due to the fact that there is no ample protection...from spectators who pass so closely by...in order to view and admire same." The resolution called the mural a "magnificent work of art" that was attracting "great and extensive interest" on the part of the public. In fact, said Roberts in his resolution, "contrary to the hopes and anticipation of the press of this State, said murals are fastly becoming endeared in the hearts of Missourians so that posterity will point with pride instead of shame to this superior work of art." He proposed the Permanent Seat of Government furnish a rail "or suitable means of protection" to keep the mural from being disfigured by an admiring public.

But Roberts' effort backfired. Representative C. P. Turley of Carter County drew applause from fellow House members when he amended the resolution the next day suggesting the Permanent Seat of Government "in order to preserve and prevent from further disfigurement the loftier portions of such murals be empowered to whitewash a belt or portion of the murals, such whitewash to commence at the base of said murals and to extend to a point six feet and four inches from the floor of the lounge and to extend around the entire lounge room."

"I know this ring of whitewash would be a monstrosity," Turley told the House, "but I've always been told that like begets like, and so this monstrosity would fit in well with the monstrosity out there on the walls."[23]

The amendment drove Roberts to put his resolution on the shelf. House journals indicate it was never brought up again during that session.

At the same time, Benton was deciding the increasing demands for speeches about the mural should be met with a fee—$100 and expenses. The *Kansas City Star* in its March 11 edition had these words of sympathy for Benton: "If a man talks his throat sore, he should be rewarded with a fee to cover at least the cost of healing. Right now, the artist is in bed with a cold, but it is not a severe cold and he hopes to be up in a day or two.''

The calls for Governor Stark to do something were blunted March 17. Benton took Stark on a guided tour of the Lounge, explaining the mural to him as they went. The artist recalled years later

...he went directly to the figure of Tom Pendergast... Looking as deadpan as possible, I said to him, ''That is a fact of Missouri's Social History.'' ''That *was* a fact,'' he laughed. He was correct but not in Kansas City before several more years had passed.[24]

Benton worried about how Stark would react to the entire work. The governor's reaction was reported in the *Kansas City Star* March 19:

I do not think it is a beautiful piece of art. But the murals are skillfully done and depict significant occurrences in the life of Missouri in the early days.

In my opinion, the artist has made a very valuable contribution to Missouri by permanently recording in pictorial form the folklore of past days.

The governor's wife had a somewhat different view from that publicly held by her husband. In his unpublished manuscript, ''The Thirties,'' Benton recalled that about a year later, when Stark told his wife an artist had been found to paint the traditional portrait of the first lady for the Executive Mansion, Mrs. Stark said, ''I hope it is not Mr. Benton, because I do want to look like a lady.''

One of the columnists for the *Kansas City Star* decided to have his own look at the controversial painting and wrote on March 21 that the great scale of the pictures, the apparent smallness of the room, and the vivid colors had an undeniable impact. ''Our first impulse was to duck,'' he wrote.

...the impression of distorted proportions in some of the larger figures sort of combine to make the spectator feel he is about to be overwhelmed and crushed, perhaps, in an avalanche that somehow seems very threatening and imminent.

But he found nothing unpleasant about the experience. After the first visual jolt, "details reach out and capture the interest in a most compelling fashion." Eventually, he wrote, the visitor finds a vantage point "from which to view something prodigious that seems about to happen."

Then he noted a second emotion that soon struck viewers of the mural: a feeling that "whatever the faults of the present generation may be, our forefathers were all noble, brave, honest and generous gentlemen, hewing through the wilderness with an ax in one hand and a Bible in the other, with a rifle leaning against a convenient tree, purely as a defensive weapon."

So, when we see, in a mural, a white man trading a passive looking Indian out of a bear hide or a silver fox fur for a cupful of very doubtful whiskey of which he has a whole jug, our sense of commercial justice is immediately outraged, and we feel that Mr. Benton is taking liberties with our ancestors.

The editor also found a third phase in which the viewer would perceive "that history is not yet finished; that the seeds of civilization planted by the pioneers (good and bad) are still growing and being harvested, and that cheating the Indians and working slaves having been found inadvisable and unprofitable, perhaps there are other things later to be found capable of improvement or abandonment." It is in this third phase, he suggested, that the viewer's resentment of Benton's technique begins to crumble in the face of "the tremendous vividness of his drawing, the compelling tempo of the dramatic action, and the startling devices which the artist has used as means to his ends."[25]

Direct criticism of the mural was one thing. But others

were drawn into the fray. *Life* magazine published a multiple-page story on the mural in its March 1 edition, showing some photographs of those in the painting and running a large color spread of the mural itself.

Two letters appeared in the March 29 issue. One was from Thomas W. Anderson, the general secretary of the Young People's Progressive League of Cleveland, who noted *Life* had traditionally been favorable to blacks.

However it seems to possess one thing in common with most magazines beneath its level: the inevitable tendency, common in white magazines, to now and then poke fun at Negro subjects.

In the issue of March 1, you use the words "a proud darky." Is there any good reason for using this or any other uncomplimentary and humiliating term in referring not only to Negroes but any member of any other minority group?

And Frank Young, the managing editor of the *Kansas City Call*, took the magazine to task for using the words "darky" and "nigger."

The first term is used freely in the South when referring to the Negro; the second, an obsolete and offensive term, has long since been dropped by all first class newspapers and larger magazines and other publications.

I believe this is an oversight on the part of the editor to allow this to get through and they do not know that the intelligent and well-meaning negroes object to it.

Life's response was a curt editor's note: "Mark Twain is *Life's* sound authority for calling the Negro in Thomas Benton's *Huckleberry Finn* mural 'Nigger Jim.'"

Benton recalled that the article, coupled with his earlier notoriety after the Indiana mural, "rapidly projected me into a countrywide prominence such as, I believe, no other American artist has ever attained." Benton had no trouble accepting the situation. After all, he noted, "For nearly ten years I lived in a generally continuous glare of spotlights."

Like movie stars, baseball players and loquacious senators, I was soon a figure recognizable in Pullman cars, hotel lobbies and night clubs. I became a regular public character. I signed my name for armies of autograph hunters. I posed with beauty queens and was entertained by overwhelming ladies...I was continuously photographed and written about by the columnists. I received fan letters by the hundreds...Under the stimulation of all this attention, enhanced occasionally by other stimulants, I spouted endlessly and frequently without regard for consequences.[26]

The consequences came later and cost him his job in Kansas City.

For those who criticized his mural because it contained no ideals, Benton had a ready answer, given at a meeting in Jefferson City on April 14. There are plenty of ideals portrayed in the painting, he said. ''The fact that Frankie shot Johnnie because he done her wrong is proof she had ideals the most respectable church people could approve.''[27]

The *Post-Dispatch* quoted him further the next day saying he didn't take ideals seriously if they did not produce results: ''You people in Jefferson City ought to know that the high ideals people express usually cover up social acts that are anything but ideal.''

Benton pointed to the art gallery in the Kansas City section as an example of what he was talking about, saying it represented ''a realistic consequence of the artistic ideal of William Rockhill Nelson.''

None of his legislative critics were at that meeting, but Benton answered some of their criticisms anyway, noting some legislators, as well as New York columnist O. O. McIntyre, had thought his colors too gaudy.

Missouri is a gaudy state. Imagine painting the social history of Missouri with a row of violets. Curiously enough, the men who think I should have painted woodland flowers are themselves salty and individualistic. You won't find any woodland flowers in the Missouri legislature.

And when asked by a person in the audience if his

opponents knew why they opposed his murals, Benton replied, "I can't tell you. But I've sometimes thought I should have painted those jackasses in the murals with open mouths."[28]

Leo Spalding, who had watched Benton paint part of the mural, wrote to the *Star* on April 19 that some of the critics were too idealistic, while Benton, "with his flashing, witty mind, successfully has defended his brain child against all comers. He has routed his adversaries."

Perhaps someone will have to paint silencers on the James boys' six-shooters, a diaper on the baby, and a lid on the famous bucket, but it won't be Benton.

More defense of the mural came from Lawrence Adams, the assistant art professor at the University of Missouri in Columbia, who had been Benton's assistant for the mural.[29] Adams helped Benton transfer his sketch to the walls of the Lounge. "There is nothing to be shocked about," he said, in a *Columbia Missourian* article April 15. "The only thing that's causing all this row over the paintings is the fact that Benton has broken with tradition and really said something."

Benton's a Missourian. He believes, as have the great muralists of history, that murals must interpret and relate the subject matter to the composition. Now take those other murals down there. You didn't see any fuss about them when they were unveiled. Why? Because they have no meaning for Missourians. They were not even painted by Missourians, and by their very idealism are innocuous.[30]

The *Missourian* noted that critics objected to Benton's portrayal of Missouri as a slave state, or as a "houn' dog" state with hunter and coonskin cap. Adams responded, "What's there to be ashamed of in that? There's nothing the matter with being a houn' dog state. Missouri should be proud of its Ozarks. And who can deny the existence of

116

slavery in Missouri? Or have they forgotten about a certain 'Dred Scott' case?''

Adams noted an observation Benton also had made—that those who viewed the mural "who stayed and absorbed the story being laid out" were the rural people. "It was the so-called 'educated' person, with enough sophistry and study of painting to corrupt his artistic tastes, who left in a huff and claimed to be 'shocked.'''

A writer identified only as E.L.J. defended Benton in the *Kansas City Star* on April 28,

Why, for example, shouldn't the woman who is changing her infant's foundation garment look as if she wondered where she left the hammer? Is she having a picnic? And why shouldn't the people listening to a Fourth-of-July orator look insensible? Did you ever listen to a Fourth-of-July political speech?

E.L.J. did good-naturedly find one error in the painting. He recalled the traditional story of Frankie and Johnny had Frankie shooting her lover in the side. "And yet, what does the artist do, I ask you. He has her shooting him in the hip, let me tell you, in a manner quite impossible if he had just stayed in his chair. It's quite wrong, and would require a lot of revision in the song....The artist ought to make Frankie load up and try again."

The *Star* reported May 6 that members of the House had finally given up trying to rest in the Lounge. Majority leader Roy Hamlin finally introduced a resolution that was adopted after a brief debate. "Because of the great amount of publicity given to the murals, the room no longer is a place for members to rest, recline and lounge, and has become a gathering place for critics of art to such an extent that the members no longer can rest, recline, lounge and use and occupy said room," the resolution said.

Representative F. J. Iffrig of St. Charles County complained, "We've had to quit resting in there because we can no longer get any rest. We've tried to hold committee meetings in the room and we can't do any business because of the constant interruption.''

House members adopted Hamlin's resolution that directed the Permanent Seat of Government to fix Room 302 on the south side of the building as a new private lounging room for House members. The 1939 House journal shows meetings were held in Room 302 by the committees on children's code, education, fish and game, and roads and highways. The Lounge was not listed for committee meetings by the House Committee on Rooms. A few years later, however, 302 went back to being the office it is today, and committee meetings were resumed in the House Lounge until another resolution was passed in 1980 that rendered the room impractical for that use.

Benton wasn't the only person defending his work in public forums by then. When the Reverend L. M. Birkhead spoke to the Kansas City Liberal Center on May 16—with Benton in the audience—he said, ''If the Missouri legislators...would deal as creatively and realistically with the political and economic problems of the state as Thomas Hart Benton has with the social history of Missouri, then we might expect Utopia to show up from around the corner.''

For those who complained of the prominence of hound dogs and mules, Birkhead claimed ''Missouri wouldn't be Missouri without its houn' dogs and its mules.''

As a Missourian whose earliest memory is that of being rocked to sleep on his father's knee to the tune of an old ballad about ''Jesse James was a thief, but he was kind to the poor,'' I can testify to the importance of the Jesse James legend in Missouri's social history. Mr. Benton was justified in putting the Jesse James panel into his murals.

''If we object to Missouri history as it has been, the thing to do is not to complain to Benton and about his realistic murals, but to improve Missouri and make her social history more beautiful,'' he said.[31]

Benton sometimes took the controversy home with him. His son, T. P., says there was "some discussion" of the arguments.

He considered the mural to be historical. He had a point of view of intellectual superiority over any criticism of it that would be backed up by professors and qualified experts on the subject of history.

The son recalls his father did not show anger about the criticism, ''only intellectual superiority.''

He thought they were dumb. Eventually the correct attitude—or the educated attitude—would prevail.[32]

The legislative session was running out, and with its end would be the end of the intense criticism in legislative halls. Not the end of political criticism, to be sure. But the intensity would abate. Representative Bill Barton of Montgomery County recalls that, down deep, much of the criticism was as much jealousy as anything.

I do...remember that, "Well, I wonder why he didn't put my picture on there. I'm a politician and I'm going to run for office. I'd like to see my name in there." That was, I guess, more of a..."I'd like to get a little more publicity."...There was some feeling that "if he's gonna use pictures, why, gee, I'd like to have mine in there."[33]

The legislature didn't meet in annual sessions then. There was no session in 1938. The comments diminished.

In mid-July, "Unofficial Greeter" Frank Canada told a reporter that children coming to the capitol wanted to see the dome or the museum. "Their parents generally ask for the Thomas Hart Benton murals," he said.[34]

Benton wrote in his first autobiography, "I think Missouri has got used to me. With my basic realism and perfect willingness to call a spade a spade, I have considerable advantages over my hecklers. I have got away with my stuff.''

I have answered every question and every objection put to me about my mural and because I answered these straight, without any beating about the bush, I think most real Missourians are beginning to like me and have come to the conclusion that I intended and made a pretty fair picture of my state.

The acceptance wasn't unanimous, though. Benton noted ''die-hards from the young Communists' nests of St. Louis'' and some of the more conservative Missourians still maintained the mural was a disgrace because it portrayed no ''idealisms.'' In fact, he noted, some of the Democrats in the legislature who helped him get the job felt he should have painted ''a sweeter picture of my home state—something a little more delicate, a little more violet-scented.'' Benton found that an odd attitude

because in my whole experience of Missouri Democrats, I've never run across any little woodland flowers (among the bucks, anyhow) and I don't believe I've ever seen a single Missouri Democratic politician, drunk or sober, who wouldn't bust you if he thought you mistook him for a violet. A great many of the objectors to the morality of my picture have been the saltiest kind of fellows in actual fact, perfect vindications by their appearance and language of the factual truth of my work.

Harry W. Flannery expressed the cooling emotions in his commentary on KMOX radio in St. Louis on February 9, 1938. Referring to Benton as ''a social historian, a man who sings folk tales, it might be said, to the accompaniment of swing music...the Carl Sandburg of the canvas, a man who looks on common people and presents them realistically with resounding force,'' Flannery noted

That's why Benton prefers to picture politicians, hillbillies, and the Ku Klux Klan instead of vases of flowers, landscapes and seascapes. That's why he put Frankie and Johnny, Huck Finn and Negro Jim, the James Brothers and Tom Pendergast in the Missouri historical murals at

120

Jefferson City, instead of presenting stuffed-shirt statesmen in imaginary heroics.

The *Missouri Social Studies Bulletin*, published in April, told visitors to the capitol who would view the mural they would "stand amazed as the vividness of the scenes strike you. You will shrink from the picture of the farmer lynched by bushwhackers."

You will stand long before a virile Jesse James as he holds up the C and A. You will smile, perhaps, at Frankie and Johnnie. You will see in startling relief all of the many stirring scenes that made Missouri. It is no disinfected and perfumed history you will read from those walls but it is real and you will carry its reality with you.

At the opposite pole was a letter to the April 14 "Public Mind" column in the *Star* from a woman who found the mural repulsive.

I believe the crudeness and lack of feeling portrayed in these murals sets a bad example. On the other hand, I desire to thank the *Star* for the sensitive and constructive articles, "Calling All Dogs," written by Albert Payson Terhune.

The same day, another letter writer said

Benton's dish is beefsteak rather than fudge...a virtue in the eyes of many. Was it not his concern to interpret history in terms of reality rather than commonplace? If it happened that a few of our ancestors helped to convert the heathen to whiskey and to defend the traditions of race prejudice by discriminating necktie parties, should these manifestations be ignored?

While the painting of this mural marked a final step in Benton's development of his artistic techniques, it also marked a milestone in critical reaction to his works. "My art moved out of the area of political controversy, with whose peripheries it had been engaged for seven years," he wrote.

The real politics in which the Missouri work was necessarily involved at its inception never came to the surface, nor did the work itself stir any

121

politically slanted ideological debate....The mural did not rid me permanently of controversy, but it did put an end to the bitter politically inspired controversy which had surrounded my earlier murals.[35]

The Missouri experience also put an end to some of the notions about the Midwest that Benton had while he was still in New York, namely that "the cultivated people of the Middle West are less intellectually provincial than those of New York or more ready for an art based upon the realities of a native culture." He wrote in *An Artist in America*

Those who affect art with a big "A" do so with their eyes on Europe just as they do in New York. They lisp the same tiresome, meaningless aesthetic jargon. In their society are to be found the same Marxist fellow travelers, the same "educated" ladies purring linguistic affectations. The same damned bores that you find in the penthouses and studios of Greenwich Village hang onto the skirts of art in the Middle West.

In the West, however, Benton found "the better part of the male gentility...seem to be secretly aware of the fact that the antics of a pink coat are not exactly in harmony with the substance of western life....This basic uneasiness keeps them quite human and I must say that, so far, I have not met a really complete ass among them. If they are a little boresome at times, they are at least not contemptible."

What is called society is, of course, like the froth on a glass of beer, of no consequence....Below the top economic foam of Missouri, the true native life lies. Although I have painted that life as I saw it and felt it, I am not yet ready to analyze it or pass judgment upon it. Taken as a whole, I like the men and women who make the real Missouri. I get along with them.

It had been a tiring experience, researching, planning, executing, and defending the Missouri mural. Benton returned to his summer home on Martha's Vinyard for the eighteenth year in 1937 to paint, refine his technique for transposing musical notes onto the scale for use by harmonica players—something the local paper said "looked like an incomprehensible caricature of some sort of unknown hieroglyphics until he explained them"—and enjoy summer on the sea. The *Martha's Vineyard Gazette* noted on July 16, 1937, that in the previous year, Benton had "painted 45,000 square feet of murals, sixty odd drawings, six lithographs, has written a 100,000 word book, 50,000 words of articles, and has delivered fifteen lectures."

In 1939, Associated American Artists published a sixty-four-page catalog of some of his works. In it Benton wrote of his feelings of artistic maturity and the comfort he had realized at last in his work: "I like painting today more than I ever liked it in my life. For many years I was in a constantly frustrated state about it. I worked and got nowhere. I worked and only got half-way to something. There was always this or that to check the free expression of what was in me."

In late years I have gained a kind of freedom. I don't stew around any more. I just go to work and do my stuff. I don't know, of course, the ultimate value of what I do. I don't care much about it. But I have a sort of inner conviction that for all the possible limitations of my mind and the distorting effects of my processes, for all the contradicting struggles and failures I have gone through with, I have come to something that is in the image of America and the American people of my time.

Benton said he did not try to paint a typical America because he had not experienced anything that could be considered typical. "The typical is a generality which does not interest me," he wrote.

My American image is made up of what I have come across, what was "there" in the time of my experience—no more, no less. My historical murals, because of this, are full of anachronisms. I paint the past through my own life experiences. I feel that an anachronism with life is better than any academically correct historical rehash.

Benton felt he had a "good grip" on his craft but could

not claim to have conquered it. "What there is in me to do I now know that I can do," he concluded.[36]

On November 15, 1939, the *Kansas City Times* noted the reconciliation of the artist and his home state seemed complete: "Benton has rediscovered Missouri and, after a bit of a fight, Missouri has discovered Benton. They get along quite nicely now, each strong, healthfully influenced by the other."

Benton stimulated Missouri by arousing a roaring, snarling art riot and Missouri gradually has given Benton a calmness and repose which distinguish his most recent work. It was after Benton and Missouri settled down together on an amicable basis that another Benton canvas was hung in the Metropolitan Museum.

Some people remained unconvinced for years, though. In fact, almost forty-five years after Benton finished painting it, the mural once again generated another controversy in the House, although it paled when compared to the rhetorical wars of 1937.

Notes

1. *An Artist in America,* 278.
2. Clipping dated January 2, 1937, in files at Nelson-Atkins Gallery of Art in Kansas City. It might be from the *Star.*
3. Christy interview (January 22, 1975). The hotel, at the corner of High and Adams streets in Jefferson City, was bought and remodeled in the 1960s to become the headquarters of the Missouri Baptist Convention.
4. Interview with the author (February 9, 1984).
5. *Daily Capital News* (January 7, 1937).
6. From the *New York World-Telegram,* excerpted in *Art Digest* magazine (April 15, 1941).
7. Burroughs, *Thomas Hart Benton, A Portrait,* 125.
8. The *Kansas City Star* (June 23, 1938) described Huselton as a "lone eagle, or lone wolf, as you prefer." It noted Huselton was deaf, a condition that prevented his working on committees or with large

groups. "But as a single-handed fighter, the town has seen few of his equal. He proved his mettle in his lone fight for Union Cemetery, forgotten in the commercialization of cemetery property. He is a veteran of such campaigns."

9. "Murals Split Art Ranks," unidentified clipping in files of State Historical Society of Missouri, Columbia (January 5, 1937).

10. "Thomas Hart Benton Takes the Stand," *Kansas City Star* (January 15, 1937).

11. Interview with the author (January 10, 1984).

12. Interview with the author (January 9, 1984).

13. Lantz interview (see endnote #27 in chapter 3).

14. Letter from Benton to Morrison (September 14, 1940). Letter and manuscript of lecture are in Western Historical Manuscripts Collection, University of Missouri-Columbia.

15. *Kansas City Star* story from Jefferson City (January 28, 1937).

16. Quoted in the *St. Louis Post-Dispatch* (February 7, 1937).

17. Charles Earle Funk, in his book, *A Hog on Ice and Other Curious Expressions* (Harper & Row, 1948) spends most of eight pages searching for the origin of the phrase and concludes it might have come from Scotland in the sixteenth century and refers to a stone used in the old game of curling.

18. Reprinted in the *Kansas City Journal-Post* (February 1937).

19. Reprinted in the *Daily Capital News* (February 19, 1937).

20. "Benton's Candor Holds," *Kansas City Times* (March 1, 1937).

21. Harold Bell Wright was a minister from Missouri's Ozarks who wrote several novels based in those areas, the most famous being *Shepherd of the Hills*, the story of a city minister who goes to the Ozarks to find his son and learns his son has died, leaving behind an illegitimate son. Without revealing his identity he becomes a minister to the hillfolk.

22. The article also noted that crowds of children "roam the capitol at will, have shouting contests, and sometimes exercise by jumping up and down on finely upholstered furniture in public rooms." The reporter complained the building was seldom cleaned, that floors were streaked with tobacco stains, and that outlets for the ventilation system were used as cuspidors, "causing the engineers for the building to request that this practice be stopped because it further befouled the air." Vandalism was evident on the freshly painted walls. Legislative chambers were poorly ventilated and showed

signs of neglect. Paper, cigar, and cigarette stubs littered the building. The governor promised corrective action.

23. Dispatch dated March 11, 1937, from the Jefferson City bureau of the *Kansas City Star*.

24. Benton, "The Thirties" (see appendix).

25. Column signed C. H. T., bylined "By Ye Ed of Roustabout," *Kansas City Star* (March 21, 1937).

26. *An Artist in America*," 278.

27. *Kansas City Times* (April 15, 1937).

28. Ibid.

29. Although Adams is generally recalled as the person who helped Benton with the mural work, others might have been involved in small ways. Mrs. Araks Tolegian of Sherman Oaks, California, recalled in a letter to the author (January 12, 1987) that her late husband, Manuel, "often spoke of helping Tom with the mural." She was unable to say what he actually did. But she said her husband, a student of Benton's at the New York Art Student's League, sometimes "baby sat" for Benton's son, T. P. She said her husband was returning to New York from visiting his parents in Los Angeles and was to take Tom back to New York. "However, he wasn't ready to go back as soon as Manuel had expected, as there were paintings that had to be done. So Tom got a hotel room for Manuel, and how long they were there, I cannot tell you." Mrs. Tolegian also wrote, "Manuel often spoke of wanting to visit Jefferson City to see the mural as he 'had worked on it with Tom.'" She says it was her husband who taught Benton how to play the harmonica.

30. In part of his statement, Adams was incorrect. Many of the lunettes and larger paintings in the capitol hallways were done by Missourians, and a Missourian was the link that brought most of the founders of the Taos Society of Artists from New Mexico to decorate the Missouri capitol. Likewise, many of the other paintings were intended to depict specific events, not a complex and general social history, as was the case with Benton's mural.

31. *Kansas City Times* (May 17, 1937). Untitled clipping in the Missouri River Room, Kansas City Public Library.

32. Interview with the author (February 24, 1987).

33. Interview with the author (February 9, 1984).

34. Associated Press story (July 12, 1937).

35. "The Thirties" (see appendix).
36. Thomas Hart Benton, *A Descriptive Catalogue of the Works of Thomas Hart Benton Spotlighting the Important Periods During the Artist's Thirty-two Years of Painting*, (New York City: Associated American Artists, 1939), 24.

Thomas Hart Benton, a small man, needed scaffolding to reach most of the mural area. On a hot summer day, he paints in details of the political rally scene showing Senator Barbour looking on as Benton's nephews fight over a broken watermelon. Not visible in the picture are the pencilled lines Benton drew on the canvas outlining the placement of people and details. (Courtesy of the Missouri Senate)

The House Lounge, pre-Benton, was a far more peaceful place. Speaker John Christy recalled that members found this decor relaxing when they wanted to escape the activity of the House floor. After the mural was painted they complained the figures seemed to jump off the walls at them. (Courtesy of the Capitol Decoration Commission)

Tom Benton relaxes in a swing in his backyard after he was fired by the Kansas City Art Institute board. Benton told a reporter he refused a demand to resign "because I have responsibilities to those kids over there in my classes." (Courtesy of Kansas City Star/Times)

The first segment of the mural is on the north wall and depicts early pioneers coming to Missouri as well as early development of the state. Commerce begins with depiction of the French trader. Development is shown in the builder's segment by the log being hewn. A slave is auctioned, and a baptismal service is held in the river. The social elements of the state are gathering. The smaller panels next to the doors show the advent of slavery, the lead mines in southeast Missouri, and the persecution of Mormons in Jackson County and northern Missouri. Above the door is Benton's salute to Missouri's most celebrated writer, Mark Twain, with a scene from *Huckleberry Finn*. (Courtesy of Missouri State Museum)

The east wall of the House Lounge is the longest segment of the mural. It portrays Missouri's social history from its days as a backwoods state through political development, turmoil of the Civil War (the smoke in the background on the left side), and the creation of the state's earliest farms. The bare bottom of the baby being changed by his mother created a small uproar among Benton's critics who thought it inappropriate to include, particularly in the foreground. To the right of the door is a modern Missouri with mechanized farms, a mature justice system, and sophisticated mining techniques.

Benton's mural flows in narrative as well as in artistic form. Note how the figures are balanced within the mural—the hunter on the far left with the miner on the far right, the political rally scene with the jury scene, and the smoke of war with the smoke of industrial pollution. Above the door is a depiction of the legend of Jesse James, who with his gang robbed banks and trains. Smaller segments on both sides of the door show the Pony Express leaving St. Joseph and the romantic steamboat days along the Mississippi River. (Courtesy of Missouri State Museum)

St. Louis (left) and Kansas City are depicted on the south wall. When the mural was painted St. Louis was still a major shoemaking city; of course, it remains a well-known center of the brewery industry. Other symbols included are the Union Station tower and a poster advertising the Veiled Prophet ball. The Kansas City mural focuses on meat packing and pharmaceutical industries, and it includes the Liberty Memorial tower and Nelson Art Gallery. Much of the controversy centered on the figure seated at lower right, Tom Pendergast, political "boss" of Kansas City. Above the door is Benton's depiction of the legend of Frankie and Johnny. Behind them on the tavern wall is the famous painting, "Custer's Last Stand," which encouraged Benton's early career as a painter. The smaller panels provide contrasting views of the Depression era: a genteel night club and a poverty-ridden railyard. (Courtesy of Missouri State Museum)

Tom Benton relaxing in Senator Barbour's office in the capitol after he conducted Governor Lloyd Stark on a tour of the mural. Stark pronounced the mural "adequate" although it was not to his own personal artistic taste. (Courtesy of *Kansas City Star/Times*)

Benton works on the night club scene in the St. Louis segment of the mural. It was about this time that he asked Glada Longdon and a friend to strike a dancing pose so he could make sure he got the figures right in the painting. Benton and his pipe were seldom far apart. Ironically, he was voted the nation's "pipe smoker of the year" in the same year he gave up smoking. (Courtesy of State Historical Society of Missouri)

Sid Larson (on scaffolding) supervises restoration of the mural in 1960, the first of several times Larson restored Benton's painting. Someday, says Larson, the entire mural will probably have to be dismantled, remounted, and anchored to rebuilt walls in the House Lounge. (Courtesy of *Kansas City Star/Times*)

Chapter 4
The Afteryears

Robert Rhodes, the Jefferson City teenager who "helped" Benton paint the mural, recalled years later Benton making drawings on some stones in the House Lounge. "I watched him draw one of the headlights of that train....It was beautifully done," he said. "He was sitting at his workbench or his worktable and he drew it out."

For a brief time, people could buy lithographs of four scenes from the mural for as little as ten to twenty dollars apiece, part of the effort by Associated American Artists to expand circulation of artistic works to the general public. But Benton the artist, the craftsman, the meticulous planner of his works, goofed in making them. By the time the mural's fiftieth anniversary was celebrated, some of those lithographs had been sold for almost as much as Benton was paid for the whole mural.

Benton decided to make lithographs of the three mythology sections of the mural—Huck Finn, Jesse James (which includes the train Rhodes saw Benton drawing), and Frankie and Johnny—and sell them for $20 each. One hundred prints were made of each work. The fourth lithograph, the farmyard scene, was published in an edition of 250 and sold for $10.

But Benton forgot that in lithography, the image is made on the stone in reverse. Instead of doing that, he made the image on the stone the same as it appears on the capitol walls. The result is that the lithographs are reverse images of the paintings visitors see in the House Lounge. A few proof copies were pulled in 1936 before a blunder compounding the mistake was noticed.

In the Jesse James lithograph, Benton had made the word "Bank" on a building in the background so that it printed backwards on the paper. And the word "boots" on a sign apparently near a shoe store also was backward. He altered the plate so the words appeared properly for the regular edition, but some of the proofs survived. Also surviving are some of the proofs for the Huck Finn print in which the name of the riverboat, *Samuel Clemens*, appears backward. In correcting the mistake for the larger edition, Benton simply removed the name of the boat. But in all of the lithographs, the images are the reverse of what is on the walls in the Missouri capitol.

In 1982, Creekmore Fath, a lawyer in Austin, Texas, who owned several of the lithographs tracked down some of the "backward" copies. He noted that a "Jesse James" lithograph had sold for $13,500 at an auction in New York and that the price in New York for the entire four-print set was about $40,000. Fath also recalled a "Frankie and Johnny" print had sold for $15,000. Simple multiplication of those figures times the number of prints made would produce a value that would rival the cost of construction of the entire Missouri capitol![1]

The mural itself was on the walls of the House Lounge to stay. But its presence as well as Benton's continued outspokenness in articles, his autobiography published soon after the mural was finished, and in interviews about art and the affairs of the world continued to irritate some people for decades.

The autobiography, published in 1937, reignited Howard Huselton's war against Benton in June 1938. Benton's contract with the Kansas City Art Institute was up for renewal then, and Huselton wanted the Institute—of which he was a member—to refuse renewal. "I have read a lot of books in my time. But for sensuality, grossness—why the little gray-haired alert woman at the bookstand told me of people returning the book, mad about the profanity, the vulgarity," Huselton sputtered. The *Star* reported on June

16 Huselton had bought seven copies of *An Artist in America* and had underlined the "good" parts with red pencil. The *Star* reported Huselton's attack did not appear to be a deciding factor although some trustees disagreed with Benton's mural portrayal of his home state. "Generally this does not extend to denying his value to the institute."

The trustees apparently regard Benton as a good, even a great, instructor, and the Institute's director characterizes the controversy-inviting artist as a great master of design and color and a splendid instructor.

Huselton took his underlined editions to the homes of the Institute directors the night before their meeting on Benton's contract. The next day the board discussed Benton and did not vote to renew his contract. It prompted Huselton to exclaim, "Glory Be!"[2]

Briefly, Huselton basked in the victory. Kansas City banker Pierre R. Porter wrote to him on June 23.

Congratulations.

Mark Twain, in "The Gilded Age," referring to some murals in the National Capitol at Washington, called them 'the *delirium tremens* of art." I have often wondered what Mark Twain would say about the Benton Murals in our State Capitol.

The same day, Robert Steele Withers of Liberty wrote Huselton that he was firmly with him. "How in the world a man so totally lacking in all that he claimed to have could have been foisted on this state as he was is beyond me," he said.

To continue him in any capacity wherein the aspirations of the youth of his generation could have been warped and degraded was preposterous....I do not think anybody in this State should be expected to stand for any man that fails so utterly to emulate the finest things we have but on the contrary revels in the opportunity to degrade them.

Huselton's victorious exclamation was premature. A

131

week after taking no action to renew the contract, the board of governors met again.

Huselton went before the board with a seven-page typewritten statement asserting that the board in its previous meeting had effectively fired Benton because it had offered a motion to reemploy him. But, he argued, by reopening the matter, the board was going to have to decide "whether a radical instructor, whose name is under a cloud because of a profane book, is worth more to the future of the Kansas City Art Institute...than a question of morals and morality;"

...whether ideals and other of the finer things in life, without cost, yet priceless, are to be scrapped in reach for dollars and a balanced budget; whether the young students of a school of art are entitled to protection as to their class surroundings, associates and teachings. The future of the institute is at stake.

Huselton argued that rehiring Benton would give him the vindication he sought, would let him boast that "he made those Missouri hicks back up,"

...that the aforementioned hicks in Kansas City, whose packing houses and slaughtering crews be so garishly glorified, both in size and color, in his murals on the walls of Missouri's Capitol...by their re-employment of him officially okayed the offensive and derogatory murals in the lounge of the House of Representatives.

Huselton suggested Benton, having won—if he was reemployed—might decide to move to a more lucrative job elsewhere. "I doubt Mr. Benton, having in mind the scorching he received over his Missouri murals and the blasting he has withstood in connection with his book and his job, will wish to remain here permanently."

He is nomadic by nature. He likes the side roads and the back country, where live the common people. He is restless in a large city....The avalanche of wide-spread and caustic criticism aroused by Mr. Benton's murals "got under his skin." While he never has admitted he felt hurt, he was greatly surprised and regretful.

And Huselton told trustees, "The Kansas City Art Institute...cannot afford to compromise with obscenity and immorality. The fathers and mothers of Kansas City will not stand for it."[3]

Despite Huselton's plea, the board of governors decided to retain Benton. A statement from the board put the Institute solidly behind Benton, the teacher.

No matter what anybody may think of Mr. Benton's book or of his painting, there has been no question regarding his ability as an instructor; and as head of his department he has given a great stimulus to his students and has achieved a high standard of instruction.

"I'm not surprised," Benton commented in the June 27 *Kansas City Star*. "I knew the board had too much sense to fire me....The whole thing was just a joke to me."

It was not a joke to Huselton, of course, or to his followers. Kansas City lawyer Ellison Neel sympathized with Huselton in a letter June [4].

What a man thinks and is comes out in his books and what a man thinks and is, will, naturally, be communicated to his pupils. It seems to me that an instructor and teacher ought to be a person of high character and good morals and, thereby, by example and precept, elevate his pupils. But that, evidently, is not the view of the majority of this Board of Directors.

Neel included a copy of a letter he had sent to the chairman of the board at the Institute, Fred Vincent. In it he referred to the book as containing "blasphemous, lewd, lascivious, immoral, degrading, sex perverted contents." He said the only effect the book could have on readers would be "to make them either sorry that they ever did so, or lower their own standards of decency and morals."

In some letters to his supporters, Huselton accused Benton's followers of asking for a hearing after the first meeting as a smokescreen "to enable the students and other friends of Mr. Benton to circulate petitions urging his reappointment, which petitions they placed in book stores, drug stores and clubs. Without knowing the significance of what they were doing, several hundred persons signed those petitions.''

Huselton asserted that less than 5 percent of those who signed the petitions had read Benton's ''erotic books.'' The result, he claimed, was that the public sentiment generated by the petitions caused two or three members of the board to switch their votes. Huselton referred to Benton's hiring as ''a calamity to the Art Institute and the art movement in Kansas City.''

One of those who wrote back to Huselton was real estate developer J.C. Nichols, a member of the Institute's advisory board. Nichols, one of the figures in the Kansas City segment of the mural, told Huselton he had made a careful inquiry about Benton's conduct in the classroom and his relations with his students and had found ''only the highest commendation.''

It happens that I knew certain students who had taken work under him, and every one of them were most enthusiastic about being able to study under him, and assured me that there has never been the slightest questionable act or word upon Mr. Benton's part in their relations with him.

Nichols noted he didn't have a vote on the board but told members he would favor renewing the contract, ''considering all elements entering into the situation.''

Things were quiet at the capitol by then. An Associated Press report from Jefferson City on July 13, 1940, quoted capitol guide E.A. Irvine, who said, ''The murals are the first thing most visitors ask to see. The tongue in cheek attitude of the visitors two years ago is gone. Instead of criticism, they praise the work.''

For the last several months, practically the only persons who have expressed a dislike for the ''muriels,'' or ''murrals,'' as they have been

134

called, are those who have a background of classic art, and just can't get used to Benton's realistic style. It's too strange for them to absorb.

Benton's contract with the Kansas City Art Institute was due for review again in 1941. That was when he chose to pop off about museums and their directors in an interview published in the *New York World-Telegram* and later reprinted in *Art Digest* April 15, 1941. "Do you want to know what's the matter with the art business in America?" he asked. "It's the third sex and museums. Even in Missouri we're full of 'em. We've had an immigration out there."

And the old ladies who've gotten so old that no man will look at 'em think that these pretty boys will do. Our museums are full of ballet dancers, retired businessmen, and boys from the Fogg Institute at Harvard where they train museum directors and art artists.

Benton told the interviewer the typical museum is "run by a pretty boy with delicate wrists and a swing in his gate. If it were left to me, I wouldn't have any museums."

That did it. Institute director Keith Martin called Benton and asked that he resign. Benton, sitting in a rope swing with his infant daughter at his home, told a reporter for the *Star* April 28, "I refused because I have responsibilities to those kids over there in my classes." The Institute's treatment of Benton had already drawn one protest. Graphic arts instructor John DeMartelly had let it be known he would not return even for some special courses because of alleged unfair treatment of Benton. "I have found out the people who are running the place are not only stupid about what is good for them, but underhanded as well," he said.

In Jefferson City the pot was beginning to boil anew, too. On April 30, a new resolution was introduced in the House referring to Benton as "the dynamic and volcanic artist who conceived and painted the murals in the House Lounge." The resolution said he "engendered a great storm" with his murals which had raged with "increasing fury...the tornadic

135

fury thereof has been greatly accelerated by his book, *An Artist in America*, and his more recent spectacular and risque utterances reflecting upon the custodians of those repositories of classic, ethical, ancient and conservative art.''

The resolution attacked two parts of the mural

wherein a naughty boy is depicted as defying his larger and stronger aggressor, and a mother as performing certain duties incident to the proper care of her young which should in all such cases, be performed in more private surroundings.

The resolution called Benton "the stormiest figure in the world of art'' and demanded he remove the mural or show why it should not be removed by someone else from the walls

which they now so flamingly, riotously and indecently adorn, or be so revised as that no figure, character or scene in said murals shall hereafter shock the nerves of aesthetic patrons of classic art—the devotees of the placid and unexciting works of more conservative painters of this and other ages.

The author of the resolution was one of the people portrayed in it—Representative David Hess of St. Louis. Hess said it was "done in fun....It was strictly a joke...not done with any malice aforethought.'' And he claimed he was put up to it by Representative Roy Hamlin of Hannibal who could not get anybody else to sponsor it. "It don't mean anything,'' Hess remembers Hamlin telling him.

I said, "Say, you're gonna put me in the middle of it. The guy's a friend of mine. Benton's a helluva...nice guy.'' And he said, "No this won't.'' I said, "I'll bet I get a call,'' and I did get a call and I told him to call Hamlin and they got it all straight. It was all a joke.

Hess recalled that Hamlin, a native of Hannibal, wanted Mark Twain painted into the Huck Finn segment of the mural. Obviously, Hamlin got nowhere.[4]

136

A few days later, the governors of the Kansas City Art Institute voted not to renew Benton's contract. He was replaced by Fletcher Martin, who had been a visiting artist at the University of Iowa.

Benton was not humbled. He admitted in the June edition of *Common Sense* that his remarks, made after a couple of highballs, had been indiscrete but had been picked up by newspapers "which are understandably tired of formal banalities." Benton asserted he had been fired "for talking" by the "stuffed shirts who raise the cash and govern the destinies" of the Institute.

Sometimes, to be sure, I talk loudly and decorate the substance of my conversation with linguistic flourishes not generally associated with serious intentions. But I was serious in New York when I let go about this museum business. The country is getting overpopulated with museums....And at the same time, by the law of cause and effect, the country is filling up with museum minds. I see this happening; I look at the young American artist growing up; and I am uneasy. I am afraid that he will again get the idea, like so many of our retired businessmen, that culture is something which must have an exotic label and must come from far away or out of the past to be genuine or worthy of attention.

Benton said young American artists for the previous few years had been "referring to actualities of American experience for their ideas out of which they made their aesthetic goods." He said it was the result of twenty years of efforts by pioneer artists who realized that American culture cannot be "bought or borrowed." He argued the trend had popularized art so much that capable artists could afford to make a living in the field.

American art has been taken from the garret into the world....The public has found something to which it can respond. Even the federal government gives out aesthetic jobs. There is hope that art may again become a living thing, of interest to plain people, rather than a collection of objects strung up on the cold walls of institutions run for aesthetic dilettantes, amateur philosophers, and generally in memory of dead vanities.

Many years later, Benton suggested his refusal to give grades to students conflicted with wishes of the trustees who wanted an accredited school which could give degrees.

I wouldn't do it. I wanted to run it as a regular old-fashioned art school and not as a goddamned adjunct to a college. I also would not engage in the school's social activities. And politically, all the trustees were very strong conservative Republicans, more conservative than you can imagine, and everything that seemed to come up, well, we disagreed on. I was glad to get out.[5]

In 1943, Representative Ralph Erdwin of Johnson County demanded the likeness of Pendergast be removed immediately. The House journal gives no indication that Erdwin introduced any resolution. Benton dismissed Erdwin's demand as "just political stuff," and told the Associated Press on January 29, "From the technical side alone, the resolution is a mighty poor one. It would be one hell of a job to erase Pendergast. I put him up there. Let someone else take him down."

That same year, Benton used his Missouri mural to support his sometimes pointed criticism of art museums. In an interview in the February edition of *Demcourier*, a publication of Demco Library Supplies, he answered the question, "How is art to be made available to the public without museums?"

I'll guarantee that ten times more Missourians have seen the murals I painted in 1936 in the Missouri State Capitol than have been in Kansas City's museum hothouse in all its history. Further, they have been more interested. Living people are interested in living art. It is because of this fact, coupled with the fact's recognition by the daily press and the national weeklies, that I am now strong enough economically to tell the truth about the decadent situation which the museums and their backers have nursed into American culture.

Whether Benton's claim that more Missourians had seen his capitol mural than had been in the art museum in Kansas City was only rhetoric is impossible to sustain. However, capitol watchman Frank Canada, who greeted visitors at the front door, told the Associated Press in July 1937 about 28,000 people had signed the guest book in the previous year, about one-tenth of the visitors to the building in his estimation. He said adult visitors usually wanted to see the Benton mural.

An interesting question that was apparently never directly raised in those rhetorically volatile times was whether the public even had the right to criticize the symbols of a mural or have it removed from a wall. The question was finally put to Benton at a meeting at Lincoln University in 1954 of the National Conference of Teachers of Art in Negro Colleges. "It boils down to whether the public has the right to destroy the work of an artist," Benton said. He went on to say that history showed institutions had the right to destroy a picture it did not like.

Current educated sentiment seems to be with the artist—that is, if the artist puts his soul into a thing, it is believed the average buyer hasn't the right to destroy it....Certainly, if the majority of the people in a community object to a mural, I really don't see what the artist can legally do to keep them from boarding it up, or tearing it down, or doing whatever they want with it.

Even as late as 1949, when Richard Chamier of Moberly was elected to the Missouri Senate, there were still some old-timers grumbling.

I left the Senate in May of 1941 to go on active duty and came back in January of '49 and I could still hear comments of people who resented what he had done. I think the work that he did for Truman's memorial did a great deal to settle the complaints that people had about him.[6]

Young Richard Webster also arrived in the legislature, as a member of the House, in 1949. He remembered thirty-five

139

years later that some of the old-timers remained from the days when Benton painted what they still referred to as the "manurials."

Usually at appropriations time when we were spending money for something of that nature for landscaping somewhere, inevitably someone would get up and say, "This is just another Benton Manurial waste of the taxpayer's money," and use that as an example of where we had spent money foolishly. And, of course, we know that was probably one of the best buys the state ever made.

Webster remembers that Representatives Tony Pickerell of Kansas City and Bill Siefert of St. Louis particularly objected to the mural. Pickerell didn't like the Kansas City segment of the mural, and Siefert opposed the Frankie and Johnny depiction.

Strangely enough, if Frankie and Johnny would have been offensive to somebody it should have been to the minority members, the black members, of the House. But they never suggested any objection to it. It always came from the white members from St. Louis....They didn't object to showing the brewery and the shoe industry but they did to showing the raucous scene where Frankie comes into the bar and shoots Johnny.[7]

Rural members didn't seem to care much about that, said Webster. But they did think the Jesse James sequence was "overplayed."

Even when the University of Missouri awarded Benton an honorary degree in 1949, old editorial animosities flared up. The *Monroe County Appeal* referred to the mural as "grotesque." The paper said Benton's works "ushered in an era of revolt that has swept the established order out of its dominating position in music, painting, sculpture, theatricals, education, literature and rules of human conduct."

A hurried humanity wants most everything sacrificed to noise and speed. It wants the action of grotesque Benton type pictures rather than the marvelous but static sort that were immortalized by Raphael, Michelangelo and those who followed in their footsteps through many centuries. It

140

prefers loud and discordant jazz music to the soft harmonies that have been handed down by masters like Johann Strauss. It will have nothing to do with books like Victor Hugo, Charles Dickens and Washington Irving wrote.

The newspaper complained that "blood and betrayals, and sex" attracted readers to modern novels, that great actors and their great stage shows had been replaced by "gangsters and cowboy types on one hand, and parlor, bedroom and bath types on the other."

It really is another day in practically every realm of human interest. Worse still, it may have come to stay. But, as Mr. Dooley used to say, what is music to one is noise to another—so why worry if Groucho and Harpo Marx are next in order for honorary degrees?[8]

By 1949, Harold Brown was in his teens and the controversy over his bare bottom, as the baby in the political scene, had long since passed.

The bare bottom in the thirties was pretty risque. And we'd heard of that earlier when I was just a teenager that this was quite a thing. But we just shoved it off as, well, it's there, so what can we do about it. We were proud of it all along, of course, because Benton even in those days, the forties and fifties, was quite well known as an artist, and I was always proud to be in there and proud my father was in there.

Schoolmates didn't poke fun at Brown for being in the mural. In fact, his presence wasn't important. If he'd say, "I'm in the murals in the House Lounge," others would ask, "Where in the heck is the House Lounge?"[9]

In April 1950, Benton visited the capitol to investigate reports that the mural had been extensively damaged. He found two holes dug in one panel but said the damage was slight and could be repaired. "You know there's always somebody who wants to find out if the paint will come off," he said, promising to return in May to make repairs. He also told Fred Appleton, with the public buildings office at the capitol that there was no need to clean the painting at that time because it would involve removal of the wax-varnish and surfacing. "Don't use any water," he advised others. "Just rub hard with a rag horizontally—that's the way the protective wax was polished by WPA workers the first time. It'll all come out with a high gloss and look as good and bright as new."

Speaker of the House John G. Christy later became a three-term mayor of Jefferson City. On one of his visits, he saw Benton eating lunch at the Governor Hotel.

He was sitting at a table right by the window by himself and I thought, "Well, maybe I'd better say something." Now, that was a good many years after. I went over to him and I said, "Mr. Benton, I'm sure you don't recall me..." and he took both hands and he threw them up in the air and..." I remember you. I remember you!"

In some ways, Christy never changed. "I just can't conceive of anybody goin' in there even today and sittin' down and just kind of relaxin', because your eyes have got to be moving around. You've got to be trying to see those things," he said. But he did grow to appreciate a work he once wanted to destroy.

Christy's inability to come to grips with the vividness of the mural for the rest of his days became a compliment, not a criticism, to Benton, who once said it was the best kind of review one of his murals could get.

I get great satisfaction of seeing some son-of-a-bitch come in the room there and say, "Jesus Christ, they're gonna walk off the wall." Well I like that kind of criticism better than I do highly specialized criticisms that tries to say *why* they appear to walk off the wall, because most people who try to do that, they can't put it into words anyhow. They just make nonsense out of it.[10]

By 1959, it was apparent the mural had become time-worn and dirty. Representative Harry Goldberg of Kansas City introduced a resolution asking Benton to clean

142

the mural. Benton agreed to supervise the work at no cost, adding that he hoped it would be done soon, while he was still spry enough to climb around on the scaffold.[11]

On February 11, 1959, Thomas Hart Benton was introduced as a distinguished guest of the House of Representatives. He received a standing ovation. Representative Robert Ellis Young of Carthage became his escort for the day.

I remember his walking in the door of the House Lounge and...he darted his finger toward one corner. What he said was, "There's old Tom." Then he said, "That's Mr. Pendergast."

The mural had become dilapidated during the years, but Young couldn't recall Benton being surprised that it needed cleaning and restoring.

The most interesting thing that he said...was to recall all the criticism that the murals received when first exhibited....He recalled, as he put it, "all the hell," if you'll pardon me, that the murals received there at first and what Mr. Benton said was that he couldn't understand why people raised all of that about the murals. He said, "All I did was unvarnish the truth a little."[12]

In the spring of 1960, Sid Larson, an art professor at what was then Christian College in Columbia, was given a $5,660 contract to clean and restore the mural. Larson had worked with Benton previously in restoring his famous painting "Persephone." This was the first of three times Larson worked on the mural during the next twenty-five years. He first had to remove the original varnish, which had become yellowed and was breaking down.

The gums in it became, somehow, sticky, and it was attracting dirt from the air. Keep in mind the room had never been air conditioned up to then; that the windows were frequently open to the...smoke from the trains down below. The paintings at the time had been soiled by droppings from the pigeons that flew in the open windows and roosted in the filligree up

143

there where the bears are. It had quite a bit of grime and a good deal of wear and tear.

The painting had been worn away at the top of the marble wainscoting where the custodians had wiped the stone. Larson remembered there was almost no paint within a foot of the light switch because people had worn it away groping for the switch.

But there was more to it than that. A vandal, or vandals, had attacked the mural. Someone had taken a ballpoint pen and stamped a horseshoe tattoo on the naked baby's rear. There were a couple of other places Larson remembers that had suffered. Someone had dug out a chunk of canvas on the rear end of a small horse in the buggy scene on the predella panel next to the doorway.

I don't know whether it's the guy with the same fixation as attacked the baby....I don't know. The other thing was that someone with a pencil had put numbers across the back of the large figure of Pendergast, that presumably was some kind of joke, an inference about his penitentiary numbers.[13]

That vandal's unfunny joke got Benton into hot water with a man who later hired him to paint another mural— Harry Truman.

Somebody told Harry Truman that I had done that. And that caused considerable coldness between Truman and me for years, until he actually got to know me and realized that I wouldn't have done such a thing.[14]

In 1965, Benton returned to Jefferson City as the principal speaker at a banquet celebrating the creation of the Missouri State Council on the Arts. Thomas Graham of Jefferson City, who was the second man to be Speaker of the House three straight terms, remembers the mistress of ceremonies introduced all of the other dignitaries first.

And after she introduced all of the wheels she came to Mr. Benton and introduced him and he got up and said, "Madam Chairman, I've never been among so many important sons-of-bitches in my whole life," and sat down. And that was the end of his speech, which I thought was something else.

The next day Benton went to Graham's office and said he wanted a drink. Graham said, "I've got bourbon and I've got scotch." Benton said, "No, I want brandy." So Graham had to send somebody out to get a bottle of brandy.

I still have the bottle. There's about three-quarters of it gone and he's the only one who ever had a drink out of it...I think everyone who was at the dinner that night came by the office to visit with him, because there wasn't much visiting with him after the banquet.

That same year, a young insurance salesman from the little northwest Missouri town of Rock Port took his seat in the House of Representatives. During Hardin Cox's first term, he searched for a pamphlet or book about the Benton mural and other capitol art at the request of his cousin, Frank Blakemore. He found nothing available about the Benton painting, so he introduced a bill to have a booklet published. When he learned another representative, Norbert Jasper of Washington, Missouri, was working on the same thing, they pooled their efforts. They got the bill through the House, but Cox remembers they had a hard time convincing a Senate committee to recommend the full Senate pass it.

We sweat out the Senate calendar and as our bill was being brought up on the floor of the Senate at 11:55—just 5 minutes before adjournment—a mistake was discovered in the omnibus bill and work was stopped on our bill.

The problems with the omnibus appropriations bill were worked out but there was no time to take up the Jasper-Cox bill.

Two years later—the legislature met every other year then—they tried again, and got the bill through the House.

But once more they ran into trouble with the Senate and on the last night of the session, the two men had one eye on the clock and the other on the Senate.

On the final night of the session we checked the progress of bills every half hour or less and slowly we worked up to our bill which was considered and passed at 11:30 only 30 minutes from the adjournment deadline.[15]

Cox recalls that Speaker Tom Graham suggested a ceremony be held when the pamphlet was printed. On October 13, 1968, a ceremony was held in the rotunda. About 500 people were there. Benton and his friend Sam Blair "had been having some libations and fun and were having a real good time," says Cox. "They wouldn't let Tom speak there, just gave him one of the first booklets printed."

They did invite all the guests to the House Lounge to see the mural and hear, for the first time, the recorded interview Benton had done in his Kansas City studio with Jim Lantz.

There they did ask Tom to speak and he gave a few words of wisdom and pointed out a few things. The thing that has always stuck in my mind, as he pointed to this mule and he said, "Yes, and I was the only damned painter to ever put a cow's tail on a mule." And everybody laughed. And when you looked at it, it was actually there.[16]

In 1968 Benton and Larson teamed up again to correct a major problem that had arisen because the room was not properly air conditioned. The director of the State Division of Planning, John Paulus, had noticed a number of cracks in the painting and persuaded the legislature to appropriate money for the repairs. The changes in temperature and humidity caused the plywood panels on which the mural had been mounted to shift. And there was a major problem that Larson thinks will someday require the Lounge walls and the mural to be dismantled. The problem stems from the

146

plywood available to Benton in 1936. Larson says it was not of the best quality or thickness. An additional problem is the way those panels were mounted to the walls. Larson says they should have been screwed to a framework of two-by-fours which then should have been toggle-bolted to the hollow double-brick capitol walls. But not enough toggle bolts were used.

They evidently used a molly-type of arrangement many times. And furthermore, in order to make a hole in them, the bricks became broken. They shattered and there was no place for them to go except down, and these broken bricks began to accumulate behind the mural and ultimately forced the bottom—since they weren't fastened good—forward into the room as much as an inch or an inch-and-a-half in some places.

Benton consulted several experts before deciding the best thing to do at the time was "snug it up" to the wall. It became exacting work which involved slicing out sections of the canvas to gain access to the wood beneath. Larson, assisted by a couple of master carpenters, tapped the wall until they found 303 places where new anchoring bolts could be installed.

At that time, with a surgeon's scalpel, I excised a poker-chip sized piece of painting out. These things were numbered and filed and then the carpenters drilled into the plywood and inserted new and additional toggle bolts, and then all that summer, turning the screw in those things a quarter or a third, at the most, turn a day, we gradually tried to draw these things back into place. To do it very fast all at once would have caused still more problems. And then when all that was done, the repairs were made, pieces put back in, the cosmetic in-painting was finished.

Today it takes a sharp eye and just the right light to find all of those places where the canvas was sliced away and replaced.

They could not draw the mural completely back to the wall because that would have set up an entirely new set of tensions. And because people continued to fiddle with the

147

environmental controls, new problems developed as the panels shifted because of changes in temperature and humidity. Larson put in a more flexible filler between the panels which would require less maintenance than a more rigid one that might chip off Benton's paint. Eventually, more sophisticated controls were installed—above a high door where meddlers couldn't tinker.

But Larson says someday the walls with their shattered bricks might have to be replaced. It's a drastic procedure he hopes will be delayed until it is absolutely necessary because of the potential danger to the painting. The supporting walls would have to be dismantled to give access to the back of the plywood panels and the removal of each canvas-covered section glued to them.

The paint surface would first be protected by temporarily covering it with built-up layers of mulberry paper, cardboard and muslin. The canvas could then be remounted on a fabricated interlocking system of rigid, honeycombed panels. The canvas would be adhered to the panel sections with a reversible adhesive. The mural then could be assembled and hung from fittings in the refurbished wall structure.[17]

In the summer of 1987, Larson was working on the mural again, retouching places where the paint had chipped or been chipped by visitors, and filling in cracks that had developed in the paint and between the panels.

Tom Benton remained crusty to the end. When he turned eighty years old, William McWhirter wrote in *Life* magazine's October 3, 1969, issue, "An artist in America may live, as Thomas Hart Benton has lived, to be 80 years old and regret nothing. That is his reward. But he will just as surely have lived that long only to be forgiven everything, and that, at last, may prove to be his undoing."

Tom Benton, who loved whiskey, chewed tobacco and hated the law, traveled, baited and painted this nation for the better part of the century. He went to war with critics, intellectuals, businessmen, politicians,

148

radicals, friends, colleagues and fellow artists, leaving home, leaving Paris, leaving the Communist revolution, leaving New York and finally returning home to the Midwest where, at least, he could be left alone. He scandalized his home state of Missouri by emblazoning a life-sized mural inside the state capitol building that placed a corrupt Kansas City political boss alongside the town's leading citizens.

But, McWhirter said, all of this had only left Tom Benton "a sanitized legend about as unsavory as your local Salvation Army Kriss Kringle or, even worse, a *senior citizen* of the arts." He wrote Benton had been "certified safe for art history, museums and children's tours."

Is nothing profane anymore?

Yes. Tom Benton is or is trying his best to be. It is not easy. The fact that he may be remembered fondly as some quaint grandpappy of American culture is our fault, not his. We prefer our artists, like our prisoners, restored and rehabilitated into the society from which they departed....But while we have gone about making our peace with Benton, no one has noticed that he has made none or very little of it with us. Thomas Hart Benton is still waging his constant war.

In 1971, Speaker of the House James Godfrey struck a blow for the mural in the Lounge when he ordered the removal of thirty small desks used by the House Appropriations Committee for budget hearings. The desks had been arranged in a squared horseshoe pattern for about three years and ran two-thirds the length of the room. Complaints were increasing from visitors that the desks blocked proper viewing of the paintings. Appropriations chairman E. J. Cantrell of Overland objected, but Godfrey overrode him.[18]

As he approached his eighty-fourth birthday, Benton still went to his studio every morning.

There, amid a clutter of lumber, canvas and beaten up furniture, he takes up his brush or a book or a pen and works for several hours.

Then he returns to the house, makes two 11 a.m. martinis (three parts gin, one part vermouth), downs them and falls to sleep. In mid-afternoon he rises and spends the rest of the day as his fancy strikes him.[19]

The fighting spirit never left Benton. In 1973, CBS correspondent Mike Wallace interviewed him at his summer home on Martha's Vineyard for the program "60 Minutes." Benton told Wallace he felt fine, that he didn't hate getting old or "give a damn" about dying. Wallace called Benton a "Missouri maverick" and said each of Benton's works had a message.

'This is, or was, part of America." But Thomas Hart Benton is known best for his murals. Benton's critics complain that his art has remained mired in Americana; popular yes, but old hat, unaware that a whole new world of color and symbolism, abstract impressionism has moved to center stage and left Tom Benton a million light years behind. But Tom Benton, unafraid of death, can hardly be expected to walk in fear of lesser adversaries, like art critics.

When Wallace reminded him that *New York Times* critic John Canaday referred to him as "a patriarchal cornball," Benton laughingly said he didn't care what Canaday, "a simple-minded art critic," said. "It's all right if he likes to see it that way," said Benton. "Canaday's only one example of a whole pack of 'em. He just writes better than most of 'em."

And was Benton a cornball? "Probably," he told Wallace. "What of it? I'm an intelligent one. What of it?"

In January 1975, Thomas Hart Benton, unafraid of death or critics, died in his studio in Kansas City after completing his last mural, depicting a history of country music. It hangs today in the Country Music Hall of Fame in Nashville, Tennessee, populated with the same things familiar to those who know his Missouri mural—a train, a riverboat, and vividly portrayed people elongated in form, alive with the virility that is the hallmark of the work of Thomas Hart Benton.

Canaday, the "simple-minded" *New York Times* critic, recalled on January 21 that Benton's regionalism of the thirties had "appealed only so long as we needed the special kind of prop it offered. The twin events of returning prosperity and a war that ended any lingering ideas that America could remain forever its old-time youthful self, or that we could ever exist again in isolation from Europe, made Benton's Americanism look provincial...."

At the moment of his death, the things he meant to stand for in art are being re-examined, although with cautiously tempered enthusiasm. If one day Thomas Benton is re-established in a high position in American art, rather than remaining in his present one as a parenthetical incident in its history, he has already had his reward in the way so many artists have to have theirs during life—in a conviction that he was right, and that his rightness must inevitably triumph.

If the dollar value of an artist's work indicates his position in American art, then Tom Benton has been re-established there. But not without controversy. And what, after all, would a discussion of Benton's art be without controversy?

In 1986, fifty years after completion of the mural in the capitol and eleven years after Benton's death, the Nelson-Atkins Gallery in Kansas City announced it was buying Benton's famous nude, "Persephone," for $2.5 million to keep it from being sold to a foreign collector. The *Kansas City Times* ran a front page story about the purchase of what some call Benton's masterpiece and accompanied the article with a color picture of it. The spirit of the 1930s anti-Benton outrage was quickly resurrected.

Baptist minister Loren R. Green, Sr., from the suburb of Mission, Kansas, wrote a letter published by the *Times* December 25, saying he was "quite shocked when I saw the front page....At first I thought I was seeing a picture out of *Playboy* or *Penthouse*."

A picture of a nude woman from the Nelson Art Gallery was almost unbelievable. It would probably have been better to relegate it to the page where X-rated movies are advertised. Oh no! You couldn't do that because I read that you had a policy where those advertisements had to be toned down in order not to be indecent or offensive to people.

Green suggested many decent people were offended by the picture. "What could make a painting like this worth $2.5 million is beyond me," he said. And he suggested the gallery spend its money "on paintings more worthwhile than this."

Thomas Vanderford of Kansas City, in a letter published five days later, said he was amazed "what comes from the pens and mouths of some of our 'religious' leaders."

Comparing it to *Playboy* or *Penthouse* is ridiculous. Had this woman been fat and pudgy like the nudes in many of the old masters, would it have shocked or excited you nearly as much?

And Russ Millin responded with a limerick published the same day:

There once was a preacher named Green
Who found Persephone obscene,
He knew what was lewd,
This psalm-singing prude,
If it doesn't wear clothes it ain't clean.

Harold Roecker wrote to the *Times* on January 4 that he was appalled at the price paid for the painting, calling it "a display of pornography." He suggested the money would be better spent on improved police protection in Kansas City.[20]

By then, *Times* columnist George Gurley had offered a series of tongue-in-cheek compromises, asking readers to consider questions raised by the controversy "dispassionately." He asked, "Will the public display of 'Persephone' contribute to the already epidemic problems of infidelity, perversion, teen-age pregnancy and sexual harassment? Will it taint KC's reputation as a wholesome place to raise children? Can the purity and innocence of Midwesterners survive exposure in 'Persephone'?"

Could anyone object if a fig leaf or some cockle shells were discreetly painted on 'Persephone" by qualified gallery technicians as a minor concession to modesty?

I don't want to take sides or offend anyone, but would "Persephone" suffer as a work of art if she had at least a bikini or some underwear on? Artists, I have to say, seem to be obsessed with nudes. They would be better off painting more trees, sailboats, barns.

Perhaps, Gurley suggested, the painting could be placed in "the kind of booth adult movies are viewed in" so decent people would not be endangered. In that January 3 column, he called on Kansas Citians to "consider these problems in a mature, sensitive way before this curvaceous female spoils our peace."

The controversy attracted the attention of people hundreds of miles away. The Naturist Society of Oshkosh, Wisconsin, asked the Nelson Gallery for copies of press releases on the issue and a picture of 'Persephone" that could be reprinted in the group's magazine, *Clothed With Sun*. It took a while for gallery officials to discover the Naturist Society was a group advocating "clothes-optional life styles." The gallery sent the information requested.[21]

Benton's mural 130 miles away in the Missouri capitol remains alive with Bentonesque virility, increasingly appreciated for the artistic and historic treasure it is. The fires of its controversy were long ago banked.

In 1980 a young state representative from St. Louis, Patrick Dougherty, decided the mural needed more protection. Dougherty had watched appropriations committee meetings that dragged on in the House Lounge until early morning hours. Perhaps seeing the "billows of smoke" generated by committee members triggered his action.

I'd mentioned it to a couple of people who more or less laughed it off and somebody suggested that I call a couple of people who were experts in murals, which I did. And the person who, I guess, enabled me to get it out was Ron Bockenkamp...for whatever reason, and [I] was able to get some support out of that committee.

153

As with everything else connected with the mural's history, this also was not accomplished easily, although Dougherty recalls his effort generated more mild laughter than resistance. Maybe it was because he was a legislative rookie. He doesn't know. But, he recalled, "nobody was really going out of their way to provide a roadblock." Debate by the entire House came late in the session.

One of the representatives got up—smoking, of course—and talked about the "Thomas Bent Harton Murials" and how we should be able to smoke, and what's wrong with that. He turned around to this picture at the back of the chamber, and said, "Well, if we're gonna do that we might as well stop smoking here."...But it was more amusement than anything else. We...had an overwhelming majority...and for a while I was very proud of that.[22]

That representative who spoke against the "Thomas Bent Harton Murials" was a former appropriations committee chairman, E.J. "Lucky" Cantrell of Overland, a St. Louis suburb. He had presided over many meetings in the Lounge until Speaker Jim Godfrey had taken his step a few years earlier.[23]

The resolution passed 124-17. Six members voted "present." Sixteen were absent.

Appropriations committee meetings are no longer held in the House Lounge. No committee meetings are. The room, now under modern climate controls that are placed high above one of the doorways to keep people from meddling with them, is seldom used for meetings. But its popularity grows as a place for visitors to come and stand in awe.

On Benton's ninety-sixth birthday, a bronze bust of the artist was unveiled in the third floor rotunda. It was the fourth bust of a famous Missourian placed there. All had been done by sculptor William J. Williams of Columbia College in Columbia.

A former student of Benton's at the Kansas City Art Institute, William McKim, looked at the bust and said, "I myself feel that probably more than any other artist in America, Tom Benton brought a consciousness to the American public to art as we know it today." McKim recalled the media seldom ran stories about art and artists when he was young.

It wasn't until Tom Benton came that we began to see an awareness on the part of the press....Over and over again, *Life* and *Time* and other publications throughout the country gave attention to the art of the times. I became aware of it because when I was a kid I liked to draw but I wasn't interested in becoming a painter because it was a world beyond me. I couldn't associate with it.

McKim met Benton when he started school and liked him "because he was like myself." Their small-town roots gave them many things in common to talk about. Because of Benton's influence, McKim took up the serious pursuit of painting and print-making. And for many years, William McKim was a professor at the Kansas City Art Institute.

What it was was his feeling for his subjects and at the same time a great deal of study along very hard and fast lines that can become very sterile if one pursues them only, namely the classic art of Europe. But he pursued that, a diligent scholar and student of those matters, at the same time without losing sight of his very personal interest in the little things, the common every day happenings, once in a while sensational things, that common people get into, and made a great art of those. And I think that that is what he is going to be remembered for as time goes on.[24]

And Benton's longtime associate, Sid Larson, noted the value of the Missouri mural probably "would be appraised today at a cost greater than the cost of this building and the ground on which it sits and all the artwork in it except for his." Larson felt those statistics tells us "something about the hard realism of Missouri," and about Benton's life and work. He said all of Benton's fame stemmed from the belief that art should be "of people and for people, recognizable, one that would touch their mind and heart."

155

When *Life* magazine served the same purpose television does today—to give us visual imagery of this country—Tom Benton was constantly, page after page, represented.

This miniature man—he was barely five feet tall—started out as a cartoonist. He was a draftsman, an easel painter, a portraitist, certainly a mural painter; he did lithographs; he did sculptures; he did drawings; he was a fantastic teacher and...had he devoted his energy to being a writer, I think he would have excelled equally as a writer.

Larson called Benton "an absolute intellectual, a man who was sophisticated and loved to pretend like he was a country boy from Neosho, and believe me he was and he was proud of it." Yes, said Larson, Benton was small, but he was also tough, strong and courageous, hard-working and hard playing, outrageous and a liberal.

His most celebrated student was Jackson Pollock and nobody could be more different. He and Harry Truman used to have dog fights in terms of who was the most expert in terms of Missouri history. If ever there was a quintessential American, and the man for whom a master pattern for what a Missourian is, that guy has to be Tom Benton.[25]

Benton's mural has withstood summer heat and winter cold, political rhetoric, neglect, vandalism and the smoke of millions of cigarettes. Sid Larson says the mural is in "remarkably good condition...still as fresh as can be."[26]

For Benton's ninety-eighth birthday, a symposium was held in Kansas City, but it was hardly a love fest. Some critics called Benton "a failure." Two said his art would not survive judgment on aesthetic terms.

One of those critics, Hilton Kramer, was taken aback by "the extremely hostile spirit which greeted the criticism of Benton's work." Kramer wrote in *Art and Antiques Magazine* in the summer of 1987 that some people who were there "to bask in the reflected glory of Benton's celebrity" were shocked by the idea that Benton "is not universally regarded as one of the towering geniuses of twentieth-century art."

156

Insults were hurled, and epithets exchanged—and these, in turn, prompted a few embarrassed local citizens to denounce the denouncers. The day ended in an atmosphere of combat and acrimony.

Kramer, who said he had always been treated courteously in previous visits to Kansas City, realized this visit was different because this was the first time he had been invited to speak about "a local deity."

He argued Benton was a failure.

I advised the audience that all their efforts on behalf of Benton's reputation would in the end prove unavailing. When the piety and the clamor subsided in the wake of the 1989 festivities, I warned, Benton would still be regarded—outside Missouri, anyway—as a minor figure.

Kramer thought "the work Benton produced in his modernist period is the only work he produced which has any aesthetic merit." But he argued Benton "abandoned what was deepest and most distinctive in his own artistic talent."

In time he became the grand old man of American art as far as Missouri was concerned. He even got to execute an immense mural in the state capital [sic] building in Jefferson City. They also named a brand of bourbon after him. It's not very good bourbon—I sampled it while I was in Kansas City—but then, the murals in Jefferson City aren't very good either. In fact, they're awful—an unrelieved panorama of pictorial cliches which seem to have been derived from old Hollywood movies.

At about the same time, Elizabeth Broun, the chief curator at the National Museum of American Art in Washington, was writing in the first issue of *Smithsonian Studies in American Art* that Benton's painting "continues to engage art historians and general audiences although there is little agreement about the merit of his work." She wrote that his critical success had diminished since the time of the Missouri mural and the works immediately after it.

His art has been considered middlebrow by the art establishment, a view that seems confirmed by the general public's consistent enthusiasm which shows no sign of diminishing....

Broun said Benton's career was one of "unfulfilled promise," based on an "essentially political and rhetorical idiom, the painterly equivalent of the country stump speeches that were a Benton family tradition." Broun argued that his art was based on its audience appeal.

His own art, after the experiments with abstraction, was high-spirited entertainment designed to catch and hold an audience with a political message neatly bracketed between humor and local color.[27]

Kansas City Times columnist George Gurley, Jr., enjoyed reading his mail about Benton. One letter from Michael Ott, a painter, suggested in Gurley's May 14 column that modernists are offended by Benton because "he knows enough 'modernese' to be dangerous."

He makes modernists feel vulnerable. When a church looks for heretics, they don't look outside the faith. It's the non-doctrinaire member that troubles the ecclesiastical authorities.

Another letter was from a former Art Institute student of Benton's who never liked him.

What an absurd premise: that Benton was "our" artist, our native genius. He was...a so-so painter with an eccentric style...with its semi-realistic, strangely bent and otherwise weirdly postured figures, always or usually bordered with a flat plain of paint, like a child's coloring book.

Gurley, in pronouncing Benton a great artist despite the disparaging criticism, said, "...it's clear that you and I KNOW WHAT WE LIKE!, and that we know as much about what's art as any effete intellectual critic."

In an effort to settle the controversy by pronouncing Benton a great artist, Gurley declared, "Nothing could be more self-evident and irrefutable."

Despite the critical division that continues about Benton,

his art, and the Missouri capitol mural in particular, those who visit the House Lounge today and hear the tour guides explain the mural and the man who painted it, might come to agree with Frank C. Tobias who wrote a poem in dialect for the *St. Louis Globe-Democrat* of March 20, 1937:

Tom Benton, son an' gran'son uv fine pioneers,
You draws an' paints scenes uv th' bygone years
An' makes th' curtain hung on mem'ry's stage
Roll up an' show us hist'ry page by page.
Gol durn my hide! Yer talent, seems ter me,
Is dratted good. W'y I kin see a flea
When pitchered houn' dog knocks a elbow on the floor
An' scratches, whines, then dashes outn door.
There's them true scenes uv pore folk's cabins, too,
An' flowin' streams an' flow'rs, jest ez true.
W'y you kin dror hog jowl an' hominy an' sich
That's far beyond view of them idle rich
That never knowed th' taste uv ash cawn pone
Ner possum baked; ner heard a table groan
With suckin' pig an' cracklin' bread, an' bowls
Uv beaten biskits that has brung th' souls
Uv toil-wore folks from sloughs uv deep despair
To high ground when God's grace has pulled a chair
Close to th' table whar they've reached an' took
A fine bankit than's in ary menu book.
Oh, Tom! Sence you have drored yourse'f to fame
They've tacked a "Thomas Hart" onto your name.
But when we see you named as "lecturin'" round
We know you allers think uv lowly ground
Whar ther is sile thet common folks lives on;
Whar God's sun rises, shines an' sets, whar airly dawn
An' evenin' shadders makes you reach an' paint
Missouri folklore; An' to dror the Saint
Uv womanhood, from th' dead past to now.
Tom Benton, we salute you an' endow
You with a title—simple, plain an' true,
"Greatest Artist that Missouri ever knew."

Notes

1. Robert Sanford, "The Time Tom Benton Got Everything Backward," *St. Louis Post-Dispatch* (October 3, 1982). The commission that supervised construction of the Missouri capitol reported the cost of the building, furnishings, and land purchases was $4,044,153.29. The special commission appointed to decorate the building reported in 1928 it had spent $1,009,003.10. The total: $5,053,156.39.

2. *Kansas City Star* (June 22, 1938).

3. Notes of Howard Huselton dated June 27, 1938, in Huselton papers of the Kansas City Art Institute. Huselton signed them, "Your brother in trouble." Letters between Huselton and several of his supporters, from the files of the Art Institute, were made available to the author at the Nelson Gallery of Art. Several are quoted in succeeding pages.

4. Interview with author (February 23, 1984).

5. Robert S. Gallagher, an interview with Thomas Hart Benton, "Before the Colors Fade: An Artist in America," *American Heritage* (June 1973), 89.

6. Interview with author (January 9, 1984).

7. Interview with author (February 29, 1984).

8. Reprinted by *Kansas City Times* (June 22, 1949).

9. Interview with the author (January 10, 1984).

10. Speech by Benton at Harry S Truman Library in Independence, Missouri (May 27, 1960), on completion of mural there.

11. *Kansas City Star* (March 22, 1960).

12. Interview with author (March 28, 1984).

13. Interview with author (December 8, 1983).

14. Gallagher, *American Heritage*, 87.

15. From a mimeographed information sheet Cox prepared and inserted in copies of the pamphlet that resulted from these efforts. The pamphlet included color photographs of the interior and exterior of the Missouri capitol and featured in the middle a brief commentary by Benton. The pamphlet has been revised and updated with each succeeding administration.

16. Cox recalled the ceremony in an interview with the author (March

160

19, 1987). The mule involved is to the right of the main entrance door as a person walks into the room.

17. Note to the author from Larson (October 1987).

18. "Murals By Benton Preserved in Capitol," *St. Louis Post-Dispatch* (August 8, 1971).

19. B. Drummond Ayers, Jr., "Benton in Home Country," *New York Times* (March 26, 1973).

20. *Kansas City Star* (January 4, 1987).

21. "They were bent on getting the picture," *Kansas City Times* (February 2, 1987).

22. Interview with the author (January 16, 1983). Ron Bockenkamp was a state representative from Jefferson County.

23. The author watched the debate.

24. Remarks recorded by the author at the unveiling ceremony (April 15, 1985).

25. Ibid.

26. Larson interview.

27. Summary of the article carried in Donald Hoffman's "Art Journal" column of the *Kansas City Star* (May 10, 1897).

Chapter 5
But What Does the Mural Mean?

The purpose of a work of art is not so much to tell what the artist's thoughts were as to stimulate thoughts in those who view it. A cartoon tells a specific story and lasts a day—a work of art tells as many stories as there are people to see it. It lasts by that power to continually stimulate as long as its material holds together. (Bad sentence, but you get the meaning.)

Thomas Hart Benton was writing to I.G. Morrison, a teacher at the University of Missouri who sometimes worked as a guide at the capitol. On September 2, 1940, Morrison delivered an interpretive lecture in the House Lounge, calling the mural "one of the most widely publicized paintings in the United States today." He sent a copy of the remarks to Benton, who replied they almost exactly matched Benton's pictorial conception. Benton marked a few places in the manuscript as questionable when he wrote back to Morrison on September 14 from his summer home at Chilmark on Martha's Vineyard. But he noted, "Where there is any difference it is of no consequence."

Years later, Benton was interviewed in his studio in Kansas City by Jim Lantz, then with KCMO radio in Kansas City. Portions of that recorded interview are now played for visitors to the Lounge. In them, Benton offers a general interpretation of the painting.

Another capitol lecturer, Ernest A. Irvine, published a small booklet in 1939, *The Benton Murals in the Missouri State Capitol.*

Benton himself wrote two manuscripts about the development, meaning, and defense of the mural. Both are in the files of the Benton Trust in Kansas City. Portions of them have been quoted throughout this book. They are presented in their entirety in the appendix.

In 1977 Benton biographer Matthew Baigell, chairman of the art department at Rutgers University, offered a newer interpretation of the mural. It focused on Benton's political philosophy of the 1930s, which he says was portrayed in the mural. This philosophy, he says, prompted the animosity toward Benton by "the radicals of the 1930s."[1]

Baigell notes that Benton had abandoned communism in the 1920s because "its adherents manipulated truth to fit specific ends" and "that Communists applied a logic...that ignored local and environmental conditions."

Benton also hated Fascism, finding it virtually equivalent with Big Business, a product of uncontrolled free enterprise, rampant individualism, and economic centralization....He found immoral the hard fact that a few businessmen could control the lives of thousands of workers.[2]

Others have sought to interpret the meaning of the figures on the walls, but the most comprehensive work is the speech by Morrison in 1940. An edited version of it is presented here, with interjections from Benton and others.

Regardless of these varying interpretations, Benton realized that each viewer of his works would, one way or another, interpret them personally. He wrote in 1974 that all he wanted from the layman "is that he, or she, find some human meaning in what is projected."

Most of the meanings are grounded in some aspect of our general American culture, of our everyday life, and should be readily discovered by any American who has the will to do so. These meanings are, of course, indeterminate, suggested rather than precisely defined, and open to free interpretation, as I believe they should be. In the end, the meanings of pictures must be found by those who view them.[3]

(Kansas City Star, December 21, 1936): The mural is so vivid in color, so true in drawing, so animated that one almost forgets it is a wall painting. It might almost be life.

Of the technical means that are responsible for its illusions of reality, Mr. Benton says that he has alternated hot and cold pigments because such treatment makes for vibration. Visitors will, of course, think of the scenes themselves and their places in history, when they see the mural, not of the distinguished art and craftsmanship that have brought them out of their dim past and made them live again. It is part of the artist's business to create such an illusion....

(Irvine): A study of the Benton Missouri Murals reveals three outstanding characteristics of his style: they are vivid in color; the rugged figures stand out from the wall as if chiseled in marble; and they have great depth. It is very doubtful if any artist at any time has achieved the profundity of three-dimensional design on a two-dimensional space as has Benton.

To heighten the impact of his characterization and design on the observer, Benton sometimes overstates, sometimes seemingly distorts, usually accentuates. For the visitor who views these murals only once in a lifetime there must be and can be no guessing at the intent. Sometimes visitors feel that the walls may "leap out" at you, or "knock you down," but neither the artist nor his murals are ever overlooked. Yet, with all this, Benton has somehow managed to keep well within the traditional and accepted bounds of the technique of his art. In answer to the complaint that the figures and the execution in general are "terrible," Benton once said, "With pride but without vanity, I can say that there is nothing wrong with the execution of that mural and I'll wager that no competent critic will say so."

(Benton, writing in the December 1928 *Creative Arts* magazine): The job for me is how, using the precise and involved techniques of deep space composition (which is for me synonymous with complete realism), I can order my recessions of form so that they really carry my content and are not mere suites of objects with a name appended. This occurred to me when I first began to work on the subject [his "American Epic" series], but it was not until 1924, when during the illness that preceded my father's death I went back to Missouri, that I got the idea of collecting individual and characteristic forms from life and using them with as little change as possible for form units in my histories.

(Kansas City Star, December 21, 1936): The mural is not a commentary. Benton has not set himself up as a judge of events or crises. He has been amused by the way people act, but he is tolerant and records their acts with as much frankness as if he were an unprejudiced and uncensored newspaper reporter. He is partial to incongruity...Painted in tempera, the mural is so vivid in color, so true in drawing, so animated that one almost forgets it is a wall painting. It might almost be life.

(Baigell): The murals add up to a serious indictment of the effects of unbridled individualism and predatory capitalism on the American people. Furthermore, the murals, one of the great statements of Populist and, ultimately, Jeffersonian sentiment ever painted by an American artist, reflected a point of view central to American culture which had gained cogency as the Depression began to permeate all levels of society....He painted the murals...during a period of intense thought about the nature of American society, its problems and its art. Perhaps for these reasons, the Missouri murals are Benton's most coherent set of murals, the one which best expressed his social philosophy.

(Ralph M. Pearson, 1937): Thomas Benton is the United States of America. His murals reveal him and his country in pristine glory as he is, as she is. No trimmings, no softening of outlines, no mellowing, no preaching about the better way, no life of the mind or spirit. Just Benton, the exuberant rugged individualist, and America, the uncouth chaos of contending forces. Take them or leave them; the

166

artist hands them to us as they can be seen by the physical eye.

Benton, the keen-visioned spectator, loves his America. He loves his native heath, Missouri. He has gone back there to live while painting the murals for the State Capitol and may stay on forever....His years in Paris never washed out of him this Missouri soil....He was the first artist in our generation thus honestly to admit his roots and draw art nourishment therefrom....Benton has always used exaggeration. Everything he paints is overstated, distorted, accentuated. There must be and can be no muffing the point. Benton will knock you down with his murals; neither he nor they are ever overlooked. (Compensation for a stubby stature, perhaps.) But, mind this point, in spite of their dynamic drive at you and into you, these murals do technically "stay on the wall." Benton knows the arc-hitecture of pictorial space. He has achieved the profundity of three-dimensional design on a two-dimensional space...and if the psychological effect of their high pictorial drama drives the trustees out of the trustee's room, as happened at the New School for Social Research, or the readers out of the library, as is said to happen at the Whitney Museum, who shall say that such events are a comparative calamity?

[The Missouri murals] again reveal Benton and the country as they are. The rough and ready spectator has looked at the daily drama and painted it, Boss Pendergast and all the rest.

Benton saw it. Now you see it.[4]

(Malcolm Vaughan, 1938): Benton is a hot-hearted, two-fisted, rip-roaring go-getter, hellbent for election and proud of it....He it is who helped revive and now leads the "I'm an American!" school of painting, a group of isolationists who maintain that by turning their backs on Europe they will see more clearly, approach more nearly, perhaps finally succeed in unveiling, the universal principles on which art is founded....What Benton is after, the thing he searches for and manifests, is plebeian America, the rude scenes and subjects associated with what we used to call "lower classes."

The impulse to paint in the backyard of life is almost as old as painting itself. It is responsible for various informal narratives that decorate Greek vases; enlivens sundry corners of otherwise saintly old Italian pictures; often animates the art of the Van Eycks and their followers—down to the last of them, Pieter Breughel, who gives his canvases entirely to the backyard happenings of sixteenth century Flanders—and finally becomes a widespread aim in the democratic painting of seventeenth century Holland.

Benton brings to the aim a stress on grossness. He has done so from the time he first turned to it, though he has now expanded his field to take in all the backyards of American civilization, from the city slum to the derelict farm. His is no desire to uplift the down-trodden by focusing attention on them. His desire is to represent life in the raw and he represents it without softening any of its harshness or crudity. To get his material at first hand, he has become perhaps the most widely traveled artist, within our borders, America has ever known.[5]

(Benton, quoted in *Kansas City Times*, April 15, 1937): My painting was and is based on Missouri behavior. The possibilities of its being influenced by my illusions and experiences are inescapable. To my mind the fact that it is realistic doesn't preclude beauty.

(Irvine): Upon entering the lounge room, the casual visitor sees a mass of color, volume and form. At first it may seem a trifle disconcerting, the color may seem to vivid, the figures overdrawn and the observer wonders what it is all about. No one sees here "just another painting"; the air is vibrant with meaning, and within this one room is caught and reflected the spirit of Missouri—past and present.

168

(Morrison): When you first entered this particular room you, no doubt, were struck first by the display of vivid color, and next by what appeared to be a conglomerate mass of figures without rhyme or reason. That first impression to many is audibly shocking. "Well where does it begin?" is often among the first inquiries.

But before I enter into anything like a detailed interpretation I want to make a few observations while you are becoming acclimated to the stimuli surrounding you.

In the first place, scores of people have asked me if the "poor, old, bony, red cow" that you see just to the right of the entrance door will live throughout the season. It is a perfectly natural question for anyone to ask who has just walked into this room for the first time.

Well, as a picture, that is a cow all right. But as a mural that is not simply a cow,...it represents the dairy industry of Missouri. In fact it is the dairy industry in operation—the man milking indicates the operation, does it not?

Now, if you want to see this as a mural, you must sit there long enough to visualize in your mind's eye the whole ice cream business of Missouri. Not just the ice cream business of your little town or city or community, but of the whole state of Missouri. You must see the whole cheese industry, from the milking of the cows on the farms to the finished product in the factory and its wholesale and retail distribution. You must visualize the condensed milk. And the bottled milk. Can you look at the figure of that old red cow and visualize literally thousands and thousands of milk wagons and trucks carrying bottled milk to hundreds of thousands of individual homes every morning? If there were a fresh snow on the ground and no other traffic at all but milk deliveries, can you visualize the maze or network their tracks would make over every section and township of Missouri? If you can do that, you are truly beginning to see this as a mural.

There is just as much difference between a mural and a picture as there is in between thinking and musing. Some people, of course, do not like to think: they just want to wile the time away diddling with what ever strikes their fancy. Such reminds me of the little third-grade girl that came running up to me one day in one of the corridors on the first floor asking, "Mr., where are the funny pictures?" To too many grown-ups these murals are just enlarged "funny pictures." Now, I am in no way criticizing our visitors. Not at all. The most of us are entirely too busy making a living these days to study the intricacies of art or to keep ourselves posted in Missouri history. History has a way of "getting away from us" unless we keep reading. You will not be able to *see* these murals today, for it takes more time than that. So when you go home and people ask you, "Did you see the Benton murals?" tell them, "No, I looked at them." There is a difference, you know.

(**Benton,** in a letter "To the Visitors" posted in the House Lounge while he was painting): This theme does not demand the representation of specific characters or events emphasized in historic record. It calls simply for a depiction of the ways people lived and the changes they effected in their environment as Missouri developed. I have been as inclusive as possible with my subject matter but although these are big walls there is much significant and interesting matter I have had to leave out.

...The objects painted on these walls are not just slapped on arbitrarily. The filling of every square quarter inch of space in this room has been planned and worked out so that the shapes, volumes and colors of things shall stand out and carry the eye over and in and out of the picture space. When you look at this painting a man's body or a tree trunk may be just a body or a tree trunk to you but they are also functioning parts of a geometrical pattern which insures that your eye shall travel easily from one place to another on

170

these walls and get a sense of unity from what is on them. The "realness" of this work depends on a lot of abstract adjustments of lines and planes and gradations of color. These adjustments cannot be disturbed without causing me a lot of work, without, in fact, making me do this thing all over.

(Morrison): Mr. Benton begins his story over in that northwest corner of the room and comes around here to this entrance door on the east portraying Missouri history of the past. Then from this entrance door on around the rest of the room he portrays our contemporary history of the present era. Those are his two main divisions. Then he makes a third division, which—strictly speaking—is not devoted to history, per se, but is devoted to portraying three Missouri legends. They are shown in the panel above each of the three doors.

The panel above the north door suggests the legends that have grown up around the stories of Mark Twain. If you will look closely you will be able to read the inscription on the steamboat, "Sam Clemens." And immediately you recognize Huck Finn and Nigger Jim standing on the raft in the foreground. It is a beautiful panel. Look at the variety and contrast of colors. I am not going into a discussion of the works of Mark Twain, but I do suggest that you reread a volume or two for pure enjoyment and appreciation. You will be surprised how much you have forgotten. The chuckles that will come to you again will enhance your appreciation of this panel more.

(Irvine): The colors in this panel are perhaps the finest in the murals. The observer is reminded that a trip to Europe to see beautiful skies is unnecessary. Here in Missouri, where the sky is blue and cloudless, and the full moon casts its sheen on the foliage of trees, smoke of the steamer, and the tranquil waters of our great Mississippi, Missouri's greatest literary genius seems to pervade the scene.

(**Baigell**): This scene also reflects Benton's mixed feelings toward this country. Huck and Jim are free on the river after escaping from different kinds of servitude. But Jim is still technically a slave, at least until the end of the novel, and we know that Huck will never permit himself to become domesticated. The two represent the conflicts between an ideal state of freedom and the constraints of civilization. In the Missouri of the mid-century period, in what might have been a modern Garden of Eden, or at least a viable modern democracy, Benton shows the effects of the introduction of social order—slavery and nefarious business practices, as well as the loss of individual freedom and liberty. He seems to be saying that if there ever was an American Dream, it never had a chance to develop.

(**Morrison**): Looking at the panel above the entrance door on the east we see the legend of the James boys and their escapades after the Civil War. Here the artist has painted a composite bank and railroad hold-up. Many people, especially elderly people, have said, "Now that is not legend. That is history. I have met Frank James, myself." Consequently this panel has been subjected to considerable criticism.

Let me call your attention to the fact that a legend must have some history back of it, or it would not be legend. If it had no history it would become a myth. A legend must have history. It must have fiction. When history and legend become so intermingled that they no longer can become separated we have a legend. So what we can prove is true about the James boys is history. What we can neither prove true nor false becomes legend. There is plenty about the Jameses that we cannot prove true. Nor can we say dogmatically that the tales are false. Those are the tales that go to make up the legends of the James boys. This panel is presented from the legendary and not the historical point of view.

172

Above the door in the south wall we have "Song of Frankie and Johnnie" [sic]. This is another panel that has aroused a lot of discussion and criticism. It also has been mistaken for history alone. It has become legendary, although I think perhaps that the artist did not search out the real origin of the song. I say that without criticism.

Many visitors do not know that "Frankie and Johnnie" is a Negro song. Many more know little of the origin. So I want to say a word about that.

The song originated some time in the late 1840s or early 1850s, in St. Louis. At that time there was a free Negro woman by the name of Frankie who shot and killed her free Negro husband by the name of Johnnie. It seems that she had evidence that her husband no longer remained true to their betrothal. The lines of the song speak of Johnnie as being a "crib man," not a shanty man. That "crib man" has a distinct social bearing on the origin of the song and places its origin at a time before free Negroes of St. Louis ever lived in "shanty style." The Negroes of the community put the episode to song; clapping their hands, stomping their feet for rhythm, and adding verse after verse as bits of gossip or fact were told. The song was not written. It became a folk song.[6]

Years passed. The song died away, only youngsters that had grown old remembered it. Then in 1899 another Negro woman of St. Louis by the peculiar name of Frankie shot and killed her husband, whose name was Allen. And I suspect that the artist, thinking this was the original song, so represented it as the last panel here. I say this because up there on the wall of the saloon where the shooting is taking place is the picture of what looks suspiciously like "Custer's Last Fight." That fight did not take place until the 1870s. At any rate the old song of "Frankie and Johnnie" was revived, with many variations. Today, according to the best authorities we have some eighty different "Frankie and Johnnie" songs with something over 300 variations.

It is partly truth, partly fiction. The two seem inseparable. It is another Missouri legend, and as such is presented by the artist.

(Benton): I believe that the myths of a country picture it almost...better than its damned politics.[7]

(Irvine): This preserves for future generations a pictorial presentation of the barroom scene which gave rise to the famous ballad....In the East and in Europe this ballad with its plaintive refrain—"He was my man but he done me wrong"—is considered typically Missourian....The whole is a splendid study in emotion showing anger, dismay, surprise, astonishment and fear. Much merriment has been caused by the two gentlemen making their hurried departure—the one at the left holding frantically to his hat while the one at the right has expended so much energy in his "get away" that one of the buttons on the rear of his trousers just couldn't "stand the strain" and has severed its connection, thus allowing one side of his suspenders to fly in the breeze.

(Baigell): This shooting differs from that in the James gang panel because it reflects upon urban problems, severe social dislocation, and the settlement of grievances by murder without any recompensing social benefits. It speaks to the horrors of oppressive slum conditions just as the juxtaposition of Pendergast and the dancer reveals the dishonored state of modern democratic procedures.

(Morrison): There is just one thing more that I want to emphasize before we go into the history— the fact that Mr. Benton was commissioned by the state legislature to paint a "Social History of Missouri." That is exactly what he has done. He has not painted a military history of our state; that will be found in other places in the building. He has not painted here an educational history, nor yet a political history; those, too, will be found other places in the building. But he *has* remained true to his assignment and painted a social history: forces at work that build a state.

174

There is the key to the whole story—forces at work that build a state. Forces that build must be virile; there is little that smacks of the dainty violet. Forces that build are promulgated by men who are men, and women who are women. Unless you are looking for the beauty that comes with strength and the virility of manhood and womanhood, I'm afraid you may be disappointed in these murals; for that is the theme of the artist from beginning to end. Missouri is a great state built by citizens of stamina, of strong bodies and sound, independent minds.

(**Baigell**): [Benton's] villains are the unfeeling entrepreneurs who, like the slaveowners and auctioneers, beat or sell workers, or like the factory owners, think of laborers as another kind of machinery. The heroes are certainly the artisans and farmers, the people who exploit, and are exploited by nobody. The most muscular and, presumably, the most handsome men are those who work the land, as if Benton were illustrating the famous passage from Jefferson's *Notes on the State of Virginia*: "Those who labor in the earth are the chosen people of God, if ever he had a chosen people...."

(**Benton**): A lot of people thought that the kind of realism I had employed had been misdirected, that it should have all been given to famous characters. But I wasn't so much interested in famous characters as I was in Missouri and the ordinary run of Missourians that I'd known in my life. The better part of that mural is stuff that I had actually experienced myself. Only the north wall and, of course, the special panels with special subject matter is stuff that I hadn't experienced. But even there I used real people that I met and knew.

(**Morrison**): Now I will call your attention to the small panel in the northwest corner of the room where Mr. Benton begins his history of Missouri. There you see the black slave being driven to work mining lead around the period of 1700.

175

Whether the slave owner is French or Spanish, I do not know. He may be of either nationality, depending on whether...you think of the early Spanish lead mines, or...of the French mines of a little later period. At any rate you will note the bucket is being lowered into or hoisted from a shallow lead mine.

In this panel the artist covers the whole exploratory period of Missouri history. Lead was mined south of what we now call St. Louis at least seventy-five years before that little military fortress was even thought of. There was not a white man's town in the land at that time. Ste. Genevieve was founded in 1735, the first white settlement in Missouri. And lead was being mined with the use of black labor before that.

But it isn't the *fact* that lead was mined in Missouri then that the artist calls to attention. Here is the whole exploratory period of the state. With a little reflection many images will flash across your mind of the trials and struggles upon the founding of a western empire. Many books have been written about this period, but Mr. Benton covers the whole subject with this one panel.

Pioneer Period

Leaving the panel covering the exploratory period, I now direct your attention to the section above it. From the door, left to the corner of the room, Mr. Benton has graphically portrayed the Pioneer Period of Missouri. In other words, he directs our attention to the 1800s, preceeding our entry into the Union. I would like to take a little more time with this section than the others, just to show you how Mr. Benton works and why it is almost impossible to see these murals in one sitting.

In the immediate foreground, with characters some ten feet high, the Frenchman is trading for furs with the Indian. The fur trade was the largest single industry of the period. It

176

was big business. It was profitable business. It was daring business. It was not always clean business. It most certainly was competitive business. Mr. Benton places his characters right out in front where they are bound to emphasize the importance of the fur trade.

You will notice that the Frenchman has a box of beads on the floor that he uses for money. And his jug of rum is his "persuader." (That is one reason we know he is a Frenchman; the Spanish were strictly forbidden to use liquor in trading with the Indians.)

The Indian is an Osage. Until the white man pushed so many tribes west across the Mississippi River, the Osage was the "Missouri Indian." This tribe owned all of the land south and much of it north of the Missouri River. They had more to do with early Missouri history than any other tribe or nation.

...If you do not know the legend of how the Osages got their name you will find an item of interest in its connection with the fur trade south of the Missouri river. The more that you know of the Osages, and the more you recall of the practices of the fur-traders of this territory during this particular period, the more this becomes a mural to you. Remember there is nothing on this wall but paint; the mural is in your head.

(Baigell): The interchange between the frontier merchant and the Indian...indicates almost at once that Benton will not revel in hymns of praise to his native state. Although we do not know his attitudes toward Indians or Indian art, we do know that he was appalled by vulturous capitalistic tactics and was sympathetic to minority groups. Thus, the first commercial scene in the murals is characterized by cunning and duplicity on the part of the entrepreneur.

(Benton): I was commissioned to make a history of Missouri, but a particular kind, a social history which meant, as we conceived it, simply a history of the life of the people...who actually made Missouri. And it begins here with the pioneer world, with the river in the background...the Missouri River, the important artery of the state, and moves into the settlers. In the very foreground you'll see a man with a jug and an Osage Indian, sitting down below him. This was the beginning of the Missouri fur trade. This is a symbolic representation. But the thing went along that way from a primitive—not a settler's beginning, but an explorer and fur trader's beginning—to, as we go over into the other panel on the right hand side of the wall, the building of the state, the construction.

(Morrison): Leaving that detail now, I call your attention to the three methods of transportation illustrated up and down the corner on the left.

Notice the small boat on the river near the top of the panel. If you look right sharply you will notice there is a rope leading from the top of the mast to the four men on the bank. There is the old pirogue, being pulled up the river by manpower. That is the way Lewis and Clark went by here in 1804. [Author's note: The Missouri capitol stands on a high bluff overlooking the south bank of the Missouri River.] Or at least that is the way that Meriwether Lewis went past on the third of June of that year. Clark was afoot on the other side of the river running a survey line. They were pulled up river by men wading, swimming, and climbing through the brush. Does not Benton here give you a social condition of the times?

Another early method of transportation is indicated below where the man is putting a pack on his burro. Note that the animal is a burro, not a mule. He is getting ready to follow the Indian trails up the river because there are no roads yet. There is nothing out here but wilderness, here and there threaded with the trails of the native Redmen. The chances are that this man floated down the river in early spring with a cargo of pelts. Now he is getting ready for the

178

long trek back afoot, laden with trinkets for his next year's buy.

Then came the wagon road, indicated with the covered wagon....The first road across Missouri was the Boonslick Trail built about 1808. It led from St. Louis to Boonslick, in what is now Howard County and across the river from where Boonville stands today. It was only a trail; for they just cut the timber, pulled the logs out of the way, and left the stumps. The land was beginning to be settled by the white man. Immigration was just starting. How deftly Benton calls this to our attention!

Just to the right of the covered wagon are three men at a shooting match. A little above them is their target—a turkey with a rope tied to its leg. The rope, more than anything else, tells the story. You see, the marksman who misses his target and kills the turkey loses the shooting match.

Sometimes they tied turkeys out at a shooting match to kill them, but they were not tied out in the open like that one. If the purpose was to kill the fowl they would tie it out behind a log, so that just his head would bob up into sight once in a while. It would take no fine shot to kill a big turkey tied out in the open. The purpose indicated here is to shoot the feathers off that fowl. That old gobbler is not going to stand still while they pluck him with rifle balls, either. They must shoot at a moving feather, 50 to 100 yards away. The artist is telling us they had to be accurate shots in those days. This is another social condition of the times. We are here today largely because of the white man's superiority in arms.

Near the upper, right-hand corner of this section is a man out tilling the soil, using a yoke of oxen. Settlement has started, but not without its perils. Notice the log fort in juxtaposition to the plowman? That is hardly a log house; it is more likely a fort. And he would not be plowing very far away from it. Do you recall seeing on the second floor the

179

lovely lunette by Oscar E. Berninghaus [sic] entitled, "The Attack on the Village of St. Louis in 1780"? Well, here is the same thing with the exception that the incident is not localized. The danger is imminent. Preparation for defense has been made. The Indian's hunting ground is yielding to the white man's plowshare at a price. Domestic activity also exacted military duty.

One more thing I want to call to your attention before we leave this pioneer period is the detail in this presentation. Notice the type of yoke he has placed across the necks of the oxen. Why did he not put a French yoke on them? The French hooked up their oxen to pull with their heads. The French mined lead in the latter part of this exploratory period and traded for furs as we see up here. The French were great business men. But who pioneered Missouri? Not the French. Just by the type of yoke he has chosen to use, Mr. Benton directs attention again to the...forces at work building a state. This room is jammed full of just such detail.

It is impossible to see all of these murals in one day—there are too many implications and details for that. I probably spent too much time on these early periods, but I wanted to give you some idea of how Benton works.

Panel Right of Door on North Wall
The Home-Building Period

The first figures that catch your attention are those of the immense character with the ax and his Negro helper. The key to the period is in the notch in this end of the timber that the Negro is holding. It is going to be used in the building of a house. Immediately above the Negro's head is a fence around the hay stack. Close by is a water-powered mill for grinding feed. Here indeed is the permanent settlement of the white man.

It is a very definite period in the history of Missouri. Frank Brangwyn uses one-fourth of his great pendants out in the dome for portraying this one period. Thomas Hart Benton uses all of this space between the door and the corner to the right for the same period. It is very important.

Near the corner, at the bottom, the blacksmith is at work with anvil and bellows. If you look on these as pictures that is all that you will see—a blacksmith at work. But if you look upon them as murals then you will look at that figure long enough to let the whole history and development of the Santa Fe Trail unfold before your mind's eye. That trail was initiated the year that Missouri became a state—1821. The Santa Fe Trail began right where the Boonslick Trail ended, at Franklin in Howard County.

(**Baigell**): Aspects of labor are shown—woodcutting and blacksmithing. The men engaged in these tasks look reasonably healthy and, by their own labor, are making their own way in the world. These are the people Benton loved—the independent yeomen whose energies created the United States. These are the figures he contrasts with the whiskey-seducing merchant on the other side of the door.

(**Morrison**): Immediately above the blacksmith a slave is being auctioned on the block. A white man has his hand on the black boy's thigh, evidently expostulating the worthiness of those limbs. Here the artist emphasizes the rapid growth of slavery during the home-building period....Actually, comparatively few slaves were shipped into Missouri to be sold; they were brought by the people who settled. The slave was always a commercial liability anywhere north of the frost line, not an asset. Missourians fought the Civil War not so much over the issue of owning slaves as on the issue of state's rights.

However, slavery was a very live question during this period, and Benton very ably brings it to our attention. A study of the home-building period would be incomplete without considering the impact of the black man.

Just to the left of the slave auction a baptism is taking

place in the water. In juxtaposition is a little Protestant church. A little to the right, the white building with a spire, is a Catholic cathedral. Here the importance of churches is brought to focus.

(**Baigell**): The St. Louis Basilica partially frames a slave on the block. Since Benton detested hypocrisy of any sort, we may read the juxtaposition of white religion and certain white business practices in the sardonic way he probably intended.

(**Morrison**): Prior to 1804 anyone who worshiped in public had to worship in the Catholic faith. Then after this land was acquired through the Louisiana Purchase, we threw the territory open for all denominations. They had quite a struggle for existence for some twenty years, but through this period the churches made their influence felt in state affairs.

(**Irvine**): The panel...tells about the days of slavery and religious development....Note the rugged strength of these slaves as well as that of the sturdy pioneer with his huge broadax. Some critics say Benton has omitted the "ideals" of our state, including religion and education. Yet, in this single section, the close observer will find three approaches to religion: Mormonism in the small panel at the bottom, Protestantism in the baptizing scene, and Catholicism in the famous Cathedral of St. Louis near the top.

(**Morrison**): The building with a dome, above the little Protestant church, is the capitol built in Jefferson City in 1837-38. It was enlarged in 1888 and burned in 1911. It stood on the bluff between the present capitol and the Missouri River.

This little panel, to the right of the door at the bottom, portrays a very dramatic scene of the same period—that of a white man being tarred and feathered....There is one man slushing hot tar onto that naked body. Another is sifting feathers onto him out of a sack. While behind the unfortunate another man is tying up his hands with a rope.

Over on the other end a Negro slave is being set free. In the center a home is ablaze and women are driven out. Grain is destroyed. The victims are Mormons. Finally, in 1838, they were driven out of Missouri. They went from here to Illinois and settled around Nauvoo. A few years later they were driven out of there for the same reason: they tried to set up a state within a state. After that many of them made the trek to Salt Lake to get clear outside of the United States and set up their own government. I mention this because...the Mormon issue is generally regarded as a religious problem. It was, in reality, much more a state problem than a religious one. I think I can say, without fear of being criticized by any competent historian, that Missouri has yet to suffer religious intolerance.[8]

(**Baigell**): In the small panels adjacent to the doorway, Benton included a slave-whipping scene in front of a lead mine, another instance of predatory capitalism as well as unbridled individualism in which one group literally enslaved another for its own economic purposes. In the other panel, a black and a white man shake hands as a Mormon family's home is burnt and a white man is being tarred. Although the full meaning of this panel is ambiguous, Benton is clearly commenting on Missouri's past and perhaps present religious prejudices.

Turn the corner to the east wall, we get into a little later period. From here to the entrance door the artist covers in great sweeps an exciting period of Missouri history that covers some sixty years. There is drama packed in every stroke of the brush.

(**Baigell**): Benton was not concerned with the kind of freedom in which people totally lacked responsibility. He was not concerned with painting man in a state of nature. Rather his ideal was that in which individuals did not dominate the lives of others, but, as artisans, laborers, and farmers, were responsible only for themselves. This at least seems also to be the message of the scenes on the long wall comprising Politics, Farming, and Law. Even though a frontiersperson opens the narrative, the episodes depict the settled society of roughly the period between 1850 and 1875. This seems to be the Golden Age for Benton, politically and psychologically but even here he finds flaws.

(**Morrison**): In the corner is a hunter and some hound dogs. Many people think the man represents Daniel Boone. They are entitled to that interpretation. Far be it from me to make a denial. He was a great and historic character, but I would like to make a few observations.

Daniel Boone, in one respect at least, was a very superstitious man. He would wear coon-skin caps, but never one with a tail on it. In all of my research I have never found that he made it a practice to hunt with hound dogs. When he was at home he did have dogs about him, but not when he was trying to dodge the trail of the Indian. And his hunting expeditions carried him into Indian country.

He was almost 70 years old when he moved his family into the Louisiana Territory around 1791. He did some hunting on his own—and trapping too—but it was mainly for his own pleasure and to satisfy that restless spirit of roving into new and unknown territory.

His real contribution to Missouri history is very ably represented in the Senate Chamber in a panel executed by Richard E. Miller, "Daniel Boone at the Judgment Tree." There he is depicted as the old Spanish syndic. He was the first American judge west of the Mississippi River. The influence he carried with that position marks his greatest contribution to Missouri history. When Lewis and Clark went by in 1804 they paused near what is now St. Charles to pay obeisance to Boone. He was at that time still the complete civil and military authority of everything north of

184

the Missouri River. He died before Missouri became a state. In fact the first legislature was attempting to formulate the proposed constitution in September of 1820 when Daniel Boone passed into the Great Beyond, and it adjourned so members could attend his last rites.[9] So, I do not interpret this character as representing Daniel Boone.

(Benton): Now hunters...are common to Missouri all the time, my time as well as this earlier time. But in this garb that ends what I would call the early or pioneer time of Missouri.

(Morrison): To me, this man with the gun represents a period in the white man's conquest of the wilderness when he went out and got his own furs instead of trading with the Indian. The implications are many and varied but this was the period when the bison and buffalo disappeared from Missouri. So did the otter and the beaver, and the Missouri bear. The white man was greedy with his game. He had no restraining game laws. Youngsters ask me almost every day why there are bears on the state seal, as if we never had any bears in the state. Indeed we did but here is the man who got rid of them. Because of his activity St. Louis became the greatest fur mart of the world. It still is, for that matter. Because of this man's activity the hunting grounds of the Indians became smaller and smaller as they were forced farther away from their native habitat. The artist has here portrayed a social force at work in the building of a new state.

There is another force at work immediately above the hunter. Notice the small steamboat in the corner? That is not the first one to come up the river here. Take a good look at the model and you will see the period in which it operated. These boats brought down the Ohio River and up the Mississippi to St. Louis something like a half million people in a period of fifteen years, landing them along the banks of the Missouri. Missouri was second to New York in

185

population for a while.[10] Great throngs of immigrants were moving into this land of plenty and freedom. That was before the railroads were laid. They came on the steamboat. That little detail shows a very distinct social force at work in the building of our commonwealth.

(**Baigell**): A river boat, rather than a keel boat, announces the taming of the river.

(**Walter G. Heren**, writing in the *Kansas City Journal-Post*, December 25, 1936): To tie the various panels together around the top of the wall, Benton has used the Missouri River, with its steamers belching streams of smoke from one panel into another, up to the period of the Civil War, when the river no longer was such a factor in transportation and the development of the state. From that point on, he uses smoke from a threshing machine engine and from factory smoke stacks to hold the panels together and to weld them into an integrated story of the progress of society in Missouri.

(**Morrison**): May I call your attention now to the courthouse? By the way, notice that the large picture of a political candidate is not on the side of the courthouse. It is stretched up on the back of the speaker's stand....

The courthouse is a substantial structure, and there is significance in that. In the "Home-Building Period," court was held out of doors under a tree. In one of the smaller lunettes down on the second floor there is a painting by Walter Ufer entitled "The First Circuit Court in Boone County" that illustrates the local administration of law during that era. State administration of law was pretty sketchy. In this panel, however, law and order have become an established state affair. The substantial building indicates that growth....

Now we come to the scene depicting political speaking. It is not hard to see this is meant for a political talkfest. Here in this section of space Benton calls attention to the period

186

of great political turmoil in Missouri, covering a period of some thirty-five years, twenty-five before the Civil War and the ten that followed it.

(Benton): As far back as I can remember I have traveled around this state....My father was a political figure in the state, and when I was a kid he used to take me on his various campaigning trips, whether he was campaigning for himself or some other candidate....I got acquainted very early with a kind of flamboyant early political life of Missouri, and that is what's represented....You see a regular country political meeting there....It happens to be, in this case, my own father making the speech. I had a portrait of him to go by. And there are other characters around there. These are all real characters....Above the speakers stand is a picture of Champ Clark....Maybe he's campaigning for Champ Clark. Back of it is the typical country town of my youth.

(Morrison): Talk about "hot politics" in Missouri the last few years![11] We do not know what "hot politics" are until we turn back to this period. Recall the "Drake Constitution" adopted in this state after the Civil War and the restrictions placed upon anyone who sympathized with the Confederate cause. Such a sympathizer could not teach school, could not preach the gospel, could not run a business of any kind, no matter how small. And he could not vote. Absolutely disfranchised. And it held on until 1875 when a new constitution was adopted. There was political turmoil alright.[12] For twenty-five years before the war men so disagreed on political issues that old parties were killed, new parties sprang up, and others split into factions. Banking was a heated issue. Railroads created problems. And, of course, slavery and states' rights became hot issues.

Yet when some people look at this scene all they see is a mother tending her baby. They get about as much history out of it as they do the old cow I mentioned a while ago. They look upon this as a picture instead of a mural.

The lady did take a back seat. She is not right down in front by the speaker's stand. But that is not the point. Here is a scene depicting the great upheaval in Missouri politics and this lady came to the political meeting. She came, even if she had to bring the baby. Look at the boys here having trouble over their watermelon. But they came to the political meeting. I do not imagine that they are guilty of listening to a single speech, but they came with their folks to the meeting. The women around the table are getting dinner ready. In those days, the meetings were quite extended. People stayed all day. They threw big dances and all of that. But the point is that they all came to the meeting. Do you see how the artist with every detail focuses your attention on the airing of political issues?

(**Irvine**): Missouri hospitality is suggested by the housewives at the ''basket dinner'' with a typical ''meddlesome Mattie'' at the end of the table, who is trying to peer into the other woman's well-filled basket, and in turn is rewarded with a haughty stare.

(**Morrison**): There's another thing that worries people a great deal in this scene. Benton has painted the likeness of Champ Clark to represent the political candidate that is seen on the canvas back of the speaker. In his original sketch he did not use this likeness. Why he did so when he painted this wall I do not know, but at any rate it has been very confusing to some visitors. They try to put the scene into Clark's time. But Clark was born on March 7, 1850, and even in the latter part of this period he would still have been a young man. Benton has used his likeness to symbolize the political candidate.

(**Baigell**): Facing the gesturing speaker is a black man standing at the rear of the audience. He is now included in the social and political systems, though not entirely accepted or integrated into them. The black man leans against a limbless tree from which, presumably, he might have been lynched if grass roots democratic processes had been less successful. Such processes had failed previously. Just above and to the right of the black man, another black is being lynched, silhouetted by flames representing the Civil War years.

(**Irvine**): The hound dogs placed directly under the picture of Champ Clark recalls to mind the presidential campaign song used by the admirers of this illustrious statesman in 1919—"You Gotta Quit Kickin' My Dawg Around."[13]

(**Morrison**): With three exceptions all characters painted on these walls were posed by living individuals....I wish that we did not know the names of any of them. Three characters were taken from photographs; the rest posed in person. Nowhere in the room does the name of the individual have anything to do with the meaning of the mural.

For instance, Governor Guy B. Park posed for the character on the speaker's platform with his arms folded. He was the governor of Missouri when these murals were painted. The mayor of Jefferson City posed for the character sitting on the platform beside him. The portly man standing on the ground with the big hat and brown coat was posed by Sid Hamilton, who was Commissioner of the Permanent Seat of Government here at the time this was painted. There is Senator Barbour, Judge Leedy of the Supreme Court, and other men of more or less importance sitting on the benches before the speaker. The names of none of them will help you interpret the making of the mural. The names may be interesting but they certainly do get into the way of true interpretation.

One must never forget the *purpose* of the artist in examining any particular section of the wall. Each detail fits into the general pattern. Interesting customs of the day are detailed in this political scene, but they must be subordinated to the all-inclusive theme. The true import of this political gathering will come to no individual without thoughtful examination, and, possibly, a little research. Here indeed is a hectic period of Missouri history about which books are still being written.

Civil War

Now I call your attention to the graphic little scene so fraught with meaning that is above the table where the women are getting dinner ready. There, in a very small space, is the conflict between the states—the Civil War.

Right in the center of the conflagration is the figure of a man dangling at the end of a rope. Immediately you recognize an execution by hanging. But why didn't the artist show a man with his back against a wall and face turned toward a firing squad? Were hangings connected with the war with Mexico? Or with the Spanish American War of a later period? No. But there is a direct Civil War social bearing.

Immediately beneath the hanging are the horses and men of the guerrillas. The Civil War in Missouri started with Kansas—that border warfare that lasted from 1856 to 1865. The names of Jim Lane, John Brown, Jennison and Charles Quantrell,[14] and a host of others come to mind.

Possibly Quantrell stands out above any of the rest. His followers were the original two-gun men, deadly shots and born to the saddle. Always on the go, they would strike a deadly blow to the enemy and then scatter like a covey of scared quail, to meet again at a predetermined spot for another assault. They gave no quarter. They asked for none. It was fight to the death and leave no wounded comrade. When they flew a flag, which was seldom, they flew the black flag of Quantrell. They were young men—all of them—including the Youngers, the Andersons, the Todds, Jim Little, and the James boys. As you look at this scene you will see the "Massacre of Centralia," "Sacking of

Lawrence," the "Attack on Independence." (Their point of view may be found in a book published in 1877 by John Edwards entitled, *Noted Missouri Guerrillas*.)

There is a detail between those two buildings that you will have to look right sharply to see. Between the building right against the blaze and the rock wall are men dressed in gray uniforms carrying a flag—the Stars and Bars of the Confederacy. They are running towards the soldiers in blue who are carrying the Stars and Stripes of the Union. The two armies in the background are often overlooked, but the guerillas are out in front. Missouri had more Civil War battles than any other state in the Union except Virginia.[15] Yet the guerrillas did more social damage to Missouri than both armies put together!

The famous painting of George Caleb Bingham entitled "Order Number 11'" made infamous (as he said it would) the military order of the same name and number....Here it is, right up here in paint. A woman with a bundle under her arm and leading a little child is squeezed in between the two armies, the guerrillas, and bushwhackers, the fire nipping at her back. Her husband is gone, their stock stolen, grain destroyed, their home burned, and nowhere to go. There is General Order No. 11. Whole counties evacuated. There is Missouri in the Civil War.

That is the cloud of the Civil War coming up back of the courthouse, back of the trees, a way early people pay no attention to it. (It reminds me of the cloud that has been coming up over the Atlantic for the past ten years and just now getting so black that people are jittery for fear that it will break into flames.) Look how black this cloud gets in the 1850s. Then breaks into the flame of 1861. It hangs like a pall over that whole period until it finally bursts into the consuming conflagration of Civil War.

Here was Missouri, a border state pounded between the North and South. The state was divided. Communities were

191

divided. Families were divided. Father fought against son, brother against brother, friend against friend, neighbor against neighbor—each fighting for a principle of self government. Missouri was a battleground indeed. The North wanted control of the Missouri River. The South wants control of it too. That river was the highway to the West—a whole empire was at stake. The first move of General Lyons[16] at the beginning of the war in Missouri was designed to gain control of the river. The same thought was in the mind of General Price. Those thoughts persisted to the end of the war. How graphically Thomas Hart Benton has brought all of this to our attention.

Recontruction Period

Then the war was over and the dark skies cleared. Look up there! You can almost see the sunshine. You sense the relief from the conflict. A new day is born. New hope has arisen. And here we have the ''reconstruction period.'' Missourians began to rebuild their state. It was not an easy task after such a conflict.

Cities and communities were devastated; graineries were empty; stock was depleted; homes were broken; bodies were wrecked. Manpower was at a premium. Old prejudices could not be lightly thrown aside. Rebuilding was complicated and hard.

(Baigell): From the flames a train emerges, driving on to the future. The image of the train, of course, recurs throughout American art and literature. For Benton, as for contemporaries such as Charles Burchfield and Sherwood Anderson, the train was a dynamic force heralding the possibility of adventure and change rather than a sad commentary on the passing of the old way of life....For Benton, railroads helped tame the land and, as much as any other single factor, contributed to the vigorous growth of a

192

rural economy which, he undoubtedly felt, was essential to the economic and psychological health of this nation.

(**Morrison**): There were two general avenues open for Missouri at the time: developing agriculture, which the artist shows in the scene at the top of the painting, and cutting down her timber, as is indicated by the men sawing wood at the bottom. Problems of the day are indicated and through it all permeates the atmosphere of self-reliance and determination, tranquil though it may be.

The very size, shape, and strength of the sawyer's bare back indicates the enormity of the lumbering industry. It shows all too well what happened to our virgin forests. There is the reason for that lone stump you see a little to the right. We denuded our timber land. We cut off too much. Uncle Sam is trying now to help us put some of it back.[17]

Before leaving this section I want to comment on that old mule. It has been criticized as much, possibly, as that old, red, milch cow over there and maybe rightly so. But there is a significance that many people miss altogether.

LaClede and his men who founded the village or fort of St. Louis imported pure-blood Arabian horses. From that time on, up to the Civil War, fine horses were bred and raised in Missouri. When the conflict broke out, there were as many fine horses within its borders as Virginia, Kentucky, or Tennessee.

When the war broke out the guerrillas you see up there—who always rode horseback—came and took their pick of the horses. They usually paid for them, but they took them whether they did or not. Then the armies came and took some more. Those that were not killed were scattered all over the Union. Missouri faced a great agricultural problem of rehabilitation with its horse-power depleted and the oxen too slow. It was then that Missouri commenced to breed the mule.[18] Do you want to remember this date? The Missouri mule came into prominence for the first time in

1867—two years after the war. Have a little more respect for that animal when you see one again. He was a social force in the building of the state, and Benton puts him in the right place.

(Baigell): In this section of the mural Benton also immortalized the Missouri mule. In addition, he emphasized the family unit. Women play an active role, either working along side their husbands or in more stereotyped activities—cooking and childcare. (Fewer blacks appear on this wall than on the others, suggesting that Benton did not know quite how to relate them to stable social settings. They remained for him symbols of economic exploitation.

(Morrison): The little panel at the bottom shows the start of the Pony Express at the western end of the Hannibal and St. Joe Railroad, where the mail started its long journey to California on horseback. There are a lot of implications tied up in that little panel. It was initiated, you remember, to save California for the Union. And did it, as far as that goes. If you turn over in your mind the history of the Pony Express as you look at this panel, you are seeing a mural. The venture ended when the telegraph wires came together and communication time again shortened.

This completes Benton's history of Missouri except for the colonial scene in the panel on the other side of the door. It is the only panel that appears out of its natural setting. I suspect the reason for it is the technical nature of the design. The past is divided from the present by this doorway. However, there is no sharp line of demarcation in any period.

(Baigell): In the panel above the doorway Benton painted Jesse James and his gang holding up a train and a bank. (Their first train robbery occurred on July 21, 1873.)[19] Although engaged in obviously antisocial acts, members of the gang were nevertheless revered as modern Robin Hoods because they often took money from still unregulated and usurious bank and railroad companies. Not surprisingly, Benton...held Jesse James in high regard. Yet the gang's habits were obviously illegal even if socially acceptable, a wry commentary on the story which begins to emerge at the right side of the long wall and in the final narrative sequence.

(**Morrison**): The artist crosses the door at the top with the Legend of the James Boys, and pulls the past and present together with the colonial scene at the bottom. There is plenty of reason to interpret this panel as a part of the social structure. Sometimes it is as hard to recognize forces at work shaping Missouri history today as it is to recall those of the past. However, they are more readily discernable here in paint.

Contemporary History

The rest of the wall is devoted to presenting forces at work today building the Missouri of Tomorrow.

(**Baigell**): Benton despised Big Business practices that developed after the Civil War. To him the robber barons were just that—thieves who stole property, goods, and controls of systems of production which rightfully belonged to the average person. Their uncontrolled rapacity, mis-named rugged individualism, virtually destroyed the America of his dreams. Benton, and such literary figures as Van Wyck Brooks and Lewis Mumford, found the quality of life during the post-Civil War decades to be the least satisfying in the history of the country. He decried the loss of aesthetic sensitivity during those bleak years...During those decades of "crude expansion, of brutal commercial exploitation, of crass parvenuism which grew out of the Reconstruction Period,"everything was calculated for profit.[20]

It follows that the post-Civil War decades fare badly in the Missouri murals. Zinc and lead mines begin to encroach on the land, polluting the atmosphere and the spaces occupied by farmers and artisans.

(**Morrison**): The first character right of the entrance is a farmer pitching small grain—perhaps wheat, barley, rye, or rice. The character is large, indicating the importance of the small-grain crops in Missouri. In the aggregate it is big business.

(**Benton**): On the other side is the big figure of the man with the mule. The man pitching the hay is, of course, not pitching it into the Jesse James picture. He's pitching it into an imaginary barn. He was put there to balance the figure on the other side....Each one of these figures not only represents a human figure but it also represents a volume in a geometric design, and you have to balance these in order to make a picture. A picture is not just like opening a slot on nature; each part has to be arranged so that they fit together and balance one another....Down below, in back of him, is the barn, silos, and a silo operation going on. Before that is the typical country life stuff with the milking of the cow, and the turkeys, and the inside of a farm kitchen where, perhaps, the son has come in and is cleaning up at the table before he's gonna eat that pie that the old lady on the other side of him is making.

(**Morrison**): In the foreground, in front of the dairy industry (portrayed by the man milking the cow) and in front of the small-grain crops, you note the turkey. Mr. Benton could well have painted an old rooster, or a gander, or any other domestic fowl I presume, but he chose to use a turkey gobbler. There is the poultry business. It is big business.[21] So the artist has painted the turkey in the foreground, where it belongs.

Also in this agricultural scene is a group of hogs. Many a wry smile and plenty of jibes are produced from reactions of spectators on viewing those hogs. Yet, withall, they present a social problem that is a very live problem in our state. I have asked hundreds of women who have entered this room—especially if I know they come from the cities—if they use vegetable compound to cook with these days or if they use lard. The verdict has been "vegetable compound." Only once in a while does a city lady tell me that she uses lard most of the time. Then I ask them if they use bacon. With a smile they almost invariably admit that they do. Well—there is the problem that Mr. Benton presents. He is showing us the relationship of lard-meat hogs to bacon-hogs. When I was a lad the farmers raised fine, fat rolly-polly Poland China hogs. Today the market has changed and the farmer is adjusting his produce to meet the demands of the market. Benton shows here a very real and present social problem—one that is being studied every day by those interested in the problems of supply and demand. Again I call attention to the theme, a social history of Missouri. Do you think that it is fun to study history by the mural method?

This scene is different from the one left of the door. Machinery has come into common usage. There is the silo, power machinery, and even a hay-track running out of the comb of that barn. Times have changed. Missouri is no longer altogether an agricultural state; it is now also industrial. A little to the right may be seen the great elevators of the cities. Back of them are flour mills, power houses, and smokestacks. Those smokestacks way back into the smoke as far as you can see are all pouring forth the smoke of industry. That great, black cloud is NOT the cloud of the first World War as some think when they recognize the cloud of the Civil War. It is the peaceful smoke of industry—Benton's way of showing the state is both agricultural and industrial today.

(**Benton**): This mass of smoke represents the coming of the smog to the cities.

(**Morrison**): Of course it balances with the Civil War

197

cloud. As far as that goes everything in the room has a balance. The mule and cow, the stump and turkey, one fence that way and another this way, a bare back over there and one over here, the hunter over in that corner and the same sized figure over here. I have never found an artist who has criticized Benton's mastery of design or his handling of color combinations. They have disagreed on philosophy, on purpose, or on whatever they choose to term the underlying motive of his work, but not on the execution. Art critics have played hob with this work from every angle. But that is to be expected. They make their living criticizing productions of art.

The red building near the top is the upper part of a typical county courthouse. The design fairly accurately fits into the general structure of our old courthouses. The type of architecture is familiar. They do not all look like that, but we do have 114 of them in the state. Here the artist suggests something of the form of state government. Remember that all state governments are not designed from the same pattern.

(Benton): This was a typical Missouri courthouse of the early days and it was the courthouse of my home town, Neosho.

(Morrison): Directly beneath the courthouse is a typical circuit courtroom scene. It is packed full of meaning—so much that you cannot exhaust its content within an hour's study.

(Irvine): Judge Kirby of Springfield is on the bench. Nat Benton, brother of the artist, is the prosecutor before the jury, which is made up of contemporary Missourians. Neither has the time honored cuspidor been overlooked in this modern courtroom scene nor the fact that the aim of some occupants has not been any too accurate.

(Morrison): The jury is a dandy cross-section of the average jury that sits in the circuit court box. You can only

198

see the faces of eleven of its members but what a story those faces tell. I've seen lawyers sit in this room and discuss for half an hour how they would go about persuading various members of the jury to their side of the case. I overheard the remark of one prominent attorney: "Now look at that one; the Almighty, himself, couldn't make that man change his mind." Various professions are indicated. Mental characteristics write themselves on every face. Positions of the body carry tell-tale effects of persuasion. Even financial successes and failures are displayed. I suspect Mr. Benton looked his men over pretty carefully to find the characteristics displayed here.

To some viewers the judge on the bench appears to be asleep. From where I stand it is plainly visible that his big brown eyes are very wide awake. But his attitude is very significant. It is an attitude of very vital concentration. (You never in your life saw a judge go to sleep on the bench anyway. He may close his eyes sometimes, better to shut out extraneous argument or emotional appeal to the jury. But asleep, never.) The judge presents a problem in the courtroom; that of divorcing the fact and the argument of law from that of persuasion. You will find it in every courtroom.

The display of the attorney making his plea to the jury carries many ramifications. Sitting down in this corner of the courtroom you see the sheriff. His attitude is indicated by his missing of the cuspidor beside him. Anyway we have problems of a social nature than can only be worked out in the courtroom. And the scene is interesting in many ways and from different angles.

(Baigell): The judge sleeps. This episode, obviously meant to contrast with the stump scene to the left of the central doorway, indicates that justice in the last quarter of the century was not nearly as vigorous as grass roots democracy earlier in the century. Honest, open debate, and proper consideration of the issues had evidently disappeared. As if to underline the change that has come over America, a miner, clutching a machine gun-like modern drill, menacingly ends the narrative of the long wall.

The Missouri Home

(**Morrison**); The dominating scene on this wall portrays a typical Missouri home. But, unless you catch the significance of the symbolism it doesn't take on much meaning. The reactions that people get are varied indeed. Some say, "Well, that must be down in the Ozarks," or "That is a poor man's home," or "That is not typical of Missouri," etc.

Allow me to digress a bit. When an author writes a history, or any other kind of book for that matter, he is entitled to present his composition from his own and maybe peculiar angle. That is his privilege. Each historian is entitled to develop his subject-matter as he sees fit.[22] This is Benton's history of Missouri. Instead of having it printed in a book he has painted it on the walls of this room. He was commissioned to paint a "Social History of Missouri." That is what he has done, and he has developed the subject-matter is his own way. The muralist must paint in symbols.[23] Those symbols mean different things to different people. That is why we have such a variety of reactions to this mural.

I take the position that in this home scene the artist epitomizes his whole story. Here is theme in a nut shell. Mr. Benton maintains that the combination or fusion of two things is required to build a state: the combination of manual labor and rugged character. So he shows the union of the two in the home. A state isn't just a parcel of land with meets and bounds only, it is made up of homes, homes, homes.

How better could Benton show the strength, stamina and importance of manual labor than in the back of that fine specimen of manhood washing his neck? There isn't a person in this room that would say that that young man spent his days in punching a typewriter, selling ladies' lingerie, or even ringing doorbells selling magazine subscriptions. No, sir. There is manual labor. The state of Missouri is built upon that man's back.

Try to imagine Missouri without manual laborers. Suppose that we take every man in the state who makes his living with his back and ship him out of the state and tell him to stay out. First of all, the farmers would all be gone. Nothing more would ever be raised to eat. We could ship nothing into the state. There would be no railroads in operation. No trucks could move. Automobiles would stop. The highways would grow up in weeds. There would be no gasoline sold. There would be no coal mined and we would go cold. There would not be an electric light in the whole state of Missouri. We couldn't even have kerosene lamps. The city sewers would clog, for there would be no running water in the mains. When our shoes wore out we would go barefooted. And when our clothes all wore out we would all be nudists from necessity. Sometimes I think our citizenry thinks all too little of the importance of work in the building of a commonwealth. Benton puts manual labor right out in front, yet I have had people ask me why he didn't put a shirt on that man or else put him in the bathroom.

In the two old folks the physical is minimized and the rugged character emphasized. There are very good reasons for using elderly characters here. One is that character shows more in the face of an older person than in the face of a younger. Strength of character is painted into every line on these two older people. The more that you study them the more you see of the essence of "quality." And by that word "quality" I do not mean money, or social position, or book-education—I am talking about the essence of manhood and womanhood that it takes to build a state.

Look at "Grandpa" for a little bit. Just look at nothing

but his hand. Does it tell you anything about that man's life? Would you call it the hand of a molly-coddle? Could you imagine it to be the hand of a "slicker"? Is it the hand of a man who wavers in his decisions? Is it the hand of a man that you really would like to know? You bet. Hands tell you a lot about people; they speak louder than words sometimes.

Look at the old gentleman's face. It tells you more. There is nothing but virile manhood in every line of it. Can you find a single line in it that would indicate that he gives up easily? Is there anything to indicate that he is a quitter? Do you see anything to indicate that he is gullible; that he believes all that he reads or all that his neighbors may tell him? Is there anything about his face that would lead you to believe that he is a man you could lead around "by the nose"? I do not believe that you could substantiate any such conclusions. On the other hand I think you will agree with me when I say that there is a man who thinks for himself. There is a man who will listen to evidence and arrive at his own independent judgement. There is a man's man; fearless, courageous, honest, determined. There is portrayed the rugged type of manhood that it takes to build a state.

Now look at "Grandma." Study her features. Study her posture. Study her mental attitude. Study the expression on her face. There is a real woman. The longer you discerningly look at her the more character you see. In that respect she may resemble your own mother-in-law; you know the first time that you met her she may not have made such a fine impression, but the longer that you studied her the more you liked her. And yet I have seen women in this room wearing great big sparklers on their fingers, make fun of those poor, old, gnarled hands of this character here. I'll bet one thing: I'll bet she never got hands like that by playing bridge—nor that kind of face either.

(Irvine): Nor is great-grandfather forgotten, for in a prominent position on the wall we behold his picture with

202

long flowing beard—a very good likeness of former Judge Woodside of Salem, Missouri.

(Morrison): Here in the Missouri Home the artist and historian shows you the union of Manual Labor and Character. But he has not dressed them up in fine clothes. He could have shown hardwood, polished floors, but he wouldn't have changed the fundamental characteristics of the home. He might have shown a bathtub instead of that basin, and all the good it would have done would be to becloud the issues, cover them up. No. You can dress those people up how you will—put fine furs, silks, any kind of flub-dubbery on them—and you will not change the message here presented.

You see, all the way around this room Benton does not show the pretty, soft side of life. Not because it isn't there, for it is. But he has shown the type of people that it takes to build a state. From the time that he shows those four men in the corner where we began, wading, swimming, climbing through the brush pulling that boat up the river that you and I might have a civilization—all the way around the room until he finishes, Mr. Benton keeps hammering on the kind of metal it takes in a people to build a state.

Over in the corner is a miner with his pneumatic drill, emphasizing the great mineral resources of Missouri. The greatest lead mines in the world are in Missouri—between Jefferson City and St. Louis. There is enough lead to supply the whole world with as much as it wants. We are, I believe, eleventh in the world production of zinc. Nearly every county between Jefferson City and the bootheel is filled with iron. Practically every county north of the river is underlaid with coal. There are others, of course, but those four are of vital importance to a state and to a nation.

(Benton): You'll see a tower which represents the mining industries of southwest Missouri and you'll find the shale piles over there. When I was a boy I worked with a surveyors outfit in that lead and zinc district around Joplin and Galena, Missouri....Below there is a modern, relatively modern—of course, it was modern when I painted the mural—modern miner working with his drill in one of the southwest Missouri mines.

(Morrison): Did you ever stop to think what position Missouri would be in if Iowa was another country instead of a state? Illinois another country, Kansas another and so on? With the great mineral resources of our state here would be the "Balkans of America," here would be the ceaseless battlegrounds of the New World. Benton shows us their importance with this miner here and the mining scene clear to the top of the wall.

St. Louis

(Benton): There is a change here. Now, most of the picture up to this panel has been devoted more or less to the rural life of Missouri. But we have two big cities in this state: St. Louis and Kansas City. And this last panel is devoted to our modern city life, or what was modern in...1936, when I painted the pictures.

(Morrison): On the south wall our two major metropolitan centers are emphasized: Kansas City on the right and Saint Louis on the left, not two cities unto themselves alone, but in connection with the contemporary history of Missouri.

(Baigell): On the third wall, the many hints previously noted finally coalesce into an indictment of the economic and political structure of Missouri and, by extension, the entire country. In this section showing urban life, the average person's freedom and individual initiation have completely disappeared. Furthermore, nothing green grows.

(Morrison): The largest breweries in Missouri are in St. Louis. In fact, the largest in the world are there. So Benton shows a striking view of a brewery from top to bottom along the left side of the door.

(Baigell): On the left, workers, no longer self-employed, aid the manufacturing processes of the shoe industry. Of the men who represent the beer industry, one very obviously drinks on the job. He, now, is in the position of abuse similar to that of the Indian in the first panel.

(Morrison): The brewing business, whether we like it personally or not, is a very important business in our state today. From a point of state revenue alone, that would be true. But there are other considerations, too.

A close second is the manufacture of leather goods, especially shoes, as indicated in the scene nearer the corner where the cutter and pressman are busy at work. Every child in the United States who has studied geography knows the importance of St. Louis as a shoe manufacturing center.

(Benton): In the foreground you'll have a typical secretary...who did the typing work and looked as pretty as she could in the office.

(Morrison): Benton has put the stenographer in the foreground, like he did the turkey over there. There is a very definite reason for that, too. You know, when I was a lad it wasn't just quite the thing to do to learn to become a ''secretary.'' (They didn't call them stenographers then.) That was considered a man's job. How about it now? We think that we can't get along without them today. She has earned her place right out in front. She is one of the social forces at work shaping Missouri of Tomorrow.

Now whether you like the way that she is fixed up is altogether personal. Maybe you do not like the way her hair is combed, or the effect of her diet, or the color of her lemonade or whatever is in that tumbler. Whether you like or dislike this young lady here is altogether personal, but the meaning that she presents as a mural fits into the scheme of present-day history.

(**Baigell**): Benton uses women in this entire section as stereotyped sex objects, precipitators of violence or as workers, no less isolated from human contact than the men. They no longer exist in "normal" social situations bound by family ties or family activities.

(**Morrison**): Near the corner, above the pressman with the white cap, is a little "out-away section," [where] women are sewing. There is the manufacturing of women's garments—great factories of them. Above, men are at work sewing. There is the tailoring business.

A little to the left is a yellow billboard reading, "The Veiled Prophet will appear in St. Louis, October" so and so. And there is emphasized that great festival they have in St. Louis every year.

Beyond that the tower of the Union Station with all it implies in the way of traffic, commerce, and transportation.

Kansas City

(**Morrison**): To the right of the door your attention is called to the greatest single industry of Kansas City. The Kansas City Stock Yards are exceeded only by those of Chicago. Livestock, not only from Missouri but from the great western plains states, is shipped to Kansas City markets. It is a packing center.

The artist is *not* calling your attention to the kind of meat that goes through the packing plants. The best meat in the world is handled there. "Kansas City Sirloin Steaks" are advertised in the best hotels and restaurants clear out to the Pacific coast—and that means good steaks.

(**Baigell**): In the stockyard scenes...a radically integrated work force moves with faceless, and presumably joyless, precision, lacking those qualities of affirmation and physical expansiveness seen in similarly large figures in other panels.

(**Morrison**): Every day I see visitors to our capitol walk under the dome on the first floor level and look up. There

206

they admire the beauty of that fine dome. They see thirteen renowned paintings of Frank Brangwyn; some of the finest murals in the world. They will look maybe for three or four minutes and they are through. Not a wheel has turned over in their heads. They will maybe say, ''Well, isn't that pretty?'' and that is all. The murals do not mean a thing. The fact of the matter is that they do present another splendid history of Missouri. Then they come to this room and immediately commence to gesticulate and become vocal. Thomas Hart Benton makes them think something when they step into this room. It may be hard to tell just what they think, but they will think something. The glass retorts at the bottom suggest chemical laboratories, especially in connection with the manufacture of flower and feeds.

(Irvine): The chemical retorts suggest Kansas City as a growing center of that industry.

(Morrison): Farther to the right is a business meeting, with men seated around tables. The "political boss" is indicated with the large character in the chair in the foreground. If it were not for the fact that one man in the group is reading a prepared address you might think this scene was staged in a night club. However, these men, who have just finished dinner and are smoking, are also listening to the paper being read. The proceedings are about over, for there is a floorshow in the background—fifteen or twenty minutes of fun and relaxation before going home. So here our attention is called to the influence of "big business" in Kansas City and Missouri.

(Benton): Now this was one of the controversial things. A lot of people sort of felt that these respectable gentlemen shouldn't be sitting in such proximity to half-naked dancing ladies....But, again, a picture like this has to put in so many things that all I was looking for was to get a general sequence and you can make up your mind about the meaning of these proximities just as you please. I did the best I can.

(**Baigell**): Tom Pendergast, the longtime currupt political boss of Kansas City, presides over a businessman's dinner. Facing him across the tables is a dancer. Political and social curruption is clearly indicated here.

(**Morrison**): The political boss indicated in the foreground is a typical figure. Many people are obsessed with the idea that there is a portrait of Mr. Pendergast. Some have fumed and given vent to uncomplimentary remarks.

If that is a portrait of Mr. Pendergast then these are not murals depicting a social history of Missouri; they cannot be murals and portraits of individuals at the same time. As I mentioned before, most of these characters were posed for by living individuals, but the names of the people have nothing to do with the meaning of the murals. The name of Mr. Pendergast has no more to do with the meaning here than the name of that baby on its mother's lap over there. And the name of the baby has nothing to do with the particular political turmoil that was generated in the period involved.

Here is another illustration. The gentleman that posed milking the cow happens to be one of my bosses, Mr. Austin Houston. He is the Assistant Commissioner of the Permanent Seat of Government. He looks after all of these millions of dollars worth of state buildings around here. If you should go downstairs and ask him if he is at the head of the dairy industry of the state he would tell you, ''No.''

Cross your fingers when you look at this scene of the political boss. Keep names out of it. We have had a political boss or bosses in Missouri from 1821 to 1940. As far as I know, in the reading of history, we have never been without one. The first political boss we ever had was the great-uncle of the man who painted these murals, Thomas Hart Benton. He was boss from 1821 on into the 1850s. His bust stands in the Hall of Fame in Washington, D.C., today representing this state. He was a grand old man, a statesman, a great politician—and the first political boss of Missouri. And we have had one ever since.

Then folks will say, "See, he put the political boss in with the business meeting." That may be true. I do not know. That turkey over there may be in the same lot with the cow, and it may not. I do not know. But he does show the close alliance of business and politics—that is a social problem. If I am not mistaken, ever since Moses descended from Mt. Sinai with his two tablets of stone, business and politics have been closely allied. There is nothing new presented to us here, but Mr. Benton again calls our attention to history as it is still being made.

(Benton): This is not a memorial to Tom Pendergast. He just happened to be, at the time that I was painting this mural, probably the most powerful figure in the state of Missouri and the most dominant figure in Kansas City. In the interest of realism I felt that he should go in the mural and so I put him in there.

(St. Louis Post-Dispatch, December 9, 1936): If the Benton murals are to symbolize our twentieth-century Missouri, the figure, one might say the transfigure, of Pendergast must, in veraciousness, contribute to this pictorial writing on the wall. The man is Missouri in the essentials of daily experience. His influence, penetrating and comprehensive, is unavoidable. He is what the Greeks call *logos*—the word, the law.

(Morrison): Above the business meeting is a white building that looks suspiciously like the Nelson Art Gallery of Kansas City and we have that influence at work in our state.

(Irvine): A teacher with her pupils is entering the building, symbolizing culture and education.

(Baigell): Unemployed workers huddle around a fire built next to Kansas City's Nelson Art Gallery.

(Morrison): Beyond that is the Liberty Memorial tower.

That is Benton's only reference to the World War. That tower was built, you know, for the Missouri boys who were sent across the pond without adequate preparation and are still over there.

Two Small Panels on South Wall

(**Morrison**): The two small panels at the bottom on either side of the door are separated from Kansas City and St. Louis by a border, just like all of the rest of the small panels in the room. On the left is a night club scene that you will find in your own home town if you live in Missouri....As far as I am aware there is only one reason for operating a night club—to entertain people who can pay for it. If you have no money stay away from a night club. Here then are the people who have money. On the other side is the opposite extreme—people who have absolutely nothing. And he shows a poor Negro picking up coal instead of a white man. There are the two extremes of social life: those who have and those who have not. This is a social history of MIssouri, forces at work building a state, and Mr. Benton brings us down to earth with these two panels.

(**Benton**): The small panel is a representation of a depression-ridden time in the cities during the early '30s. Now, I don't know very much of that's left today. But in thosedays along the railroad tracks and in the less fortunate areas of the city, people even had to...gather their fuel along the tracks. This represents that kind of poverty. Once again, lots of people didn't want to have such things represented as occurring in the state of Missouri. But I felt that I had to put it in, and besides I had the kind of contract that said if I could prove the fact then I could put it in the picture, which I used very frequently.

(**Baigell**): Nowhere on this wall do we find a trust in, let alone a hope for, the future. We see workers divorced, both from the products and from the control of their labor. We see a murder scene, a corrupt political boss, scavengers, and institutionalized culture unresponsive to societal needs.

(**Morrison**): This pretty well completes the trip around the room except for these four long, narrow panels on the west side between the windows. Great stalks of corn are shown representing agriculture. Power lines and so forth represent public utilities and business. Two panels of each indicate the close balance between the two today.

(**Baigell**): The landscape is largely bare of vegetation. The corn stalks look parched and drooping, and it is startling to realize that the last image in the entire mural cycle is a cut-down corn stalk.

(**Irvine**): Two transmission towers...may well suggest the extension of the comforts and conveniences of the city to rural areas through the program of rural electrification.[24]

(**Author's note**): The panels between the windows also portray a train, its firebox glowing red. Is it, as Baigell suggests, a symbol of Missouri rushing to the future?

(**Benton** in *An Artist in America*) : For the nomadic urges of our western people, the prime symbol of adventurous life has for years been the railroad train. No doubt before its advent, the Conestoga wagon, the six-horse stage, and the riverboat held a place equally suggestive. With the coming of the automobile, the railroad train is losing its high place, but all during my boyhood it was the prime space cutter and therefore the great symbol of change. Above all other things it had the power to break down the barriers of locality. Its steam pushed promises, shook up the roots of generations, and moved the hearts of men and women with all the confused mixtures of joy and pain that accompany the thought of separation and departure. For all bitten with the urge to pull up stakes and be done with familiar boredoms (and that urge...is deep in the American spirit) the steam train bearing down on a station or roaring out of a curve of

211

the hills, or disappearing over a distant ridge, was a thing replete with suggestive motion.

It is not so long ago that when the passenger train came into a western town everybody who could went down to meet it. As soon as I was able to get loose from my mother's skirts, I followed the boys of Neosho to the railroad station and watched with the yearning loafers of the town the evening passenger roll in. I soon learned that the proper way to receive a train waswith a nonchalant familiarity; that it was "in form" to speak of her as "Number so-and-so," knowingly to inspect the unloading of her mailbags and express packages, and to lay great stress on the number of seconds or minutes she was before or behind time. This is the way we covered our emotions. It occurred to no one, young or old, that our very presence at the station was an indication of impractical romanticism and that our knowing ways with technicalities were swaggering fakes.

(Morrison): I have not pointed out all of the little details of these murals. There is too much on these walls to attempt to grasp all of the meaning in one day. It cannot be done. But I hope at least that you will get a better understanding of Benton's "Social History of Missouri."

(Benton): There are just a few more things I'd like to say. One is most murals are painted with one subject and this mural is different in that it deals with a multiplicity of subjects. And it was a considerable technical problem to get them all in here. Also the case came up and was argued with me and my backers time and again and that was how much we should include of what we would call the "history book history" of Missouri—the great men and so forth. Considerable effort was make, pressure was put upon me to put my great-grandfather25 Thomas H. Benton, in the picture, and later to put General John J. Pershing, in the picture. Well, I didn't want to fill the picture full of Bentons. I had already gotten my brother in there and my nephews, things of that sort. But I didn't see how I could put General Pershing in the picture, or other notable Missourians who had no direct effect on the life of Missouri. Pershing had not lived in the state or had any effect on its life. So my problem with this picture and these various proximities which I was talking about was to get all those things in here in some kind of sequence so that when you look at the picture, you're not just stopped but your eye moves over into another part of the picture. If you will look at this picture from that point of view, you will find that your eye moves very easily from one point to another. Now this is all because of the technical arrangement, with the lines and forms in the mural and that is the real big problem in making a mural is to get it to hang together.

(Irvine): Many competent critics have remarked that had the paintings no other merit save its extraordinary balance of form and color, it would still remain a most wonderful piece of art. Only a visit to the room can give any adequate conception of the superb coloring, the wonderful technique of the artist and his masterful design.

(Benton, in *Kansas City Journal-Post*, December 25, 1936): My work is incomplete as to Missouri's history. I would like to have ten times the wall space I had here. I can think of a lot of things that should be preserved on the walls of this and other public buildings in Missouri. This is just as near complete as I could make it.

(Earle Davis, in the foreword to *An American in Art*): He has painted what he thinks is important about our country, the life and condition of the poorer classes, themines, the steel mills, the industry centers of the nation, the plains, the hillbilly mountain regions, the folksy countryside, the farms and cattle country, the religion of the simple people rather than the rich, the Negro and Indian, in other words, "the people and the land." He depicts everything from folk ballads to universal myths, from Persephone to Susannah,

213

from Huck Finn to Frankie and Johnny. The comparison to Sandburg is inevitable; his subject has been "The People, Yes."

For the nonspecial audience Benton's selection of material has been the beginning of argument. His murals have sometimes attracted aroused attention because he focused on subjects which many viewers would rather ignore or forget. In the Middle West anyone who is old enough to remember must recall the hullabaloo which followed the exhibition of his mural in the Capitol of Missouri at Jefferson City, the placing of Huck Finn and Nigger Jim, Frankie and Johnny, even Boss Pendergast in prominent places on the wall commemorating Missouri's history. What most people claimed to want was a monument, not a challenge, certainly not the living soul of Missouri.

(**Benton** in *An American in Art)*: My original purpose [of painting American history] was to present a people's history in contrast to the conventional histories which generally spotlighted great men, political and military events, and successions of ideas. I wanted to show that the people's behaviors, their action on the opening land, was the primary reality of American life....I would go in my history from the frontiers, where the people controlled operations, to the labor lines of the machine age, where they decidedly did not.

(**Baigell**): What, then, can we say about the Missouri murals? The theme seems to be the social bankruptcy of modern American economic systems. Rather than confront this problem in terms of the needs of modern society, Benton wanted to return to an idealized past....Benton's mural cycle...ended on a pessimistic note, implying that there was little hope for the individual worker in modern society....Benton's work certainly had nationalistic overtones. He wanted to recreate a past, an essentially pre-industrial American past, to which many first-

214

generation Americans had no ties and, with Hitler's Germany as the feared model, one from which they would be excluded and even eliminated. But I think it may be argued that Benton's position was based not necessarily on exclusion, but on fear. He was afraid of a totalitarian takeover by either the left or the right. He did not want to exclude people from his America as much as he wanted to exclude those economic and political systems that owuld prevent his American dream from coming true. In his American dream nobody would exploit anybody else. This could only occur, he said, through a return to Jeffersonian principles.26

(Kansas City Star, December 21, 1936): Many attributes contribute to the satisfaction one feels in looking at the mural. The artist has interpreted his facts with subtlety and force. His humor is eminently good natured. His drawing is sound, his color natural and often intense as the color in this region and climate is apt to be. His characters are convincing. He is above everything human and sympathetic without being sentimental. His viewpoint is that of the artist who sees the pageant of life and is absorbed in his job of setting down the facts as he sees them about the world in which he lives.

(**Thomas Craven**, in *Scribner's* magazine, October 1937): The issues precipitated by the murals are not only of the first importance to art but to all fields where clear thinking is indispensable. Benton, a thorough-going Missourian in many respects, refused to be bound by conventions or acceptable patterns of thinking. He proved himself capable of making accurate and incisive distinctions in a world running rapidly to large-scale confusions of ideas.

(**Vaughan**, 1938): Benton's agitated rhythms and distorted forms, his twisting contours, fluttering outlines and exaggerated poses, each unit knit efficiently into enormous structures that seem to write in broken curves and angles structures that seem to write in broken curves and angles across the walls, are usually superbly organized compositions. But the compositions appear alien, unrelated to his subject matter. In other words, they seem to have little or nothing to do with America. A relationship has, however, been claimed for them. Their champion tells us that they reflect the restlessness and confusion, the violence, the chaos of modern America.

Unfortunately we have no man of the hour in American painting. Benton's worth lies less in his pictures than in the example he has set for other painters: the example that calls them to shun esthetic phantasies and find their strength in life near the soil, the teeming life of industry, the life of cities—in brief, whatever actualities of native life surround them.

(**Benton**): I did the best I could.

Notes

1. Matthew Baigell, with Allen Kaufman, "The Missouri Murals: Another Look at Benton," *Art Journal* (Summer 1977), 314-321. Kaufman was a graduate student in history at Rutgers. Assisting Kaufman in "the basic reading of the murals" was Howard Green, also a graduate student in history at Rutgers.

2. Ibid, 320.

3. Thomas Hart Benton, from catalogue for exhibit, "Thomas Hart Benton: An Artist's Selection, 1908-1974," The Nelson Gallery & Atkins Museum *Bulletin* vol. 5, no. 2 (Kansas City, Missouri).

4. Ralph M. Pearson, "The Artist's Point of View: Thomas Benton Paints Missouri," *Forum* (January-June 1937), 367.

5. Malcolm Vaughan, "Up from Missouri," *The North American Review* (Spring 1938), 87-88.

6. Benton wrote a question mark in the left margin of the page next to this paragraph, indicating some disagreement with Morrison's accounting of the history of the song.

7. Robert S. Gallagher, "Before the Colors Fade: An Artist in America," *American Heritage* (June 1973), 87.

8. Benton underlined the words earlier in this paragraph—"trouble

that we had with the Mormons. Finally we had the Mormon war.''—and the last few words of the paragraph, ''that Missouri has yet to suffer religious intolerance.'' In the margin he wrote, in strong disagreement, ''Rats!''

9. Benton put a question mark in the margin next to this statement.

10. Benton put a question mark next to this part of the paragraph.

11. In the few years leading up to the delivery of this speech, Missourians had seen the indictment and imprisonment of the state insurance superintendent for taking kickbacks, had seen the crumbling of the power of Kansas City political boss Tom Pendergast who ultimately went to prison on tax evasion charges, and had seen a Republican elected governor, only to have the Democratically dominated legislature block his inauguration for six weeks.

12. Benton put two question marks next to this paragraph. In 1945, four years after this speech was made, Missourians adopted a new constitution which is still in effect.

13. Actually, the Champ Clark campaign that featured that song on behalf of him was in 1912.

14. Actually, it was William Clarke Quantrill.

15. Benton has a question mark in the margin next to this statement.

16. General Nathaniel Lyon was commander of the Union forces in the early days of the Civil War in Missouri. He was killed in the battle of Wilson's Creek, south of Springfield, on August 10, 1861, the fortieth anniversary of the day Missouri entered the union. Morrison, in his speech, added an ''s'' to Lyon's name.

17. At the time Benton painted the mural, efforts were starting to protect the state's remaining forest land. Eighty percent of the land was in virgin forest when the first white settlers went to Missouri. By the middle of the nineteenth century, random and intensive commercial cutting of timber was well underway. In 1899 almost 724 million board feet were cut. But by 1931 only 75,000 board feet were cut. The first serious reforestation effort in Missouri began that year when the legislature allowed the federal government to buy land for forests. In 1934 the limit on the amount of land that could be purchased was lifted. Now, more than one-third of Missouri is forests again, and Reynolds, Shannon, and Carter counties are more than 80 percent forest.

18. Benton put a question mark next to the rest of this paragraph.

19. The gang's first train robbery was near Council Bluffs, Iowa. The James gang's first train robbery in Missouri was at Gad's Hill, a small place south of St. Louis on January 31, 1874. Their first bank robbery had been at Liberty, near Kansas City, on February 13, 1866. The engineer of the train was killed in the Iowa robbery (the gang had pulled a rail loose, causing the train to derail), and a college student was shot to death during the holdup in Liberty. Nobody died at Gad's Hill.

20. Baigell was quoting from *An Artist in America*, 29.

21. Another Benton question mark in the margin.

22. Benton underlined the next five sentences in the original typescript.

23. Benton underlined these sentences in Morrison's script.

24. Although the federal law authorizing rural electric cooperatives had been passed earlier, the first mile of line energized in Missouri was in July 1937 in Lewis County, in the northeast part of the state.

25. Benton later corrected himself, "If I said it I didn't mean to say it. I've read that so many times I think it's gotten into my head. Actually he was my great-uncle. I'm a descendent of his brother."

26. In the August 1937 issue of *Common Sense*, Benton defined that attitude as a return to "individualistic agrarianism and to [Jefferson's] notions of free and independent economic units with little or no governmental control."

Appendix 1

In researching a series of lectures for the Missouri Committee for the Humanities in 1983-84, the author and Douglas Wixson from the University of Missouri-Rolla found in the files of the Benton Trust in Kansas City two manuscripts in which Benton discusses the Missouri capitol mural. The manuscripts—one of which was incomplete—are printed here to provide readers with a greater understanding not only of the art but the man who created it. In the first manuscript, apparently written several years after the Missouri mural was completed, the footnotes are Benton's.

The Thirties

The crash of the stock market and the general breakdown of the business and industrial structure in the United States was not reflected in my own life. The growth of interest in my paintings, which began in 1927, continued and sales of these, though at low figures, so improved that Rita and I were able to move into a commodious studio apartment just off Fifth Avenue on thirteenth street. We were able to afford an enlargement of our home on Martha's Vineyard and the building of a studio there. We bought our first automobile, a great lumbering Stutz, from a busted broker friend who was no longer able to keep it going. As the business world went down we went up.

This was also true of some others. Among these were Alvin Johnson and his associates who after years of effort, finally raised enough money to build the new School for Social Research on West 12th St. I have told in other writings[1] about how this led to my first mural and how, with Johnson's encouragement, I made that a "realistic" depiction of our contemporary American life. I have also told about the criticism which the mural received at its completion.

In the preceding account of "the twenties" I outlined the growth of the muralistic history of the United States which was shown at the annual Architectural League exhibitions. I do not believe, however, that I gave enough emphasis to the changes which began to occur in my attitudes toward the History as during my travels about the country I accumulated more and more drawings of its contemporary life. The History as an evolutionary progression would eventually lead to that life but I began to be somewhat impatient to get there. It was this which occasioned the muralistic painting of the "Bootleggers" in 1927; my first attempt to handle a contemporary scene on a large scale. After completion of this painting, interest in the History, which had not yet reached the Revolution, began to fade. There was also the looming problem of what to do with it, how to take care of its growing stack of large pictures.

When the commission for the New School mural was tendered to me in 1929, I was psychologically ready to put its subject matter in the present, to forget past history, and make it a record of the American life that I had myself directly experienced.

Although I had had two gallery exhibitions of easel paintings, drawings and water colors devoted to the contemporary American scene, one in 1926 and one in 1928,[2] which should have prepared the art world for the Americanist content of the mural, they had not done so, or at least had not done so sufficiently to acclimate either artists or critics to its large scale rendition. The formalistic methods of my painting, whether approved or not, were well known at this time but their application at the New School to the common facts of American life, giving a muralistic impact to what was traditionally regarded as "genre" subject matter, aroused highly negative reactions even among people who had heretofore looked with favor on my experiments.

There is no need to review here the criticism which followed the mural's presentation to the public.[3] But something should be said about the personal situations that developed. A number of friends, artists, writers and Marxist leaning intellectuals who had looked with favor on my history paintings, both for their "abstract" form and their symbolism reacted with contempt to what they called the "vulgarity" and triviality of the New School mural. The "radical" friends were outspoken, too outspoken, about its lack of "social direction," of "social meaning." As a result of all of this there began to be casualties among my friendships.

The first to go was "Huby" (Leo Huberman)[4] who although he posed for one of the figures in the mural promptly sided with the radical Marxist groups when they declared it a reactionary exercise in "chauvinism." The second, and more surprising, was "Mike" Robinson (Boardman) who had heretofore been one of my strongest supporters. It was through Robinson's influence it will be remembered that I had obtained my teaching position at the Art Students League and it was he also who made the connections which led to the exhibition of my earlier mural experiments at the Architectural League.

Another was Ralph Pierson. Pierson, as much as anyone, was responsible for the commission to do the New School Mural.[5] He had brought Alvin Johnson's attention to my work and had persuaded him that if a mural space was to be given to the Mexican Orosco, one should also be given me, "the one American muralist," as he put it. Nevertheless when the mural was finished he followed the "commie" crowd's judgments about its subject matter and the Stieglitz group's sneers at its aesthetic properties. When, after I had done the next mural for the Whitney Library in '32 and the Indiana mural in '33, the controversies about these began giving me prominence in the press, other friends shifted their attitudes, not only toward my work but toward me personally. Lewis Mumford, who had been a companion not only in New York but at Martha's Vineyard, was one of these. Lewis had supported my Architectural League experiments and was one of the critics I counted on to help persuade the architects to accept my ideas about breaking the planes of their walls with three dimensional compositions. However Lewis, like the Marxist and Stieglitz groups, took the view that my "Americanism" was leading me astray. Another friend who changed was E.E. Cummings.

Cummings, and his wife Ann, were much liked by Rita and myself. They visited with us frequently and we with them. Cummings was a most entertaining commentator on the literary and artistic world of Greenwich Village. His witty cuts at its characters were always good for a laugh. But now, for reasons that I never fathomed, he began directing such cuts toward me. I became "the great American Artist," "the American Genius," "the Saviour of American Painting," so often that I ceased seeing him. Did Cummings regard himself as a rival painter? Or did he just begin to resent the public attention I was getting?

Was this public attention the real reason for some of the other shifts of attitude on the part of my friends and were the aesthetic and political reasons they advanced mere rationalizations of a very commonplace form of jealousy?

Tom Craven, the only writer who stuck by me during these days claimed that this was so. He almost persuaded me to believe it and would have surely succeeded were it not for the fact that I knew all my artist friends, at least, were too profoundly convinced of the superiority of their own "geniuses" over mine to make such a jealousy plausible. For the writer friends, where no competitive situation existed, there was possibly some resentment that a mere painter should be receiving the publicity which, because of the superior importance of writing to painting, was due to them. Our English traditions and specifically those affected by Puritanism and similar biblical cults have always cast the

222

role of the visual image maker well below that of the verbal one.[6] It is perhaps because of this that Anglo-Saxon-American visual art has never received the public support given it in Latin countries. There has often been a considerable condescension on the part of English writers when they discussed the visual arts. Our political and practical worlds, both English and American, have reflected this.

It is possible that a jealousy of Tom Craven's success was deflected to me by the writers of my circle. Craven's espousal of my cause, and later that of all the Regionalists, his sometimes aspersive treatment of the American disciples of Parisian modernism, brought him a lot of attention. His articles were widely read and created enemies right and left. It would be quite natural that those resenting his success should have carried part of that over to me, so frequently the subject of his eulogies. I am convinced something of this sort occurred with Lewis Mumford and it may have occurred with Cummings. Both disliked Craven heartily.

Among the painters and critics it is unquestionable that Craven's espousal of my Americanist view point created prejudices against it in 1930-31, just as later his espousal of its "Regionalist" outlook made that suspect. Craven never minced words and often in the interests of strong statement would go clear overboard. He hated the language and the pretensions of all our self-styled aesthetes and let that be clearly known. The effect of this was that many of these assumed that my own art had no aesthetic but was merely crude illustration—crude and "chauvinistic." Even such a critic as Forbes Watson, who surely knew better, finally adopted that viewpoint.

Whatever the causes, I lost contact with a lot of old associates after the New School and Whitney Museum murals. This resulted in the creation of new intimacies with my students, or with those among them who remained loyal

223

to me after the critics began multiplying my deficiencies. From 1932 until I left New York in 1935, it was these younger artists who made up the core of the Benton social circle. I had, it is true, already experimented very happily with a young companion when I toured the South and West with Bill Hayden in 1928.[7] But it was not until the thirties that such associations became habitual. Looking back on this change, this shift toward men ten, twelve, fifteen years younger than myself, I regard it as one of the most fortunate happenings of my life. Not only did it compensate for the friendships I lost but set a pattern for the future which would enable me to keep active and maintain a youthful outlook late in life.

When I moved to Kansas City I continued to seek out younger people, and as the years went by these became, relative to my own age, younger and younger so that when most men retire to a sedentary life I was still adventuring in the mountains, and on the rivers and seas, with the young feeling quite as vigorous in spirit as those I adventured with.

Although the two New York murals were controversial and unacceptable to many they so established my position as a muralist that it was easy to secure the commission to paint the mural for the Indiana Exhibit at the Chicago World's Fair in 1933. This commission came to me because of a situation which had developed in the State between rival groups of artists and planners. It had been determined some three years before that a mural which would represent the cultural and economic development of Indiana would be preferable to the usual state exhibits of commercial enterprise and of agricultural and other resource items. The State had some pride in its "cultural" life which was shared by its legislators and there was little disagreement about how to proceed with it. There were a number of artists resident in the State, some known to the Eastern Academy exhibitions, but none had had any experience with mural

224

designing. The State's historians and various local commissions and these artists got themselves into such a contradictory mess of plans that they could not extricate themselves. When, seven months before the Chicago Fair was to open, no progress on the mural project had been made the legislature put control of it into the hands of Richard Lieber [Von Lieber] who, a celebrated conservationist of the Theodore Roosevelt-Gifford Pinchot persuasion, had been rehabilitating Indiana's State Parks. Lieber, a cultivated, energetic Indiana old-style German took dictatorial action. Convinced after a few interviews with the Indiana planners and artists that they had nothing feasible to offer, or the technical competence to implement it if they did, Lieber called for advice on Tom Hibben, then acting as State architect for his park improvements.

I had met Tom a number of years before at his brother Paxton Hibben's apartment in New York. Paxton was at the time one of the better known writers and poets. Tom had followed my mural experiments exhibited at the Architectural League during the twenties and had been one of the few architects who looked with wholehearted favor on them. So when Lieber asked him if he thought there was an artist in the country who could plan and execute a proper mural in six months, Tom named me and was sent to New York to interview me.

When he outlined the Indiana project I was appalled by its size and more still by the limited time given to handle it. However, when he offered ten thousand dollars for the work I promptly accepted it.

It must be remembered here that I had painted the New School mural for expenses and the Whitney Museum for very little more.[8] Tom's offer of real money for mural work was the first I had received. Also we were still deep in the depression and ten thousand dollars looked very big in my eyes.

I went promptly out to Indianapolis to begin research on my subject. It was the middle of December and the mural, two hundred feet long and twelve feet high, had to be ready for installation at Chicago by June 3rd. The moment I arrived in the city I ran into a storm of protest.

The New York controversies about my two murals there were known to Indiana artists and their protagonists. As soon as the Press announced that the commission to execute the World's Fair mural for Indiana had been awarded to me, photographs of these New York murals were obtained and circulated among the various commissioners. Richard Lieber had succeeded and among members of the Indiana legislature, accompanied by the question, "Do you want this artist, already judged incompetent by New York to represent our State in the World's Fair?" However, either through Lieber's persuasions, backed by Tom Hibben's known architectural competence, or simply because the legislators were indifferent to my supposed aesthetic deficiencies the contract between me and the State was approved. Then the cabal against me took another tack and this time in a direction that could have been made embarrassing had it been energetically pursued.

Though the designation "Regionalist" had not yet been applied to my work it had nevertheless taken on some of the philosophy which later characterized that movement. My own defense of it and those of others, who like Tom Craven joined me, involved certain premises which were now brought into play in Indiana. These premises stated that Art was improper primarily as a cultured expression, the expression of a certain kind of life and civilization and that it took its significance through the representation of these. It followed, naturally, that those who lived that life and participated directly in its culture would be most likely to provide the truest and most adequate representations of these. Therefore the state of Indiana was denying itself and

226

its own midwestern culture when it hired a "foreign" New York to do what Indiana artists, by the "foreigner's" own arguments, could do better. This localist problem was actually discussed in my presence by a legislative committee, though somewhat humorously. It was quickly solved, when Lieber presented my family background. As a native Missourian, the son of a Missouri congressman and U.S. District Attorney General, and grand-nephew of the great Missouri Senator Thomas H. Benton, it was decided that I was a good enough midwesterner for the State of Indiana to hire. My credentials as a midwestern artist were thus established for the first time. They led a couple of years later to my mural in the State Capitol in Missouri and my permanent return to the Midwest.

Research for the subject matter of the Indiana mural was by no means confined to books. One of the Park department employees was assigned to drive me over the State, provide introductions and help me get Indiana characters to pose. Even though it was winter and often very cold and windy the time spent at this gave me a good "feel" of the State and its people. My driver knew his way about and how to best forward my interests. Coming into a small town or city he would look up the Mayor and any others in the town who might have information to give. Once he explained my purposes we got the most complete cooperation. Indiana is a great State for historical hoarding and I was able to find all kinds of old implements and costumes of all periods of the State's history. At night we would visit the pool halls, bowling alleys and often on Wednesday night the churches of the places we visited. All of this revived my small town Missouri memories and before my researches were half done I found myself psychologically attuned to my midwestern task.

I have told in *An Artist in America* how I got my Indiana work completed but did not much explore the effects on my social attitudes which occurred during the process. The Indiana environment, as I said above, revived memories of a similar one in the Missouri country of my youth but it did more. The ease with which I adjusted to the people it thrust upon me very quickly gave me the feeling, not only that I was one of them, but that there had never been any break in my being so. I began to feel as if the people at the New York art world, with whom I had so long sojourned and whom I had so lately left, were a sort of dream memory and that there had been no real break in continuity between the midwest of my youth and the one I was now experiencing.

Almost from the moment of my arrival in Indianapolis, I was thrown in intimate contact with members of the State Legislature, not in formal meetings at the State House, but in convivial hotel room gatherings which I think we called the "children's hour." After Richard Lieber had revealed the ties of my family to midwestern politics and my relation to Senator Benton a considerable curiosity was aroused about me among the Democratic politicians who had, with the Roosevelt landslide, taken possession of usually Republican Indiana. Uninvolved as I was with studies of Indiana history and in direct observations of the State's prevailing social conditions (preparatory to my mural work) I was able to talk with these new acquaintances with some understanding. This created a will to understand me and the way I was envisaging the mural project and contributed greatly to ending all effective opposition to it. So well did I get along with those Indiana Democrats that they even supported me against Richard Lieber when differences arose between us on the propriety of representing the Ku Klux Klan as a factor in Indiana history in the mural.

It is a widely accepted belief, forwarded by the intellectualist magazines and often by editorial comment in big city newspapers, that the country politician is an ignorant, prejudiced and venal promoter of narrow interests,

228

more often than not his own. There are, of course, such men in every state legislature, but the men with whom I drank "Brown County" whiskey at the "children's hour" gatherings in Indianapolis hotel rooms were mostly pretty well educated, knowledgeable in history, not only local but national and sometimes universal, and were able to weigh current social questions with a minimum of prejudice. The conversations I had with them led me to conclude there was much more narrowness of vision among my intellectualist acquaintances in New York.

In spite of the violent opposition expressed by the Marxist groups in the east to my conceptions of muralistic history a few people in Indianapolis, following one of the disgruntled artists whose ambitions had been thwarted when Lieber put the Indiana mural in my hands, began circulating a story about my communist affiliations. It was alleged that though I might try to hide it, I always had been and was still a fellow traveler with the Communists. At this time when even Franklin Roosevelt represented an extreme radicalism to many people the charge of favoring Communists could have disastrous effects on those in whose hands the power to allocate public money was invested—on those, in particular who were presently spending Indiana's money on me. The charge never reached any legislative committees that I know of, but it put a scare into Richard Lieber who, a Republican hangover in the new Democratic power circles, felt highly sensitive to it. As a Republican liberal (of the Theodore Roosevelt-Gifford Pinchot variety) he knew there were plenty of Democrats in Indiana who might regard him as too "liberal." He had already had enough trouble with his conservationist projects in the State Parks to create enemies among these as well as among members of his own Republican party.

Anyhow, and at the urging of one of Lieber's friends, the question of my Communism was agitated in the "children's hour" gatherings with members of the legislature. It was here I learned how open-minded these supposedly narrow minded politicos could be.

I made no effort to conceal the fact that Marxist economics and political theories had interested me from 1915 to about 1930 and openly told of my association with Bob Minor and other Communists and how in the early twenties I had conspired with Bob to provide secret meeting places for the persecuted members of the commie party, one of which included my own apartment in New York. With Tom Hibben's help I explained the widespread doubts about the efficacy of the capitalist system and the possibility of sustaining it which had grown up among young people during and after the war [World War I] and how these doubts were aggravated by the collapse of twenty-nine and the depression following. All this was perfectly understood and, if not sympathized with, was accepted without any of the violent adverse judgments that the mythology of country political prejudices would have predicted. The explanation of how I had been moved away from my belief in the present applicability of the communist system to the American situation by my travels about the country during the twenties was also understood and accepted. When I also explained that the very neatness and all-inclusiveness of Marxism, its centering of all human life about one motivation, became too much of an intellectual artifice for my American mind, I touched a point with which all my interlocutors heartily agreed.

The dialogues covering this subject did not occur at one sitting nor were they sustained without the entrance of other topics but they were bruited around and invitations to our gatherings were much sought after at the State House. This made them quite costly because Tom Hibben and I were supplying the yet illicit whiskey, so in the end, using the pressures of my work as an excuse, we had to ease them off.

But they got me off the communist hook for good. The allegations never reached the newspapers even though reporters often attended our gatherings.

This was the first time I had ever discussed political theory, or philosophized about its meanings, with men in whose hands enough actual political power rested to cause me difficulties. The discussions at Barn House during the twenties[9] were purely intellectual. There were no consequences possible. But here there was always a slight smell of danger. It was not that I had any real fear that my revelations would jeopardize my job. I knew that these Democratic country lawyers, which most of the legislators were, understood that we were playing with ideas and that an artist like myself could not possibly implement any of them in terms of political action, even had I such intentions. The danger, if there was any, lay in the possibility that some of the passionately anti-Roosevelt factions might use a mere willingness to discuss communist and socialist theories as a weapon, not against me, but against those members of the legislature who gave me their friendship. People of the business community in large numbers and some of their supporters in the Press were already beginning to regard Roosevelt's election as a move toward socialism and were quite jittery enough about this to see a convivial talk fest as a conspiracy. However, as indicated above, nothing of the sort happened. What did happen, also before noted, was the growth in me of a sense of psychological attunement to midwestern attitudes and a feeling that all the years I had spent in great cities in the pursuit of art had not greatly changed my basic small-town midwesternism.

As early as 1918, when during my term in the Navy I had been thrust among southern and western young people, I discovered much the same feelings though they were not then reinforced by any exploration of ideas. Again in my travels about the back country in the twenties time and again such feelings came up but I never stayed long enough in one place for them to crystalize as they did during the "children's hour" sessions in Indianapolis during the early winter of 1933.

It is possible that the political climate of the time where our whole system was everywhere under question, made my reintegration with the midwestern mind much easier than it might have been earlier—or even a little later. Ideas questioning the nature of our culture, though they might put a scare into wealthy people, had massive support in the dissatisfactions of farmers, workers and small businessmen and their political representatives all over the Midwest. This created an atmosphere where a new willingness to experiment politically put such novelty as my own ideas might have in the natural order of things. I had no difficulty whatever in justifying them with the politicians who had control of Indiana. As it turned out I had more objections to overcome with the man who had hired me, Richard Lieber, than with any of these. Lieber was what we called a man of "culture" in the old-fashioned sense. He was highly educated and liberal minded toward artistic experiment but possessed of a strong sense of social propriety. He had readily agreed when I suggested that our mural represent the culture of Indiana from the pre-historic moundbuilders to the present, but he had a different conception of culture from what I had in mind. Where I saw it was a total "life of the people," he saw it as a chain of high achievements. He wanted the mural to picture a succession of these as they arrived in Indiana history. Otherwise he wanted the conventional State House or Public Library mural. However, his liberalism, pushed by Tom Hibben, prevailed over his conventionalism, and he finally consented to put the whole mural project, subject matter as well as style, into my hands. After that he made only one sustained protest which was about the inclusion of Indiana's Ku Klux Klan episode.

I outmaneuvered him on that by getting the support of our "children's hour" Democrats who agreed with me that it should be shown. As Democrats they took some pleasure pointing out that it was an episode for which Lieber's Republican party was responsible.[10]

The dickering, the exchanges of ideas, the explanations of my artistic intentions were made with men for whom aesthetic propositions were almost unknown. Even Lieber was not familiar with their modern forms. He rested, as his Teutonic education and Junker background dictated, with philosophic generalities of the grand, the sublime, the typical and the vulgar, the latter represented by the very type of mural "genre" I advocated. So it was necessary to use a language that was plain, direct, and devoid of any of the fancy specialisms of Art in order to put over and keep control of my mural project. I learned to do this very quickly and could even make clear why I put so much valuable time into making a clay model of the mural when Lieber and his advisors thought I should get on with its painting. Translating the reasons for this purely formal exercise into acceptable common sense language was a task. But I managed it and in the process found my own thinking clarified. I learned the lessons here that were later to help me come through the political atmosphere of the Missouri State Capitol: how to advance artistic reasons so that they appeared commonly American and how to make aesthetic necessities seem the outgrowth of practical ones. The Indiana mural provided a political training ground for the future.

When I completed the mural, and after a six week sojourn in Martha's Vineyard returned to New York, I was like an empty sack. I had my teaching position at the Art Students League and the renewal of my contacts it provided with the young, but the stimulation I had received in Indiana from dealing with actual, political power was absent and

233

regretted. To recapture some of the essence of this I visited one of the Tammany Clubs in our Greenwich Village neighborhood, hoping I might renew touch with an area of real political action in New York. The repudiation of my efforts was so immediate and so contemptuous that I made an instant retreat into the Art World. These small time, poker playing, dice throwing Ghetto politicos were just like those who surrounded Benny the Alderman back in the early twenties.[11] They thought I was looking for a soft spot in the W.P.A. or something similar and subjected me to the most humiliating treatment I had ever had. Comparing them with the small town politicians and lawyers of Indiana I decided then and there where my America was.

As my connections with Leo Huberman and the Marxist-intellectualist fellow traveler crowd had already been severed, and as my brother teachers at the Art Students League had formed a sort of cabal against me,[12] I was in a pretty isolated position. I was also without creative ideas. The three big murals I had undertaken had cleaned me out.

At this time, late September 1933, I received a note from the composer Carl Ruggles suggesting a visit to his place in Arlington, Vermont, and saying that the autumn foliage was beginning to be right. I had known Carl since the early twenties when Edgar Varese had organized the International Composers Guild and he was one of my favorite masters of "cussing" as well as a most interesting musician. I also thought that a walk through the autumnal hills of New England might recharge my empty spirits. So I went to see Carl. I got recharged all right but it was not the scenery that did it but Carl himself. Not more than an hour after I arrived, while he was banging out Wagnerian chords on the piano, I started making drawings of him. Finally I hit one that fired me up, and my creativity was restimulated. After some tramping about the country I returned to New York and started composing the "Suntreader," a portrait of Carl at his piano. I have always thought this to be one of the best portrait compositions I ever made, and many agreed this was so when I first exhibited it in New York in the spring of '34.

Shortly after I finished the portrait of Carl, I was approached by Dr. and Mrs. (Audrey) McMahon with an interesting proposition. Dr. McMahon, well known at the time, was head of certain art and aesthetic studies at Columbia University, and Mrs. McMahon, a very forceful lady, was under Harry Hopkins, furthering national extension of the art projects of the W.P.A., then beginning to be fully operative in New York City. She was having difficulties, it appeared, with state politicians all over the Middle West who looked upon such projects with vast suspicion.

It was proposed that I, now pretty well known nationally because of the squabbles over my murals, and known also as an artist who was ''really'' American, should try to open the minds of the midwestern people to the value of her art promotions by a series of lectures over the country. My known attitudes might offset the belief, aroused in many places by the vociferousness of New York's young communist artists, that art had become a disloyal enterprise. I was not to talk specifically about the W.P.A. projects, or engage in controversies about them, but to try to encourage public interest in American art in general. Reports of the way I had handled myself with the State legislators and the Press in Indiana had reached the McMahons and they were convinced I was the best choice among New York artists for such a venture.

Still somewhat restless and *desoeuvre* [''idle''] after my murals and remembering how much enjoyment I had had with the ''children's hour'' discussions in Indianapolis, I acceded to the McMahon's proposal. Getting a six weeks leave of absence from my Art Students League classes, now well reinstituted, I set out on my tour, following a schedule

235

set up by Mrs. McMahon. This took me from Pittsburgh over the Mississippi valley and westward to Lubbock, Texas. Although I had a prepared talk, I found the questions which followed it generated so much more audience interest that I soon abandoned it and depended almost wholly on the questions to keep things moving. I found these generally interesting but so inclined to run in the same patterns that after a few lectures I could predict them. This was especially true at universities and colleges where I soon learned to anticipate almost every query thrown at me. I could tell instantly what were the directions taken by the professors in their teaching, what modern schools and theories they were attached to and what their attitudes toward the environmentalist art I professed was likely to be. I soon realized that this latter was more suspected by the teachers than by the students.

All in all, the tour was a success. It resulted in two momentous meetings, one with Grant Wood at the University of Iowa, which set up a long friendship and another with some politicians at Jefferson City, Missouri, which led to the commission for the Missouri State Capitol mural and to my permanent return to the Midwest.[13]

A few days after I returned to New York I was approached by Forbes Watson, Ed Rowan and Ned Bruce with a new mural proposition. In addition to Harry Hopkins' W.P.A. Art projects, another had been set up under the Treasury Department. This was not a relief project like the W.P.A., but one in which mural commissions were to be given out for various public buildings by a Treasury committee headed by Watson, Rowan, and Bruce. The commissions were to be alloted not according to the depression needs of the artists selected but because of their supposed competency for mural work. I was the first artist considered for the project.

It was suggested that because of the susceptibility of

236

public murals to political criticism, and, because of the delicate position of the selecting committee in the political atmosphere of Washington where the murals were to be placed, that I be as conservative as possible in the handling of subject matter. It was also suggested that any statements I made to writers of the press about the mural should be screened by the committee. Public controversy about my mural might jeopardize the whole Treasury project, I was told, and every precaution must be taken to avoid that. I was also required to submit my designs to the committee for approval and make such changes in them as it deemed necessary.

The idea of working under supervision and a gag rule did not appeal to me, but after a few days of doubt the honor of having a governmental commission won me over and I took on the mural. It was for the new Postal Department Building in Washington and had for its subject ''Postal Transportation.'' I soon found this theme to be unrewarding, difficult in terms of interesting imagery, especially in the handling of its modern aspects, but I managed to come up with designs which met the approval of the building's architects.

While I was working on this mural project, I was asked by the Director of the Art Students League to repeat one of my midwestern lectures for the League's student body. When I agreed to this and it became known, so large a number of people asked to attend that the talk had to be transferred from the League's quarters to Vanderbilt Hall in a nearby building on 57th Street.

A considerable amount of publicity about my Indiana work had reached New York and this, coupled with that about my two earlier murals, had me now highly spotlighted in the city's eye. Because of this the audience I faced was only partially composed of art students. Besides people from the general lay public the John Reed Club sent a whole battalion of Communists and fellow travelers and I caught sight of some well-known left-wing lecture baiters who had caused me trouble before. I guessed from the start that I would have no tame audience. This was promptly corroborated. I had hardly begun with a few sentences about what I took to be the relations of the country's art to its going culture, a simple paraphrase of Taine, before four young men, led by a former member of one of my classes, marched up the steps to the stage and demanded to be seated there. When I asked why, they said, "This is a Forum. We have the same right to be heard as you." I told them I had not been asked to debate anything in a Forum but only to describe an American view of art to the League's student body and explain some of the motivations of that. I said this loudly, so the audience could hear and asked its members whether they wanted to do what I had been invited to do or turn the stage over to the young men to conduct a Forum. I got a solid applauding hand, as I expected, but it had no effect on the would-be Forumists who refused to budge. They stood, grim and sure in their young self-righteousness, and stared at me. I did not know what to do. Finally Cliff, the Art Students League maintenance man, walked up with a couple of burly janitors and nudged the interlopers off the stage. As they passed by me to the steps, my former student leaned toward me. "I always knew you were a dirty anti-Semite Benton," he said.

This remark, without rhyme or reason, crude, deliberately offensive, knocked me off balance with anger. When I turned to the audience, I had nothing to say. I could think only of the young man and the bitterness of his face as he cast his slur. "What have I done to the bastard?" I thought. Three or four years before, he, with two young Jewish girls, had registered for my class at the League. They sat together aloof from the other students, the girls holding the boy in obvious adoration. On an oversize drawing pad he would trace spindly lines with different colored pencils paying

238

little or no attention to the model in front of him. Once a line was made he contemplated it, pondered it before he made another. The girls imitated him.

I generally attended my League class twice a week to look over the students' work, but I never made criticisms or suggestions unless I was asked to do so. When a student was having anatomical problems in his drawing he would call me over and we would study the model together. If he thought he was doing all right I left him alone. As the new student and his girl friends seemed satisfied with themselves I paid no attention to them. Finally about the end of their second week in class the young man addressed me, "You haven't said anything about my work." "How can I?" I asked him, "You're not studying the model. I can't see any way to help you." "I didn't ask for help," he said, "It's just that, as a teacher, you should notice me." "I've already done that," I told him. Some of the students who overheard this exchange snickered. At this the young man took his pad off the easel, put his box of colored pencils in his pocket, and, followed by his girl friends, walked out of the class. I guess they were transferred to another one because they did not come back. This was the only personal contact I ever had with the young fellow, though I saw him later at the John Reed Club when, after the completion of the Whitney Library Mural, I had undertaken a talk there.

With the stage cleared I managed to pull myself together and re-started my lecture. As I led into the reasons behind my choice of Americanist subject matter an outburst of boos and footstomping occurred and a chant began, "We want to be heard. We demand to be heard." I knew from experience that this kind of behavior was to be expected from the John Reed Club boys and other "fellow traveling" groups about New York when at their own meetings they did not like the ideas of a speaker, but I was surprised to find it exhibited in so mixed an audience as the one now before us. Trying a humorous approach to the situation I yelled out: "Well, you're being heard all right. It's like the zoo at feed time in here. What is it you want us to hear besides your howling and stomping?" A fellow right below the stage, one of the habitual lecture baiters I'd noticed, rose up, stretched out a clenched fist and shouted, "They want these people to know there is a different way for American art than the Fascist one you stand for." With this there was sustained cheering and clapping from the "commie" crowd while people from other groups in the audience yelled, "Shut up." "Keep quiet."

The Fascist accusation angered me again and I let fly some pretty intemperate remarks about the ignorance of America, and American meanings that prevailed in the artistic and intellectual "ghettoes" of New York. I don't remember what I said because it was said in anger but I learned later from people sympathetic to me that it was pretty rough.

This outburst of recriminatory yelling across the heads of the audience climaxed the disorderly trend of the meeting. My opponents, satisfied apparently with having my Fascism publicly declared, ceased their outcries and I myself calmed down. But the lecture I had prepared was sidetracked. I couldn't pick it up. However calling for questions I managed an improvised half hour or so which ended with applause enough to indicate I had the sympathy of the better part of the audience.

This was my last attempt at a public lecture in New York. But the fellow travelers were not through with me. Some time later a delegation from the John Reed Club asked me to come there and answer more questions for a paper they were publishing. The group was very polite and seemed so genuinely disposed to explore my views seriously that I told them if they would write their questions I would write answers to them. This they agreed to. When, however, a typewritten transcript of the questions and my answers to them, plus answers to my answers, was shown me I discovered so much editing, and consequent distorting, of my views that I refused to agree to publication. I knew that I had been caught in a trap where the last word would always rest with people who wanted to damage me, but I thought I might extricate myself if I were allowed to revise my original answers and elaborate on them. The John Reed Club boys went along with this and said further they would publish these revisions without editing. In this way I figured that though they would still have all the advantages I could make a good enough showing to clarify my position with unbiased readers. One thing which was not told me was that the artist Stuart Davis was the editor-in-chief of the proposed publication. Had I known this I would have had second thoughts about having anything to do with it. Stuart had been a loud and vindictive critic of all my efforts since the Forum Exhibition of 1916. He had joined a small group of artists who then took particular exception to the inclusion of my work in that showing but, unlike the others, he had remained bitter after the exhibition had dropped into history. People often asked me what Stuart had against me. I always answered that I didn't know. This was untrue because I did know. Only I was ashamed to recall it because it involved a piece of very stupid behaviour on my own part.

In the summer of 1912 when, after three years in Paris, I was making my first efforts to find a footing in New York, I was much in the company of Sam Halpert who had also recently returned from a long sojourn in Paris.[14] I had a small studio adjoining that of Sam's in the Lincoln Square Arcade at 65th Street and Broadway and we visited each other frequently to reminisce about Paris and its art world, which we still greatly missed. Paris had the effect in those days of inducing a sort of snobbery in people who had had the privilege to study there and both Sam and I felt ourselves superior to artists who had not had the experience. One day coming into Sam's studio I found the floor covered with drawings and above them a young and enthusiastic artist showing them off. In a bored sort of way Sam introduced him as Stuart Davis. The young man, apparently twenty or twenty-one years old, was very full of himself, proud of his abilities, and very aggressive about his drawings which were rough, Robert Henri-like improvisations in charcoal. When he began insistently calling my attention to their qualities, my sense of Parisian superiority prompted me to suggest that he was a little presumptuous in pushing himself before a couple of Parisian veterans. I said he should "go to Paris and try to learn something." I regretted this remark the moment I caught its effect on Stuart's face and felt ashamed of its snobbery but it was too late. Stuart with his strong self-pride would never forget it.

The John Reed Club group, like other groups with Marxist leanings, were advocates of a form of art which had come to be called "Social Realism." As I also advocated a sort of social realism for my own art, I thought it possible an exchange between us might forward an understanding. I thought I could make it clear that what separated us was not our basic attitudes toward the depression-ridden people of America, or even the morality of the Capitalist system, but only a theory about what should be done to improve the situations of these. I thought an exploration of our definitions of realism might show that I was socially more realistic than they, at least in regard to American society. Surely a reasonably conducted dialogue between us would dissipate their belief in my Fascism and put the controversies about what my art represented on a more intelligent basis than they presently were.

I have explained before[15] how my travels about the country made me skeptical about the application of the Marxian world scheme to our American society and how when I expressed my doubts I came to be regarded by a number of my friends as a reactionary, even, among some, as a sort of traitor. Let me elaborate further on this .

My first acquaintance with Marxist doctrine came about when in the winter of 1914-15 I met John Weischal and became involved in his dreams of a "People's Art Guild." The majority of those interested in this project for redirecting art toward a greater concern with the lives and aspirations of the "working class" were idealistic young Jews coming mostly from families recently immigrated to America and belonging to those social groups later described by Mike Gold in his "Jews Without Money." Life in the ghettos of New York had not provided these groups with what the myths of "Golden America" promised, and those who had not come over with revolutionary doctrines soon adopted them. So the young people who interested themselves in John Weischel's ideas, either as artists or as intellectuals, were conditioned by their backgrounds toward "radical" changes in our social order. My own views, based on their political aspects on the midwestern populism of the nineties and affected by Hippolyte Taine's writings on the social motivations of art, were not too opposed to what I found in these young social activists. This was true enough though I was still strongly attached in my technical experiments to the "art for arts' sake" movements of Paris.

When the war broke out in Europe I found it easy to agree with John Weischel and his young socialist followers that it was only a struggle by great capitalists for control of the resources of the world. When later, in 1919, I returned from my own participation in that war with a determination to direct my art toward more social meanings than heretofore, I had the support of most of the young Jewish radicals. My early interest in, and sympathy with, the aims of the Russian revolution solidified this support as did my friendship with

Bob Minor, then working at firmly establishing a Communist party center in New York. There were, through the mid-twenties, no suspicions generated that what I meant by "social meanings" was different from what my radical friends meant by such meanings. I do not believe that I myself made any differentiations.

At this time, convinced as I had become both by the persuasions of companionship and that of my reading that Marx's economic determinism was the only "scientific" explanation of history, and its only true description, there was no reason for me to suspect, or others to suspect, that I did not fit in with the patterns of thought generally accepted by the Communist-oriented artists and intellectuals of New York. Although I felt selfconscious and quite silly when I was addressed as "Comrade Benton," as occasionally happened, I accepted the appellation.

Karl Radek's dictum that "the new Soviet reality required a realistic art," accepted everywhere in fellow-traveling artistic circles, could be applied just as well to the new democratic reality which liberal thinkers of all persuasions envisaged for America as the twenties neared their catastrophic end. Weren't we all comrades in the face of that disaster and the looming death throes of the society it ended or which it appeared to be ending?

I do not clearly remember when Radek's call for a realistic socially oriented art became defined as "Social Realism" and took on that propogandistic pattern which made it a political instrument in the service of Russian and Chinese Communism. But by the opening of the thirties it had the force of a religious dogma among literary and artistic radicals in New York. Its announced program was to point up the evils of American capitalism and contrast them with the virtues of communism. The American worker must be seen as a downtrodden and persecuted proletarian, the American farmer as a starving peasant, the American politician, especially the "liberal" politician, and labor sympathizer as a servant of predatory capitalists, and the whole of American history as a fraudulent myth concocted by capitalistic overlords to reconcile the American people to their "serfdom."

There were writers among the communist groups who were able to arrange and interpret the facts of American history that such an outlook appeared plausible. All that was necessary was to select cases of violence, fraud and oppression, and there were of course plenty, emphasize them and fit them into a Marxist progression.[16] Opposition to such rationalizations, even to any parts of them, soon became evidence of an immoral alliance with the evil and "anti-progressive" forces of society. With the rise of Hitler, such opposition could be readily interpreted as anti-Semitism and with the rise of the United Front at the outbreak of the Spanish War as a sign of pro-Fascism. My differences with the Social realists were subjected to both interpretations.

This was the situation in New York in the early thirties when I painted my first two murals. It directed and determined the temper of the criticisms leveled at them by the communist groups. The complete absence in these murals of the propogandist imagery of "Social Realism" was taken as proof of their reactionary character and justified the bitterness of the criticisms. At least that is my guess. Only some utterly certain conviction of my "anti-social" character could have turned into "that son-of-a-bitch Benton" for so many young idealists. Looking back it is amazing to think how much violence and hate could have been generated by mere political attitudes. No political *powers* of any consequence were at stake at any time. The Communist party had little real power even in Socialist labor politics, the fellow travelers had none at all. Yet the feelings generated were as if we had lined ourselves up on actual and violent revolutionary firing lines.

Nevertheless, in spite of all this passionate partisanship and the disruptive tactics it displayed at my Art Student's League lecture, I still thought that answering the John Reed Club questions might ease my position with its members. Perhaps it would had it not been for the entrance of Stuart Davis into the exchange of ideas. I said before I had not expected this entrance. Stuart, who had finally made his trip to Paris, had returned a convinced and passionate "abstractionist" somewhat in the order of Bracque and Picasso and it was difficult to see how he could reconcile this new direction of his painting with the tenets of "Social Realism." However, for the question and answers battle set up by the John Reed Club, he managed to do this and became the most vehement questioner, commentator, and detractor of my views of the whole outfit.

As this verbal fracas has been recorded in the John Reed Club publication, in the *Art Digest*, and otherwhere, there is no need of reproducing it here. While it did not improve my relations with the fellow-traveling world, it did add considerably to the number of those sympathetic with my Americanist intentions and my art. And, moreover, it defended my position at just the right time, at a time when the rigidities and intolerance of the Marxist cliques began turning even radical-minded reformists against them. Their all-or-nothing attitudes had made them politically useless. The new liberalist directions, taken by actual political powers after Franklin Roosevelt's election to the Presidency, turned their pretensions to social leadership into an academic gesture. The new Democratic liberals were plainly taking over that leadership. The entrenched conservatives of the country transferred their fears of communist activities to the more immediately consequential ones of Roosevelt. In this new situation, Democratic and Americanist in its outlook, my art found itself largely justified. By the spring of 1935, most of the vehemence of the left wing cabal against it petered out. When an attempt was made by a few die-hards to organize a picket line at an exhibition of my paintings not enough people would join to make it worthwhile.[17]

Shortly after I met Grant Wood during my lecture tour of 1934, our names and that of John Steuart Curry began to be regularly associated. The Regionalist movement was born. As indicated in other writings[18], I do not know exactly how this occurred. But in the new atmosphere of Democratic liberalism, where a growing interest in American meanings was promoted by a flood of Americanist historical studies, the Americanist nature of our subject matter and attitudes pushed our arts into wide public attention. They fitted with the times.

Though the more rabid politically motivated criticisms which I had received in New York were now largely a thing of the past dying out as faith in Marxist solutions for American problems began to weaken, the Regionalist movement, with its flavor of midwestern localism, drew another kind of criticism. To the abstractionist schools, divorced as they were from representational meanings and for whom art had, from 1910, been associated with a Paris-centered cult of aesthetic internationalism, the localist character and nationalist flavor of Regionalist art made it seem not only a chauvinistic and reactionary gesture but a ''provincial'' one as well, a rustic and boorish repudiation of all artistic sensitivity. Spearheaded in New York, first by Alfred Stieglitz and his coterie, and then by Mr. Rockefeller's and Alfred Barr's Museum of Modern Art, and later by a string of dealers, art professors, critics, and museum directors, the abstractionist groups emphasized a pattern of aesthetic thinking where all the significant meanings of art lay interiorly in the processes of art itself instead of

247

outwardly through what these processes represented. That such thinking enclosed a fair measure of artistic truth is unquestionable and I, along with Wood and Curry, and other Regionalists recognized the fact. That a work of art is first of all an agglomeration of aesthetic properties and that these must always constitute its core is so obvious that even to state it seems a redundancy. But the abstractionists and their protagonists state it over and over again and in every possible kind of verbiage, when they started hurling their criticisms at the Regionalist movement. Those who tried to defend the movements were often put in a position where they appeared to deny the very elementary conditions of art.

In 1924 in the *Arts Magazine*, I had published an article called "Form and Subject" in which I tried to bring out the functional place of the subject in creating artistic forms. There was nothing new in this. It was simply an attempt to revive an historically accepted principle; an ancient link between the artist and society which had been ignored to the point of repudiation by the new exotic painting movements by American artists, including for a while myself, had been dominating New York exhibitions since 1916. I thought a new look at these aesthetics was in order. Admittedly I was propelled by the veering of my own painting toward a concern with subject matter, which occurred shortly after the war in 1919, so the writing was in some measure a defense of this. But its propositions were valid enough in general to enlist the sympathies of such varying people as Forbes Watson, John Weischel, Tom Craven, Lewis Mumford, E.E. Cummings, and Boardman Robinson. And there were others. Though the Marxist groups were yet unorganized, Marxist Social Realism yet unborn as a movement, radical thought among artists, influenced probably by Diego Rivera in Mexico, was turning against the Parisian schools. Many besides John Weischel objected to their lack of communicable "meanings." So my article found a fairly wide and receptive audience.

Later, however, when I turned the "subject" from a generality to the more specifically American art form, practically all this support was (as before indicated) withdrawn. I never regained it even though I made no changes whatever in the basic principles which I originally set forth. I simply applied them to an environmental case, following quite precisely the guidelines of Hippolyte Taine, the French philosopher whose writings had first aroused environmentalist ideas in 1910. Perhaps if I had mentioned this French influence my Francophile critics, who looked to Paris for all their ideas, would have been easier on me. In any case when the "subject" became an "American subject" it also became an aesthetic "booberie," and increasingly so when a decade later it became a motivating factor in midwestern Regionalism. The standard critique of Regionalism rested, after the mid-thirties, more on its supposed indifference to intellectual and aesthetic values than on any political shortcomings. Its major differences, or what were taken to be such, arose from its rapport with the common everyday facts of American life, from its concern, as one young college art critic put it to me in a loaded question at one of my lectures. "Why," he asked, "do you deal only with the lowest common denominators of American life?" Regionalism for such elites was only a new "know nothingism."

I have said that my lecture tour of 1934 under Audrey McMahon's supervision led to the commission for the Missouri State Capitol mural and my return to residence in Missouri. I have also described in *An Artist in America* how the idea for this mural was first broached at a highly convivial hotel party by State Senator Ed Barbour, a close crony of my brother's and how, to my great surprise, he got it authorized by the State legislature a little later. Since making this description certain facts have been brought to my attention which make the passage of the bill for the mural more extraordinary than it seemed to me at the time it occurred. My lecture sponsor, Audrey McMahon, though she did not mention it to me, had been out to Missouri to extend her W.P.A. art projects. She came there, according to the story I was told, unverified but probable, with the airs of an Eastern imperative talking to a bunch of slick politicos.

One of her auditors, a State official who had "imperator" propulsions of his own, resented her pretensions and the injection also of a bunch of unknown and unpredictable artists into what was proving to be a useful vote controlling gimmick. Mr. Harry Hopkins' W.P.A. projects, left for implementation in the hands of the Missouri politicians in power, were a patronage bonanza. They could be something less if "Lady Audrey" got her hand in. So the Missouri "imperator" put a check on the designs of the New York "imperatrine" using the trivial and useless character of art as well as its vote-getting inconsequence to convince the largely Democratic Missouri legislature of his correctness in doing so. Federal work money, as he pointed out, should not be wasted on crazy artists-not in Missouri anyhow. With those Republicans who remained in office after the Roosevelt victory joining heartily with the "imperator's" conclusions, there was a decidedly anti-art atmosphere prevailing in the Missouri State Capitol when the bill authorizing the Benton mural was introduced. How then was that bill passed, and when, after its passage, I demanded modifications in its contractural requirements, were these so easily obtained? Before approaching this mystery I must go back to the Treasury commission on which I was working in New York when I received news of the success of the Benton mural proposal in the Missouri legislature.

After the government architects had approved my sketches for the Post Office mural, the Treasury committee, the final arbiters of the work, began criticizing them, finding fault with one detail after another. As I have said, the theme of the work was difficult and I felt I had managed well to get everything at all out of it. So I was much disturbed by the criticisms. If I yielded to them I would have to make completely new designs, which would involve the reconstruction of the clay models on which they were based and the re-doing of all the studies I had made from life. Should I go through with all this I would still have no assurances that what I came up with would be acceptable. I knew that the members of the committee, when they made provisions to gag me, had been fearful about the consequences of hiring me and I now felt because of the pettiness of their criticisms that they were trying to rid themselves of me by harassment. The recent fracas at the Art Students League lecture had not, I knew, reduced my reputation for exciting controversies.

While I was wondering how to act in this matter, a telegram came from my brother announcing the Missouri legislature's passage of Senator Barbour's bill. I promptly wrote a letter to the Treasury Department committee withdrawing from the Post office project.[19] The committee members made no protest about this. They were, no doubt, relieved to get me off their hands.

As soon as I realized that Senator Barbour was serious about his Benton mural project and was actually moving to get legislative sanction for it, I wrote to my brother and laid out the terms for a contract which would be acceptable to me. I named the theme ''A Social History of Missouri'' and insisted that selection and organization of the subject matter be left entirely in my hands. All this was agreed to by the Senator. However, when the contract for the mural was sent for my signature I discovered a small article which stated that I was to work with the approval of the Missouri State Art Commission. Had I known that such a commission existed I would have stipulated in my original contractural

251

plan that I be freed from its supervision. But now with its unforseen entrance into the contract I was caught in the same kind of situation which had led to my withdrawal from the Post Office project. I was pretty certain that a Missouri Art Commission would be quite as fearful of my way of seeing things as was the Treasury Department Committee and in matters of art I would likely be much more conservative. When I had designated my mural theme as "A Social History of Missouri," I had in mind not only a picture of actual life in Missouri but also representations of the hardy mythology which had come out of that life. Missouri stories like Jesse James and Frankie and Johnny were coming to mind as mural material along with other subjects too unconventional to submit to the timorous judgments of any official art commission.

The mural contract carried a fee of $16,000, a very large sum for a painter at the time, and I hated to put it in jeopardy by questioning what would surely seem a proper safeguard to any State legislator. But, on the other hand, I looked at the mural itself as the greatest opportunity I had yet to realize my artistic dreams. Unlike the Post Office mural its theme offered immensely interesting and congenial subjects, many so familiar from boyhood memories that their representation would automatically have the qualities of that specifically Missouri spirit I wanted my mural to express. I could make it almost like a painted autobiography if I had freedom to act as I saw fit. Without that freedom I could be channeled into producing a commonplace official work full of trite and mushy symbols.

Weighing the dreadful chance of losing the sixteen thousand dollars against that of having my mural ideas emasculated, I screwed up courage and returned the contract to Sen. Barbour with a note saying I could not undertake the work unless the article putting me under supervision was deleted. A week later the contract was returned to me. The troublesome clause was gone and I was completely free.

Looking back on these times, barely out of the worst effects of the depression when political power in Missouri was largely in the hands of Kansas City's Pendergast faction whose social projects here based entirely on the amount of patronage opportunities they offered, it is, as I said before, a mystery that the mural commission was given me and given finally, so that I had absolute control over it. Unlike Indiana which had prior commitments for a mural before I was called in, there was no situation existing in Missouri where muralistic propositions had any relevance whatever. The proposal for a Benton mural was made up out of whole cloth, created apart from any remote semblance of need (the Capitol building was already loaded with official paintings), and accepted in an atmosphere made at least partially hostile to art by the specter of Audrey McMahon's W.P.A. projects.

Senator Ed Barbour, who initiated the mural proposal and pushed it through the Legislature, came from a divided political district and had no political favors to offer for the votes he rounded up. His power, shaky enough in his own traditionally Republican district, hardly reached far enough into the ruling Democratic political block in Kansas City to be persuasive. And yet without the consent of those representing that block, which as I have said, had a strong grip on the State Legislature, he could never have got his mural bill passed. The temper of that block toward things artistic had been expressed earlier by a germane spirit named Miles Bulger who had pithily said for all to hear that "art was on the bum in Kansas City." Keep it "on the bum" out-state as well would surely have been the ruling sentiment of any Kansas City delegation to the legislature. And yet the mural bill passed and the contract for it was amended to my satisfaction in about six weeks after it was conceived!

253

Whenever I questioned him about this marvel, Senator Ed always asserted that he and he alone had been responsible for it. "I got you that 'mioriel,' Tom, and nobody else," was the only explanation I ever got from him. At first I took this to be a defense of the lawyer's fee of five hundred dollars he charged me for "representing my interests before the legislature," but as my brother backed up his claims I pushed my curiosity about them aside. However I got the Missouri job, it was the greatest thing that had so far happened to me. I rested content with that.

Later on, however, when the mural was about half finished, my curiosity about its inception was rearoused. In one small section of the work, which dealt with the past history of Missouri, I had depicted a group of black slaves working under the whip of an overseer in some primitive lead works. A Negro political faction in St. Louis took offense at this representation and sent a delegation to the governor asking to have it effaced. The governor, an old fellow named Guy Park, politically close to the Pendergast organization of Kansas City, had become a friend and admirer of my father's way back in the days when my father had been United States Attorney for the Western District of Missouri. Because of this I had got along famously with Governor Guy while working in the Capitol. He came in every few days to look at the progress of my mural and often invited me to his office for an after work sip of bourbon. The day that the St. Louis delegation put its request before him, he called me to his office and told me about it. "Tom," he said, "this business puts me in a jam. I don't like to ask this of you but I think you'll have to change that part of your picture."

"Governor," I told him, "my contract calls for a 'Social History of Missouri.' Isn't that lead mine episode a social fact? Isn't it true to history?"

"Tom," he came back with, "that's right. And according

to your contract I can't make you take it out. But you'll be smart if you do. These St. Louis blacks are very important to our organization in the Eastern part of the State for the coming election (Roosevelt vs. Landon—1936). It was our organization that gave you this 'muriel' job and you can do it a little favor like I'm asking for in return. Be good for your future anyhow." I had a quick realization of what I was up against. If I made a change in response to this political pressure I might start a chain of other such pressures asking for similar responses and my whole mural concept would be ruined. Who could guess what might come up in politically motivated minds?

Almost as soon, however, as these fears hit me a hopeful idea eased them back a little.

"Governor," I asked, "how important is the leader of this St. Louis crowd?"

"The most important black vote 'getouter' in the town," he replied "and he knows it. Plumb full of himself. That's why this business is touchy."

"Could I meet him?" I asked, "And talk with him by myself?"

"Why yes, Tom," said the governor, and he opened the door to his reception room and beckoned in a burly, flashily dressed Negro as Mr. Sharkey, the "St. Louis leader."[20] I said to him, "Governor Park has told me about your complaint and I can see that its reasonable. But there's a side to it you don't know about. Have you seen the painting?" "No," he answered, "but what I've been told is enough." "Well, let's go look at it," I said. "I want your advice about that part of it I said you didn't know about."

Remembering a saying of my Father's, "If you want a feller to help you, make him feel important," I continued: "You may be just the man to solve a problem that's been bothering me." Bowing to the governor and asking his

255

retinue to wait a minute, Mr. Sharkey followed me to my painting.

I was at the moment working on a representation of an old-fashioned outdoor Missouri political meeting, where my father, as speaker, addressed a country town audience. Standing as a listener in a very prominent position was a figure for which I had not yet found an appropriate face. I pointed out this figure and said, "Mr. Sharkey, I've been looking for a face of a prominent politician of your race for this figure. I want to show the progress of Missouri's colored people from their unhappy beginnings, shown by the lead mine scene, to their present position of political importance in the State. The lead mine scene is a bad part of our history, I'll admit, but it's necessary to show how the colored people overcame their misfortunes and rose up to the position of power that you represent. How about my putting your face on that figure? You'll be up there on this State House wall as a permanent record of the colored man's accomplishments in our state."

"Why, Mister Artist," he replied, "I think that would be all right."

I made a quick but accurate drawing of him. "Bring your delegation here anytime after ten in the morning and you'll see yourself up there," I said.

The next day he and his friends came and whispered and chuckled to see his image standing out so prominently in the big painting. That ended the one and only protest I had to consider while the mural was in process.

In the afternoon Governor Guy called me in for a highball. "They say you are an artist, Tom," he laughed, "but you're a better politician." A somewhat dubious compliment, but I received it with much satisfaction because it meant I was free again.

But the governor's statement, "it was our organization that gave you the "murial job'" kept coming to mind. "Our

256

organization" meant without doubt the Pendergast organization in Kansas City because the governor, coming from Clay County just north of Kansas City, could have gotten nowhere without its support.

I remembered that during his active political life my father was a frequent visitor to Kansas City. This fact was burned into my memory because he had his pocket picked there, several times; one time even his watch and chain were taken off his belly. These visits occurred around the turn of the century before the rise of the Pendergast factions, but some political interest in him must have been inherited by them because when he was made president of the State Constitutional Convention in 1922 the Democrats of Kansas City supported the honor.[21]

Further proof of the affection accorded my father by the ruling Missouri Democrats came in 1924 when he lay dying of cancer in a Springfield, Missouri, hospital. The annual State Democratic convention in Springfield was in progress at the time and strings of delegates came to the hospital to see him. I had come out from New York to stay by his sick bed and had to receive these visitors in a little anteroom next to where he lay. One day a Kansas City group headed by Tom Pendergast, then in his stalwart prime, came to see the dying man. They were a silent lot going in to his room one by one to shake his hand. Pendergast was the last. When he came back into the anteroom he reached a big half-closed fist out to me. When I grasped it I felt a hard object left in my palm. "This is from his friends for any little things he might need," Pendergast said and walked out. The hard object was a tight roll of bills, eight hundred dollars in all.

I was dumbfounded and much disconcerted. I dared not tell my father about it. Long out of practice or political perquisites he was at the end of his financial rope. I was broke and my brother, as a cub attorney, was earning little. But my father would be profoundly humiliated if he thought people suspected our situation. He had been a leader in the State. To let him think he was an object of charity as he ended his life was impossible. I knew my brother would also feel humiliated. But having to account for possession of the money I told him about it.

"Why the hell did you take it?" he asked. I told him I didn't suspect what it was till too late. It was done so quickly. And then I said it was undoubtedly a well-meant gift. It would have been more embarrassing to refuse it than accept it.

"Well," my brother said, "we can damn well use the money, but for Christ's sake don't ever say a word about it to anybody."

Does the mystery of why Ed Barbour's mural bill was so quickly and fully supported in the Missouri legislature lie in some now forgotten political debt owed to my father and paid off to his son? It is possible. The loyalties of politics often reach far, passing on to new men and through new situations, even corrupt ones.

In any case, during the summer and autumn of 1936 when I worked on my mural, doors were open to all who wanted to see what I was doing, not one word of objection to any of its conceptions came my way. Except for the instance of the colored delegation from St. Louis, I was left completely undisturbed. Politicians, judges, preachers, newsmen, farmers and town and city folk came in and looked. I often talked with them. I sketched them when I needed faces, and when they looked interesting enough or appropriate for the subject I was painting. All in all I felt I was in complete harmony with the Missouri culture being pictured. Tom Pendergast, now aging and ill, had himself posed for a sketch to be incorporated in the mural. Bankers, real estate operators, plough boys, black boys, and bedizened secretaries offered themselves eagerly as subjects for my brush. Everything was as smooth as a happy dream.

When the mural was finished, however, in late December of 1936, this calm was broken by roars of protest[22] about the propriety of its subject matter. These were initiated for the most part by conservative groups in St. Louis and Kansas City whose antipathies to my conceptions had been held in leash probably by their greater antipathies for those of Franklin Roosevelt. Once that Presidential campaign of '36 was over and Roosevelt installed again in the White House some of the exasperation felt about that was redirected toward me. The newspaper reporters and their editors fanned the dissatisfactions, mostly I think with tongue in cheek and for the fun of having something to write about besides politics.

Although the Democrats had won the national elections, Kansas City's Pendergast Democrats lost their hold over state politics. My old friend Governor Guy was replaced by Lloyd Stark, a very anti-Pendergast Democrat from the Northeastern part of the State. When Stark came to visit the mural he went directly to the figure of Tom Pendergast which dominated that section of the work devoted to Kansas City. Looking as dead pan as possible, I said to him, "That is a fact of Missouri's Social History." "That *was* a fact," he laughed. He was correct but not in Kansas City before several more years had passed.

I wonder how he would react to the protests about the propriety of the mural. Whether or not he sided with them he never said anything publicly. Two or three new legislators aired a proposition to whitewash the painting but they were not serious enough to make any moves to that end. In about a month the storm of criticisms blew itself out. The mural was safe.

The only intimation I ever had about how the new governor might feel about my work came a year later when it was announced to his wife that an artist had been found to do her Mansion House portrait. (It is customary in Missouri for each governor's wife to leave a portrait of herself in the Governor's Mansion.) Mrs. Stark reacted to the announcement with concern, ''I hope it is not Mr. Benton,'' she said, ''because I do want to look like a lady.''

With the creation of the Missouri mural my art moved out of the area of political controversy, with whose peripheries it had been engaged for seven years. The real politics in which the Missouri work was necessarily involved at its inception never came to the surface, nor did the work itself stir any politically slanted ideological debate. The incident of the St. Louis Negro protest could have been worked up into such a debate had it not been privately settled, but I did not, as in Indiana, once have to justify or explain away, or even acknowledge, any kind of political beliefs. Although its subject matter could have laid it open to the same kind of ''fellow-traveling'' criticism hurled at my New York murals, it did not do so in any noticeable way. A few artists and writers in St. Louis, ''provincial'' members of New York's Artist and Writers Congress, did once try to inveigle me into a discussion in St. Louis, but that would have been so out of place in a Missouri context that I easily brushed it aside. Later when the mural drew its extreme conservative criticism, these fellows were all on my side anyway. The mural did not rid me permanently of controversy, but it did put an end to the bitter politically inspired controversy which had surrounded my earlier murals.

In early 1937, I made a series of drawings on the great Ohio-Mississippi flood which so damaged southeast Missouri. These were done for the *St. Louis Post-Dispatch* and the *Kansas City Star*. Several paintings came out of them, the most notable being ''Missouri Spring,'' now in the collection of Harpo Marx, the celebrated movie comedian.

In the summer I reported on the Michigan ''sit down'' strikes with another series for *Life* magazine and later for the same publication with still another series on Hollywood's

260

cinema activities. Out of the latter came the painting, "Hollywood."

In 1938 and '39, I painted the two nudes "Persephone" and "Susannah and the Elders," besides a number of smaller pictures. Both nudes became controversial but not in any political way.

The changes which came to my painting in the late thirties, changes in my directions, were very largely technical, but technical in a narrower sense than those which had occupied me earlier.

Influenced considerably by Grant Wood I....

Notes

1. *An Artist in America* and *An American in Art*.
2. The formalistic methods of my painting, whether approved or not, were well known at this time, but their application at the New School to the common facts of American life, giving a muralistic impact to what was traditionally regarded as "genre" subject matter, aroused highly negative reactions, even among people who had heretofore looked with favor on my experiments.
3. See *An American in Art*.
4. See "The Twenties."
5. See *An American in Art*.
6. Maybe an unconscious reaction to the Second Commandment.
7. See *An Artist in America*.
8. See *An Artist in America* and *An American in Art*.
9. See "The Twenties." The Barn House is on Martha's Vineyard.
10. See *An Artist in America*.
11. See *An Artist in America*.
12. See *An Artist in America*.
13. See *An Artist in America*.
14. See *An American in Art*.
15. See "The Twenties."
16. Leo Huberman's *We, the People* and *Man's Worldly Goods* are two of the better and more intelligent examples of this kind of writing.

17. Social Realism itself began to change character. Instead of an out-and-out propogandist instrument for world communism, it moved into a more limited but more actualistic portrayal of the luckless children of our American democracy. It became not a call for the future but a statement about the present. In this new aspect it was not far from my own art.

18. *An Artist in America, An American in Art.*

19. See Francis O'Connor, *History of W.P.A. and Treasury Projects*, for a copy of the letter.

20. A fictitious name. I've forgotten his real one though it could probably be ascertained by looking up St. Louis political records and checking these with his portraits.

21. This is pretty well certified by the statement made by U.S. Congressman Joe Shannon of Kansas City when he wrote me for permission to introduce my war-time "Year of Peril" (See *An Artist in America*) into the *Congressional Record*. He said, "We always honored your father as the first Democrat in Missouri. I want to honor his son as the first artist."

22. See *An Artist in America.*

The Missouri Mural and its Critics

Mural art through long periods of time has been accorded a position different from that of the other plastic arts. It is a public art and has been the special servant of established powers, of church and State, time and again. It has been regarded and used as an instrument of propoganda, as a means of acclaiming and idealizing the beliefs and assumptions of reigning powers. The Pharoahs of Egypt and the Kings of Assyria glorified their deeds with mural carvings. Religious orders taught their doctrines with carved reliefs and paintings on the walls of their sanctuaries. Wherein power has been absolute mural art has been lined up among its servants. Wherein doctrine has attained supremacy its proponents have tied the artist to their purposes.

The Fathers of the Early Christian Church saw their mural paintings as vehicles for carrying doctrinal messages. They cared little about Art as a "mirror held up to life." They cared little about life itself which they saw as an evil nearing its doom. They felt that an art which dealt with life, as did the dispersed pagan art of the Greeks, was obscene, perverse and fit for Hell fire.

The art of the muralist, whether carver or painter, has been constantly shackled by those who saw it as an instrument of purpose. But the mural art like all other arts does best when it is free, and a survey of the arts of the ancient empires and Religions shows that it was in periods where absolute powers, doctrinal or temporal, were in abeyance that those arts took on vitality and health. The artist is one for whom the visible world is of paramount importance and he must be allowed to deal with it if he is to produce anything real or moving.

Moralists, doctrinaires, those bitten with power complexes tend to deny all value to life save as it fits in with their ends. Such denial reached one of its highest points for the artist when the Fathers of the Early Christian Church maintained that the function of art was to mortify life. For a long time painters under the Church found themselves burdened with lifeless symbolic forms which the Fathers regarded as essential requirements of good art.

To the Italian painters Cimabue and Giotto are accorded the reputations of having first successfully broken the power of orthodox symbolism over the mural arts of the west. Although these artists dealt with orthodox subject matter, depicting accepted religious myths, they abandoned the symbolical conventions of the church and sought the life around them for their actual pictorial matter. In so doing they prepared the ground for that great flowering of robust and healthy human art which marks the renaissance as one of the richest periods in the representation of human values and emotions. The artist turned loose into life brought life to his forms.

In the dying renaissance, mural painting under the hands of Lords and Kings who were intent upon idealizing their positions left again its study of life and returned to symbolism and allegory. There, in spite of the rise of democratic powers and their accompanying views in reference to individual freedom and responsibility, it has remained. Official mural art under the democracies has remained tied to precedents of stale idealism which had their origin in the minds of Kings and nobles who did not dare look at life because of the bitter contradictions it drove into their assumptions that all was as it should be. Here in the United States as in the European democracies the walls of public buildings are full of vague and wordless shadows of dead orthodoxy.

The mural art which I began developing eighteen years ago and whose latest example is in the House lounge at Jefferson City is in revolt against such a condition of affairs. Years ago I joined with the Mexican artists Rivera and

264

Orozco against the perpetuation of stale forms on public walls. I have since parted company with these artists on the issue of communistic propoganda which with its doctrinal rigidity I see as leading to another artistic orthodoxy destined like those of the past to deny the artists' right to refer to life except through grooves of predetermined purpose.

I see mural painting as no different from any other painting in its responsibilities to experience. Because of its size and the extensions of its forms it is technically different from the average easel painting and demands more ingenuity in organization but in its subject matter, its references, its spirit it is not so. To have a living character, to be interesting it must, like any other vital expression, be motivated by interesting and unstereotyped experience. It must find its meanings and its matter not in the stale conventions of orthodox opinion, radical or conservative, but in the flow of life, in life as it is lived rather than thought.

The things that men do and "do with" are more important in the development of a society than the opinions or ideas to which they give lip service.

In the growth of a state like Missouri, no famed individual, whatever his line, can have had the fundamental social consequences of the two-handed saw or the broad ax. Nor can such individuals be as significant in their efforts on the environment, to which the artist must refer for his material, as the obscene people who used the instruments. You cannot stand General Pershing, for instance, up against a buck saw or its user where the actual life of Missouri is concerned, or my great-uncle, Senator Benton, up against a mule or its driver. The actions of Frankie and Johnny back on the St. Louis waterfront, although they are not of the present, illustrate better the realities of life as it is actually lived than do anybody's opinions about the Constitution. Ideas and ideals are important in that they frequently have consequences in action but it is the action itself that is significant. Especially is this so for a painter who must draw on what is visible for the stuff with which he works. Of course, Ozark sunsets are visible in Missouri and so are violets in the woods, but no adequate picture of the land of Missouri could be made with sunsets and no true picture of its people could be made with a row of violets. I suspect that even those legislators who have objected to my painting of Missouri would resent being pictured as a bunch of violets. Certainly none that I have yet come across have the shrinking qualities of little flowers.

In the substance of that cyclone of criticism which my painting of Missouri has turned loose I am but little interested. It is for the most part of a stereotyped character and not worth detailed attention. But the phenomena itself is interesting and I want to express a few opinions about it, not in defense of my picture, which will eventually defend itself through the satisfactions and amusements it will give people who are interested in life, but just as a matter of philosophy.

The function of criticism seems to be more to reveal the mental habits and character of the critic than to prove faults in the thing criticized. Criticism is a quite normal and constant human reaction to the unfamiliar. Human beings, creatures of routine and habit think, as a rule, by combining little patterns of words, which they have memorized. When these patterns fail to encompass or describe new things the first human impulse is to assault these things and declare them unreal or untrue or immoral or perverse. There is nothing particularly malicious about this. It is simply the result of that pitiful human inertia which ties the best of us to habit and which can only be overcome by a considerable effort of will. This effort few are willing to make. It is too comfortable in the warm pigsty of familiar ways.

In all the criticisms of my Missouri mural I have not seen one that did not indicate the critics surrender to stale verbal habit. That is not always because of lack of normal intelligence either. It is simply because the critic tried to formulate his reactions to an unfamiliar thing too quickly. In doing this he inevitably forced a clash between his habitual formulation and the new stuff he faced. The unpleasant feeling aroused, he then automatically read out into the object which caused it.

All this is old stuff with me. I have faced it.

Most of my life as an artist, not only among laymen but among informed students of the history of Art.[sic] For twenty years the majority of the critics of the East, people with a reputation for knowledge and judgment, have found fault with my work. This used to hurt me. It doesn't any more, partly because I have become used to it and partly because I have learned to understand it and the simple human frailty behind it.

Words are wonderful things but they have an insidious life of their own. They trip up folks who use them without care. The habit of making quick verbal formulations is a dangerous one. In the long run such a habit always puts folks in the wrong because when new things come into their ken and they try to label them with habitually used words and phrases, which, of course, never fit, they break out with stupidities and make asses of themselves.

People who have jobs or professions which do not call for or do not allow of hasty verbal formulations are more fortunate than those whose tongues have to wag. They are generally more realistic toward new things than those who feel constrained to get their reactions promptly into words. As a consequence trained scientific men, who do not dare to formulate without lengthy investigations, and farmers, plain working men--and the majority of women who simply live and do their work without bothering about it, are likely to approach new things in a fairly objective way and take them simply for what they are. I am not trying to make a universal rule here, but experience has taught me that this is generally true.

While I was working on the Missouri mural thousands of people came to see me from all over this state and from other states. Most of them were just plain people not given much to spouting opinions. No doubt if they had been forced to express opinions these would have fallen into standardized categories and been as stale as most of those I have read. But my visitors playing to no audience were not forced to say anything. They just looked at my pictures, saw it as one of the world they lived in and liked it. They did not bother about whether the picture was painted in an unaccustomed style or whether the colors were pale or bright or whether the subject matter fitted in to any special pattern of propriety. They apparently saw my pictured procession of things and people as I saw them in the real life from which I took them, just as interesting and characteristic aspects of the human struggle that was and is Missouri.

Some of the stuff I painted in Jeff City is to be laughed at; some of it with a sufficiently developed social conscience ought to be wept over. I myself do not insist either on laughter or tears. My picture is neither a comedy or a moral essay. It is just simply a picture of what was and is. And apart from its technical values which are the concern of specialists, it is mainly a picture for plain people like the farmers and their wives and kids who came to see me paint it last summer. It is for them and those representatives of theirs, who like them, do not see all things stacked up against a lot of habitual phrases which belie the human saltiness of the real characters and doings. My picture is for realistic minded people or better for people when they are in a realistic frame of mind and prepared to accept the beauty that goes with what is true. As the question of the truth of my mural has been injected into much of the criticism I have received it is in order that I should say something about it.

The whole business of Truth is a little different but serious consideration points to it as a value rather than as a thing.

Truth appears to be an attitude taken toward a thing.

It is wholly dependent upon your perceptions of a thing and does not rest in the thing itself. Any lawyer who had dealt with witnesses to a crime or accident must recognize the peculiar nature of Truth. Any student of politics, anyone even who witnessed our last presidential campaign must see that Truth is not only an attitude but a highly conditioned one. Any student of scientific truth must readily acknowledge that Truth is simply a temporary value that we give to our perceptions. A fact, when by the grace of God you can find it, is a fact, but the Truth is a conviction or feeling attached to that fact. The word Truth is seldom applied to simple, directly ascertainable facts. An apple is an apple— But what is a true apple? The word True is always applied to a complex fact and is directed generally to relatives that are perceived to exist between them. In the perceiving of relations human beings, even with the finest instruments, do not reach absolute Truth. If they reach and sustain the value of an approximate Truth they are lucky indeed.

Now as to the Truth of my mural. The facts upon which it is based are as true as facts can be. The historical facts involved are not living facts. They are facts of record but they pass as True for the specialist in History and that is enough for me to work on. The mural however is not historical in the accepted sense as a stream of events. It does not portray specific historical events but the social conditions in which they occurred. These conditions when they were behind the span of my own life, I took second hand from people who lived before me and who wrote about what they perceived. Recognizing the shaky nature of perception I read, where I could, more than one account. This second hand fact however is not quite the stuff with which an artist can work. The kind of facts with which he can work are, as intimated above, those which he perceives directly, which impress his own senses. So in dealing with what happened before my time I tried where possible those things which I had myself experienced and which were approximately the same as I might have experienced had I lived earlier. The truth of my approximations were determined by the accounts I read which were recommended by authorities on the History of the State.

My mural, then, for the most part deals with facts directly perceived by me. I have said enough above to show how personal is perception and how conditioned must be its Truth. But suppose for a moment that my perceptions of any given fact or complex of facts was absolutely and scientifically true. Suppose that I saw truly and my pencil recorded accurately. I would still have to get what I saw and recorded into relation with a mass of other such seen and recorded facts for the social progression I was to paint in the mural. I would have to fit them into some kind of a logical scheme or there would be nothing but confusion on the walls.

When a lawyer makes out his case he tries to make a well knit convincing story in which each part fits neatly and logically with the other. If he can't make such a story he loses his case. In order to make that story he suppresses certain aspects of the facts with which he deals and magnifies others. For his opponent and his opponents' client he distorts things. Of course he does. But where would he be without the selective processes involved in that distortion. Law suits are won by those who distort logically and reasonably. Convincing or moving statements are made by those who know how to adapt facts to design. This is sad maybe, but it is the way things go in the world and in that reflection of the world which is Art.

I tried my level best in the House lounge mural to make an all around true and honest picture of Missouri. Under the frankly admitted conditions of my perceptions and under the logical procedures of my craft, where the necessity for establishing sequential relations between the many objects depicted imposed their own conditions, I have done all I could to be accurate.

I myself see where I have failed in some places but I still think that in the whole I did a pretty good job and one which will assuredly outlast the kind of criticism given it so far.

Appendix 2

On August 15, 1940, Betty Chamberlain of *Time* magazine sent a telegram to Benton saying the magazine was planning a story on the exhibit of Hollywood stars, "with special emphasis [on] your paintings." She asked Benton for a detailed story about his use of plaster models and asked a series of additional questions including, "Have any complications arisen from this method of procedure such as dogs or drunks sitting on models, heat melting plastilene etc." The following is a copy of Benton's handwritten, rough-draft reply. The original is in the files of the Nelson-Atkins Museum of Art in Kansas City.

Benton the Model Maker

I began making clay models in 1917 as a study of anatomical detail and of the play of light and shade on the forms of muscles and draperies. This was suggested by the references of Vasari and other commentators to such practices by Italian Renaissance painters. I made also a number of bas-reliefs which I painted in color.

In 1919 I made my first experiments with models designed in the perspectives of painting. Since my student days in Paris I had been concerned with the Renaissance problem of deep space, and perspective. I wanted to design my pictures in depth by superimposing solid objects so as to produce the effect of lines of form going back into space as well as playing on the picture surface.

I would ink this kind of design out on paper with geometrical forms, with cubic, conic and cylindrical shapes plus perspective lines but I could never turn these abstractions into convincing realities when it came to painting them.

It was the problem of turning my theoretical conception into a reality that set me to modeling my diagrams in 1917. I was looking for some kind of logic that would unite the diverse shapes of my composition and make them appear to belong together when painted. I found it in the pattern of light and shade which occured when my designs were modeled in clay. This procedure determined my style. I had no style nor could I make a convincing painting before I began working out my conceptions in clay.

The first successful painting I made with the use of a model was bought by Mr. Thomas Kelly of New York and Philadelphia. The second was bought by Dr. A.C. Barnes of Philadelphia. Both were figure compositions. It took two years of experiment with clay to make them. They are labored but still passable paintings. They, along with my first American History pictures, represent the beginnings of my present style.

In 1923 I began painting my models with different shades of black, grey, and white. In this way I added to my basic form a pattern of tone. For ten years I worked at the problem of turning this form and tone into the color or painting. I had lots of trouble with my color during this time. This was because there was no basic relation between my form and color. In 1933 it occurred to me that I might work my color schemes out by painting them on the actual model. I am not dumb, but it took me ten years to think of this simple way of assuring a relation between form and color. It is the way of natu re, but I didn't think of it.

After the basic relations of form and color were solved and I could paint easily in the colors I liked there yet remained the question of texture. This I settled in 1937. I studied the linear configurations of textures in nature and cut these into the surfaces of my work. In addition I kept the actual textures near me for reference.

The above with the use of egg tempera for all underpainting shows development of my manual technique. My intellectual interest remains as it began a concern with lines of form operating in deep space.

My emotional interests are with American life in its actuality. I make models for nearly everything I do.

Occasionally I make simple still life studies, or paint a portrait head without a model, but if the picture is complicated I always work it out in clay. My drawings and sketches from nature determine the subject matter and the linear perspective of the models.

I work fast with clay. I can make a model in an hour if I have worked out my composition exactly on paper. Very complicated designs such as the Persephone may take several days. The biggest model and most complicated was for the Missouri mural. This was 15 feet long and 20 inches high. It took two months to complete. I intended to give this model to the Missouri State Museum but souvenir hunters picked nearly all the figures off it while I was away.

People who have no interest in painting are often interested immensely in my models. I myself do not consider them works of art. I do not keep them. They are only steps in my painting technique. When I am through with them I bust them up and use the clay again. I use plastilene. In order to make a painting surface I coat the finished model with half and half egg yolk and water. Then I paint it white and work into the color with egg tempera.

I get a great kick making these models. I feel my paintings in my hands. I like especially to paint the color on them.

My models keep well. Sometimes I have an idea and make a model and don't get at painting from it for a couple of years. Often I take Kodachrome photographs of the models.

To be effective these models must be seen in the same light in which they were made. If not both the form and perspective is discordant. When I photograph them in color I work out of doors with the sun striking the model at the exactly correct angle. I use a tissue paper screen to diffuse the light and eliminate cast shadows. The models are so designed in the studio that no shadow is ever cast across a form. One of the purposes of the model is to eliminate the form destroying accidents of light and shade which occur in nature. They make light and shade an element of design. This control of light on superimposed forms is what makes for the three-dimensional effect of my paintings.

We don't let dogs or drunks in the studio. We keep them in the living room.

INDEX